SOUND RECORDING TECHN
AMERICAN LITERAT

Phonographs, tapes, stereo LPs, digital remix – how did these remarkable technologies impact American writing? This book explores how twentieth-century writers shaped the ways we listen in our multimedia present. Uncovering a rich new archive of materials, this book offers a resonant reading of how writers across several genres, such as John Dos Passos, Langston Hughes, William S. Burroughs, and others, navigated the intermedial spaces between texts and recordings. Numerous scholars have taken up *remix* – a term co-opted from DJs and sound engineers – as the defining aesthetic of twenty-first-century art and literature. Others have examined modernism's debt to the phonograph. But in the gap between these moments, one finds that the reciprocal relationship between the literary arts and sonic technologies continued to evolve. A mix of American literary history, sound studies, and media archaeology, this interdisciplinary study will appeal to scholars, students, and audiophiles.

JESSICA E. TEAGUE is an Assistant Professor of English at the University of Nevada, Las Vegas. The intersections between literature, sound, and technology are the focus of her research. Her work has been published in journals such as *American Quarterly* and *Sound Studies*.

CAMBRIDGE STUDIES IN AMERICAN LITERATURE AND CULTURE

Editor
Leonard Cassuto, *Fordham University*

Founding Editor
Albert Gelpi, *Stanford University*

Advisory Board
Robert Levine, *University of Maryland*
Ross Posnock, *Columbia University*
Branka Arsić, *Columbia University*
Wai Chee Dimock, *Yale University*
Tim Armstrong, *Royal Holloway, University of London*
Walter Benn Michaels, *University of Illinois, Chicago*
Kenneth Warren, *University of Chicago*

Recent Books in this Series

(Continued after the Index)

SOUND RECORDING TECHNOLOGY AND AMERICAN LITERATURE

From the Phonograph to the Remix

JESSICA E. TEAGUE

University of Nevada, Las Vegas

Shaftesbury Road, Cambridge CB2 8EA, United Kingdom

One Liberty Plaza, 20th Floor, New York, NY 10006, USA

477 Williamstown Road, Port Melbourne, VIC 3207, Australia

314–321, 3rd Floor, Plot 3, Splendor Forum, Jasola District Centre, New Delhi – 110025, India

103 Penang Road, #05–06/07, Visioncrest Commercial, Singapore 238467

Cambridge University Press is part of Cambridge University Press & Assessment, a department of the University of Cambridge.

We share the University's mission to contribute to society through the pursuit of education, learning and research at the highest international levels of excellence.

www.cambridge.org
Information on this title: www.cambridge.org/9781108793797

DOI: 10.1017/9781108879002

First published 2021
First paperback edition 2022

A catalogue record for this publication is available from the British Library

Library of Congress Cataloging-in-Publication data
NAMES: Teague, Jessica, 1982– author.
TITLE: Sound recording technology and American literature from the phonograph to the remix / Jessica Teague.
DESCRIPTION: Cambridge, UK ; New York : Cambridge University Press, 2021. | Series: Cambridge studies in American literature and culture | Based on the author's dissertation (doctoral) – Columbia University, 2013. | Includes bibliographical references and index.
IDENTIFIERS: LCCN 2020046970 (print) | LCCN 2020046971 (ebook) | ISBN 9781108840132 (hardback) | ISBN 9781108879002 (ebook)
SUBJECTS: LCSH: American literature – 20th century – History and critcism. | Sound in literature. | Literature and technology – History. | Sound – Recording and reproducing.
CLASSIFICATION: LCC PS228.S64 T43 2021 (print) | LCC PS228.S64 (ebook) | DDC 810.9/356–dc23
LC record available at https://lccn.loc.gov/2020046970
LC ebook record available at https://lccn.loc.gov/2020046971

ISBN   978-1-108-84013-2   Hardback
ISBN   978-1-108-79379-7   Paperback

For my parents

Contents

Figures

Acknowledgments

To record oneself – one's voice – and then to listen back to it is always a bit disorienting. My own voice sounds too high. It lacks the resonant quality of hearing it from within my own body. It is familiar and yet all wrong. Writing a book can also feel this way, at times. The ideas in one's head can feel thin and brittle when finally committed to the page, but I have been fortunate to have many interlocutors over the years who have echoed my voice back to me with kindness and encouragement. This work is dedicated to them.

In the dissertation phase of this project at Columbia University, I was privileged to have a team of brilliant, thoughtful advisors whose contributions to this book cannot be overstated. Brent Edwards was a guiding force throughout my graduate studies, and I am so grateful for his generosity of time and intellect. His willingness to think alongside me and to ask the hard questions helped me develop intellectual autonomy. Robert O'Meally has been a booster of this project since the beginning, and he introduced me to intellectual communities inside and outside academe. Our conversations over the years always felt more like jam sessions and gave fuel to the fire whenever I was in need of inspiration. In Michael Golston, I found the kind of careful reader and critic who pushed me to work harder and made me a better writer. I could not ask for better mentors. This project also benefited greatly from my participation in the Jazz Study Group at the Center for Jazz Studies, where so many scholars so graciously shared their work and debated the discipline. While at Columbia, I was also lucky to receive guidance and feedback from a number of other faculty and affiliates, including Katherine Biers, Sarah Cole, Krin Gabbard, Austin Graham, Ross Posnock, Martin Puchner, and John Szwed. Equally important are the many friends among my cohort who read drafts, walked and talked in the park, debated over drinks, and commiserated over coffee. Cheers to the members of the 20/21 Colloquium, the Americanist Colloquium, and SynDissCo. It would be impossible to name them all, but special thanks are due to Deborah Aschkenes, Jean-Christophe Cloutier, Tim Donohue, Emily Hayman, Jang Wook Huh, Alastair Morrison, Imani Owens, Hiie Saumaa, and Adam Spry, who read early drafts of this work.

I am particularly grateful for the support I have received from my home institution, UNLV. Since my arrival in Las Vegas, I have found myself surrounded by the best kind of colleagues – the kind who become valued friends as well as intellectual collaborators. At UNLV, our interdisciplinary Americanist Colloquium and reading group has been absolutely central to my ongoing work – special thanks are due to Julia Lee, Brandon Manning, and Vincent Perez for helping to get this group off the ground. I am particularly indebted to those who have been willing to read and offer feedback on my manuscript at various stages or who assisted with research questions, including Gary Totten, Anne Stevens, Emily Setina, Susanna Newbury, Heather Lusty, Eryn Green, and Hanna Andrews. I am also appreciative of my mentor, Kelly Mays, for the encouragement to stay the course. Gratitude is also due to Deans Jennifer Keene and Chris Heavey, the UNLV College of Liberal Arts, and the English Department for institutional support that has made my research possible, including financial support for research trips and two incredible research assistants, RC Wonderly and Anthony Farris. Beyond the walls of my home university, I am thankful for the friendships and connections I've made at various conferences. Shout-outs are due to Jennifer Lynn Stoever, Julie Beth Napolin, and Lisa Hollenbach, who organized special sessions on sound studies that helped me clarify my own relationship to the field.

For a project that is as archivally driven as mine has been, it would be impossible to overstate the value of institutional support and fellowships. Columbia's Marjorie Hope Nicolson Fellowship and a Mellon/ACLS Dissertation Completion Fellowship gave me the time and space I needed to get this project off the ground. A Lillian Gary Taylor Fellowship in American Literature at the University of Virginia Libraries allowed me to extend my work on John Dos Passos and significantly revise portions of the manuscript. Additional thanks are due to the various archives that made their collections available to me: Tulane University's Hogan Jazz Archive (and the helpful Bruce Raeburn), Yale's Beinecke Rare Book and Manuscript Library, the Berg Collection of English and American Literature and the Theatre on Film and Tape Archive at the New York Public Library, and the Audiovisual Department at the Bibliothèque Nationale de France in Paris (with special thanks to Anne Legrand).

Long before I started researching literature and sound recording technology in a more formal way, I benefited from the intellectual and musical camaraderie of family, friends, and teachers who introduced to me to new writers, new art, and new music. My parents fostered a love of music and theatre in me from a very early age, and I was the beneficiary of my dad's and my Uncle Mike's audiophile tendencies. My high school music teacher, Anne-Marie Katemopolous, deserves much credit for teaching me how to listen to and write about music, and my crate-digging friends, Brandon Mitchell, Barbara Jwanouskos, and Jason Sklar, helped open my ears at a formative moment.

Last, but certainly not least, this book would not exist without my partner in literature and in life, John Hay. He continues to be my first and my last reader, my sounding board, and my most important collaborator. He encouraged me to keep working on this project at the moments when I most needed it and has shown an enthusiasm for the subject that probably no one but myself could muster. Our son, Leo, came into this world just as this book was entering its final stages, and it has been a joy to write these very different chapters together with you, John.

Resonant Reading
Listening to American Literature after the Phonograph

When Gertrude Stein published *Three Lives*, her first book-length work, in 1909, readers were struck by her peculiar, repetitive style. As one dust jacket review put it, Stein's prose was like a "stubborn phonograph." Taken in passing, the comparison might seem unremarkable, but in 1909, when the phonograph was still a relatively new technology, the dust jacket remark penned by Georgiana Goddard King (a Reader in English at Bryn Mawr College) reveals how at least one early reader *heard* Gertrude Stein. According to King, Stein had "pushed the method of realism as far as it would go," and "the patient iteration, the odd style, with all its stops and starts, like a stubborn phonograph, are a part of the incantation. The reader must take it or leave it, – but always, taken or left, it remains astonishing."

The insistence that one not just read but hear Gertrude Stein's writing was one of the ways that her early admirers attempted to explain her unusual approach to language to potential readers. The art patroness Mabel Dodge, Stein's close friend, suggested that one must read Stein aloud; she contended that by "listening one feels that from the combination of repeated sounds, varied ever so little, that there emerges gradually a perception of some meaning quite other than that of the contents of the phrases" (Hoffman 30). Similarly, Carl Van Vechten raved that Stein "has really turned language into music, really made its sound more important than its sense" (Hoffman 34). While each of these directives instructs readers to *listen* to Stein, it is King's comparison of Stein's style to a "stubborn phonograph" that suggests what Stein might have sounded like to her contemporary readers. Indirectly, King offers an analogy for *how* to listen to Stein: not simply to the sound of the voices or to the prose's musical qualities, but to its aural-mechanical aspects. King's analogy implies that Stein's writing has phonographic qualities; but what is more, she suggests that listening to the phonograph prepares one to read Stein. Interestingly, King's analogy links Stein's writing to a mechanical glitch. Sometimes called a "broken record" or a skip, the "stubborn phonograph" refers to that all-too-common moment when the needle jumps out of the groove and the same few seconds of a record loop and repeat again and again until a person lifts the arm of the phonograph and resets the needle in the groove. It is a suspension of the forward motion of musical time. The error reveals what is mechanical about the machine and exaggerates the very thing that distinguishes phonographic sounds from other kinds of sound production: repeatability. A record repeating in this way is called broken, but language too can break when submitted to repetition – a phenomenon Stein was well aware of and put to use in a number of her works, including "Melanctha" from *Three Lives*. With characters whose repeated professions of "I love you" never quite convey the emotional heft the words imply, relationships quickly break down.[1]

This particular anecdote about an early reader's encounter with Gertrude Stein's prose is a helpful representation of the ways that, even in the early years of the phonograph, sound recording technology was shaping the ways that readers were hearing and making sense of sound, and in particular of how it was shaping the way they read. By making sounds repeatable, the phonograph ripped sound from the strictures of space and time and made sound an object. But while the trope of the broken record was adopted as a commonplace insult in the twentieth century, it actually points to a very specific aspect of the early phonographic technology's limitations. By the end of the twentieth century, recordings were no longer made on wax cylinders, or shellac discs, or even on vinyl – and yet the stubborn phonograph's aural-mechanical qualities such as the skip, the scratch, and the loop have persisted as aesthetic markers. Engineers and DJs use digital processes to add back the nostalgic sounds of recording technology from an earlier era. While Thomas Edison's invention of the phonograph certainly had major implications for how people thought about sound and its repeatability, as sound recording technologies developed over the course of the next century, so too did the responses of listeners, readers, and writers. These responses and experiments are the subject of this book.

What is the relationship between listening and literature in the era of recorded sound? How have American writers navigated the intermedial spaces between texts and recordings in order to shape our listening practices? These questions motivate my investigation of the sustained engagement between American literature and sound reproduction technologies during the noisy twentieth century and into the twenty-first. Through an analysis of texts and recordings by writers from John Dos Passos to Kevin

Young, I explore how authors across several genres extended formal techniques in response to the advent of electrical recording, ethnographic recording practices, long-play stereo albums, magnetic tape, and digital remix. I contend that the development of sound recording technology not only shaped many of the stylistic innovations that we now associate with literary modernism, but also compelled writers to theorize sound in ways that continue to inflect our listening practices. For instance, Langston Hughes's "LP Book," *Ask Your Mama: 12 Moods for Jazz* (1961), conceptualizes the spatial dimensions of stereophonic sound. Jack Kerouac experimented with an early version of the tape recorder in the 1950s while writing his novels *Visions of Cody* (1972) and *On the Road* (1957) in ways that parallel the compositional works of John Cage.

Numerous scholars have taken up *remix* – a term co-opted from DJs and sound engineers – as the defining aesthetic of twenty-first century art and literature.[2] Others have examined modernist literature's debt to the phonograph.[3] My book explores the gap between these moments, revealing that the reciprocal relationship between the literary arts and sound technologies continued to evolve over the twentieth century. Ultimately, I contend that while literary innovations were certainly shaped by phonographic technologies, writers have often led the way in imagining new uses for sound technologies, and their texts have played a key role in tutoring the ear to listen within a modern multimedia environment.

The historical scope of the book runs from the 1920s to the present, or from the first electrified recordings to the digital era, with an emphasis on mid-century modernist texts. Each of the five chapters pairs literary texts with a key development in sound recording technology. The purpose of this organization is not to make a techno-determinist argument about sound technology's influence on writing, but rather to reveal the reciprocal relationship between texts and recordings, and to acknowledge the ways writers have in fact shaped the uses of sound technology. In the field of sound studies, the tendency has been to arrange the history of sound recording in relationship to the music industry, but this approach has limited the ways that we think about sound's material and cultural contexts. As examples like the one taken from Gertrude Stein's dust jacket illustrate, the culture of readers, writers, and listeners was actively influencing how Americans recorded and listened to themselves.

More than any of Stein's other works, "Melanctha" – the story of a young African American woman from Baltimore – influenced a number of modernist writers who were inspired by Stein's ability to capture speech rhythms, including Ernest Hemingway, Nella Larsen, William Carlos Williams, and Richard Wright.[4] To be sure, Stein's attempt to represent Black characters is not without problems. However, while admirers like Wright and Larsen noted Stein's ability to represent Black voices, their reflections on Stein instead pointed to their own ability to *hear* the voices. Wright admitted that *Three Lives* helped him to "hear" English as he had never heard it before; he commented in his journals, "I heard English as Negroes spoke it," and "'Melanctha' was written in such a manner that I could actually stand outside of the English language and hear it" (qtd. in Weiss 16). What Wright refers to as "standing outside" language illustrates the paradoxical desire to have one's native language made to sound foreign, that is, for language to be dissociated from itself, and for the voice to be abstracted from language.[5] On some level, what Stein performs for Wright is a phonographic move; by divorcing sound from its speaker and the sounds of language from its sense, Stein enables a listening moment on the page that is analogous to listening to a phonograph. She makes the sensual qualities of speech and language something to be heard. In challenging readers to hear the sounds of language anew, Stein helped readers become aware of their listening as an active process.

The kinds of questions that sound recording raised about the phenomenology of sound – about its relationship to temporality, space, liveness, identity, and voice – illustrate how sound recording became a metaphor for understanding our relationship to modernity. Furthermore, many of the conceptual issues made prominent by recording technology are ones embedded in the technology of writing as well (writing being, in many ways, our earliest sound recording technology). In this sense, the phonograph and the technologies of sound reproduction that came after have continued to reinvigorate the idea of writing as a technology for experimentation. Poetry has always worked along the sonic line between literature and music, but in the twentieth century, these sonic traces were bleeding into literature across genres, including novels, autobiographies, and plays. That line between literature and music became even more blurred when writers like Gertrude Stein started making their own recordings.

During her infamous 1934–35 American tour, Gertrude Stein gave a series of lectures, promoted *Four Saints in Three Acts* (her opera with Virgil Thomson), and made several appearances on the radio. It was the first time American readers heard Stein in her own words. The tour also marked the first time that Stein enjoyed the kind of celebrity that she had felt her writing had always deserved. The recent publication of *The Autobiography of Alice B. Toklas* (1933) had given readers a more accessible glimpse of her world; the success of *Four Saints in Three Acts* on Broadway, however, put her playful approach to language in a new, performative context. As one journalist described Stein's lecture series, "To hear Miss Stein read her own work is to understand it – I speak for myself – for the first time. ... You see why she writes as she does; you see how from sentence to sentence, which seem so much alike, she introduces differences of tone, or perhaps of accent. And then when you think she has been saying the same thing four or five times, you suddenly know that she has carefully, link by link, been leading you to a new thing."[6] The combination of public appearances and lectures, the performances of her work, and radio brought Stein's sound to new ears.[7]

In addition to her radio appearances and lectures, Stein also visited the speech lab of lexicologists George W. Hibbitt and W. Cabell Greet at Columbia University in order to make recordings of her writings, including an excerpt from *The Making of Americans* and several of her "portraits." As Chris Mustazza documents, these recordings were made as part of Hibbitt and Greet's studies of American dialect and became part of the first audio archive of poetry. In 1956, they were edited and released in a popular format by Caedmon Audio – the first record label to specialize in spoken-word recordings and to promote recordings of contemporary poets (Mustazza). These recordings, now available to stream and download on PennSound, have helped Stein continue to reach the ears of students in classrooms, and have also been given new life by contemporary remix artists such as DJ Spooky (the stage name of Paul D. Miller). In DJ Spooky's 2004 remix of "If I told him, a completed portrait of Picasso," the rhythms of her repetitions are accentuated by the ways they idiosyncratically sync (and don't sync) with the samples and beats with which the original recording has been mixed. As Stein raps on the idea of what it might mean to make an "exact resemblance" of Picasso, we hear the exact resemblance of her voice on the remixed recording, bobbing and weaving with and against the DJ's beats:

> Who came first, Napoleon first.
> Presently.
> Exactly do they do.
> First exactly.
> Exactly do they do too.
> First exactly.
> And first exactly.
> Exactly do they do.

And first exactly and exactly.
And do they do
(*Portraits and Prayers* 21)

If DJ Spooky's remix does not exactly make Stein danceable, his resetting of one of her more popular portraits highlights the connections between her dexterous language and that of contemporary rappers. And of course, the remix also draws attention to the ways contemporary digital recording and remix practices resonate with the aesthetics of modernist collage and cubism. Examples like these illustrate the brilliantly recursive ways that recording technologies and American letters have continued to inform and shape one another.[8] In order to sketch how one might listen to American literature *after* the phonograph, the sections that follow offer both historical and critical contexts for the emergence of phonographic technologies as well as several early examples of cross-pollination between literature and the phonograph. By attending to the conceptual links between writing and sound recording, I detail how resonant reading practices can help readers approach the varied sounds of texts in the twentieth and twenty-first centuries.

Writing Sound

If writing has always been a technology for recording speech, its primary limitation has been its inability to reproduce speech sounds. Since at least the eighteenth century, tinkerers and inventors had attempted to create automata that could produce human speech, but the majority of these experiments focused on recreating the mechanics of the vocal apparatus.[9] However, as the science related to the physics of sound and the anatomy of the human ear developed in the nineteenth century, attitudes toward sound and its production shifted from mouth to ear. As media scholar and cultural historian Jonathan Sterne has noted, sound reproduction as we know it today was the outgrowth of a number of scientific and technological developments at the end of the nineteenth century, including new discoveries in medicine, and inventions such as the stethoscope and electric telegraph. Hermann Helmholtz's studies of the inner ear and the tympanic membrane in the 1860s, for instance, led him to treat sound as an effect, and he developed a theory of hearing based on sympathetic vibration (Sterne 66). This discovery was critical for how future inventors would conceive of sound reproduction, and as a result, the mechanics of the ear itself became a model. Deafness studies drove the work of nineteenth-century inventors like Édouard-Léon Scott de Martinville (who created the phonautograph in 1857) and later Alexander Graham Bell (the telephone in 1876), who developed machines that would "write" (i.e., visualize) speech with the goal of helping the deaf learn to speak (Kittler 74). Thomas Edison's 1877 phonograph drew upon recent innovations in telephone technology and was modeled on the sympathetic vibrations of the *tympanum membrani* or ear drum. By attaching a stylus to a small diaphragm and pulling it along a piece of wax paper (and later a piece of tinfoil) while speaking into a mouthpiece, Edison could record the vibrations produced by the voice. By pulling that same stylus through the resulting groove, the sounds could be reproduced. Both Scott's phonautograph and Edison's phonograph were inscriptive technologies, but only the phonograph could *read* the scribbles it produced.[10] Although the phonograph itself bore little physical resemblance to the human form, the ear and its tympanic function would forever be embedded inside it.

Of the many legends perpetuated by Thomas Edison about the 1877 invention of the phonograph, one of the most often repeated is that the first words the phonograph ever spoke were "Mary had a little lamb." The story has become so well known that recording historians tend to take the relationship between the phonograph and the nursery rhyme for granted, thinking little about the choice to record those particular words or their origins in an 1830 American poem by Sarah Josepha Hale. Edison may have felt the decision to recite "Mary had a little lamb" to be an unimportant one; within Edison's laboratory, the nursery rhyme had been used as the test phrase to ensure the consistency and clarity of the various tympanic diaphragms that he had been developing for the telegraph and telephone.[11] However, there is something prophetic about the choice to record Hale's poem, anchoring the phonograph's origins to American literature. In the development of tympanic diaphragms, the rhyme was spoken again and again until the phonograph could repeat the phrase with sufficient fidelity. However, speech that was recognizable as such was challenging to reproduce. Edison's assistant, Charles Batchelor, recalled that when they replayed the first test recording, "Out came 'ary ad ell am.' It was not fine talking, but the shape of it was there" (qtd. in Stross 494). As media theorist Friedrich Kittler observed, the phonograph is "a machine that records noises regardless of so-called meaning" (85). Not surprisingly, this lack of distinction meant that the early iterations of sound reproduction technologies produced sounds that were *shaped* like speech, but the words themselves were fragmented and unintelligible. Like the lamb who copies Mary's movements without knowing where she goes, the phonograph copies the voice without knowing that it speaks; the job of listeners was to learn how to hear it.

While Edison loved to claim in the 1880s that he had "perfected" the phonograph, human ears still strained to hear the machine talk – it "took practice to recognize speech," and the first phonographs were not suitable for use by the average listener (Millard 27). Even in 1889, *The Atlantic Monthly* called the so-called talking machine "a caricature upon the human voice" (Hubert). No doubt aware of the phonograph's limitations, Edison looked for ways to frame the sounds emitted by his device and the Edison Phonograph Company hosted public demonstrations or "tone tests" that helped new listeners hear the phonograph's voice, as seen in Figure 0.1. Here again, the choice of "Mary had a little lamb" (and other familiar phrases and songs) in these performances was not arbitrary. The cadence of the nursery rhyme along with its cultural ubiquity meant that audiences would be able to hear and understand the words transmitted by the phonograph if only because they had heard the words before.

For those who have written the histories of sound recording, perhaps the most confounding aspect is that the name "phonograph" does not conform to teleological expectations about the development of the technology as a machine for musical enjoyment. An etymological study of the term phonograph usually brings one to its Greek roots: *phonē* (sound, voice) and *graphē* (writing). The term phonograph is often dubbed a misnomer by music historians who resist the notion that the machine *writes* sound – but writing has, and continues to be, interrelated with sound technology and its development.[12] As it so happened, the word *phonograph* was not new; it had existed as a verb since at least 1837, not as some obscure passing concept, but as a popular form of shorthand stenography. To phonograph meant to write down speech phonetically – specifically using Benjamin Pitman's method of shorthand, which was the most popular form of shorthand during the nineteenth century.[13] Because English has "sounds that the Latin tongue never possessed," Pitman felt that the Roman alphabet was a limited way to capture English speech and anticipated that his phonography would expand the expressive possibilities for writing (Pitman 11). Edison himself had picked up a copy of Pitman's *Manual of Phonography* while working as a young telegrapher during the Civil War (Gitelman, *Scripts* 62). Phonetic (or "verbatim") stenography had started to become standard practice in courtrooms and congressional proceedings in the 1860s and was popular among newspaper reporters as well (44–49).

Edison himself helped to perpetuate the view of the phonograph as a reading and writing machine, and early encounters with the technology

Figure 0.1 "The Edison Concert Phonograph: Have You Heard It?," c. 1899

stressed these functions. In the first article to announce the invention to the public (the December 22, 1877, issue of *Scientific American*), the writers described the machine in terms of its abilities both to write and to "read":

> Now there is no doubt that by practice, and the aid of a magnifier, it would be possible to read phonetically Mr. Edison's record of dots and dashes, but he saves us that trouble by literally making it read itself. The distinction is

> the same as if, instead of perusing a book ourselves, we drop it into
> a machine, set the latter in motion, and behold! the voice of the author is
> heard repeating his own composition. (384)

From the tone of the article, one might assume that the phonograph encroached on the terrain of readers and writers. While that threat never came to fruition, the possible uses of the phonograph as a writing and reading machine continued to occupy Edison. In an article Edison penned in *The North American Review* in 1888 announcing his "perfected" phonograph, he stressed the dictation function of the device and spoke of the storage capacity of the new wax cylinders in terms of word count: "Each wax blank will receive from 800 to 1,000 words; and of course several blanks may be used for one document, if needed" (648). Even as late as 1934, Theodor Adorno described the phonograph's curves as "a delicately scribbled, utterly illegible writing" ("Form of the Phonograph" 56). Recorded music, we find, was just one among many imagined uses for the phonograph (including talking clocks and dolls that could speak). If writers of the period felt that this technology was made for them, it was a result of Edison's own marketing schemes.

In the context of late nineteenth-century American literature, the invention of sound recording technology coincided with a growing interest in capturing the sounds of speech and regional dialect on the page – or one might say, there was an interest in writing phonographically. As I elaborate in my second chapter, early ethnographers, especially those interested in preserving Native American languages and regional American folklore, were some of the first to make use of phonographic technology. Authors of regionalist fiction like Mark Twain, Joel Chandler Harris, and Charles Chesnutt were known for their elaborate use of dialect writing – intentional misspellings (usually phonetic representations), grammatical mistakes, and vernacular language – as one of the key strategies to represent how people from different regions actually spoke. Twain considered his representation of dialect as constitutive to character development (rather than merely decorative) in novels such as *Adventures of Huckleberry Finn* (1884). As he remarks in his explanatory note, *Huckleberry Finn* contains several variations of Pike County dialect, and "the shadings have not been done in a haphazard fashion, or by guesswork; but painstakingly, and with the trustworthy guidance and support of personal familiarity with these several forms of speech." For Twain, who was perhaps just as well known for his oratory as for his published works, the sounds of speech were central to his style as well as his celebrity.

Intrigued by the possibilities of Edison's phonograph as a tool for writing, Twain sent a telegram to Edison in May of 1888 to request a meeting and to inquire about getting a phonograph of his own to write his next novel.[14] Despite scheduling conflicts, the two would go on to meet at Edison's laboratory in June. According to Edison, Twain made a number of recordings during his visit (which were later lost in a 1914 fire). Although Twain was not able to get a phonograph that summer, in 1891 he rented two machines in order to dictate parts of his novel, *The American Claimant* (1892). In letters to William Dean Howells from April 1891, Twain remarked that he "filled four dozen cylinders in two sittings"; however, he "then found I could have said about as much with the pen and said it a deal better. Then I resigned." The phonograph was useful to Twain while dealing with rheumatoid arthritis that kept him from his pen, but he was not yet convinced of the machine's literary value "because it hasn't any ideas and it hasn't any gift for elaboration, or smartness of talk, or vigor of action, or felicity of expression, but is just matter-of-fact, compressive, unornamental, and as grave and unsmiling as the devil" ("Edison and Mark Twain"). In other words, the so-called talking machine was not nearly as witty or charming as Twain himself. Or maybe this was simply an early instance of someone not liking the sound of their own recorded voice. Twain's critique sounds suspiciously similar to Socrates's lament that writing, like a painting, cannot respond when addressed; but Twain's misgivings about the "unsmiling" phonograph may have had as much to do with its *sound* as with its abilities as a writing machine. Edison declared the phonograph "perfected" in 1888, but the sounds it produced still lacked lifelike fidelity.

Although the phonograph did not prove to be the writing tool Twain hoped it might be, encounters with the phonograph soon found their way into literary settings.[15] One of the first instances in which the phonograph appeared in literature concerned the role of a phonograph in a courtroom – an unsurprising choice given the phonograph's early associations with stenography. In George William Hill's 1883 play *The Phonograph Witness: A Drama in Five Acts*, which is a parlor drama set in the "future" of the early twentieth century, the phonograph is made to serve as a key witness in a murder trial in a dramatic courtroom scene. More famously, many of the chapters in Bram Stoker's *Dracula* (1897) are written as-told-to a phonograph, which Dr. Seward uses to record his diary and field notes.[16] Victorian interests in using the phonograph to preserve the voices of the dead made Count Dracula (as a member of the un-dead) the perfect phonographic subject. Interest in phonetics, diction, and the desire to eradicate linguistic differences was also an abiding interest of the British playwright George Bernard Shaw and became the theme of his popular play *Pygmalion* (1913), which employed phonographic technology to train Eliza Doolittle to speak like a lady.

Joel Chandler Harris, who was best known for his Uncle Remus stories, was also interested in the implications of the phonograph for literature. Well aware of the ways in which his own Uncle Remus stories were already phonographic, Harris wrote a short story titled "A Queer Experience with the Phonograph" for his 1892 sequel, *Uncle Remus and His Friends: Old Plantation Stories, Songs, and Ballads.* In this story, an emancipated Uncle Remus is still working for Miss Sally, who decides to play a prank on him using the family's new phonograph. First, she invites Uncle Remus to listen to the "comic solos, some pieces by a military band, a banjo solo, the chimes of Trinity Church" via the listening tubes (292). While Miss Sally tries to explain that the sounds come from the wax cylinders, Uncle Remus insists that it's a trick: "Uh-uh, Miss Sally! Dey may fool you but I done been yer too long fer dat; dey can't fool me. De t'er een' er deze yer pipes ain't so mighty fer fum de circus" (295–96). However, the real prank comes when Aunt Sally plays a cylinder on which she has recorded her own vocal imitations of their cook telling scandalous stories about Uncle Remus. Sally's imitations are all too convincing for Remus, who proceeds to pick a fight with the cook. Reading Harris's representations of Black voices today, it is hard not to cringe at the racism inherent in these exaggerated parodies of the voice. But beyond the joke made at Remus's expense, readers and listeners of the time might have recognized the larger joke Harris was making as he performs his own feat of phonographing the voices of Uncle Remus and his friends on the page. The joke is not so much that Uncle Remus is fooled into believing that the voice he hears is that of the cook, but the fact that he can recognize a voice *at all.* The phonograph's low fidelity obscures the inevitable flaws of Miss Sally's own vocal caricature; it does not hide those of Harris. As I will discuss in more detail in Chapter 1, some of the most popular early phonograph recordings trafficked in a similar brand of humor – adapting then-popular minstrel show comedy routines to the recorded medium along with vaudeville jokes that parodied the accents of Irish, Italian, and Jewish immigrants. Mishearings and misunderstandings were treated as comedic fodder by record companies seeking to draw attention to the marketable new medium.

But just as the phonograph quickly became a subject of fiction, fiction was also an important tool for teaching marketing strategies to phonograph salesmen. In early issues of *Talking Machine World*, a trade magazine for phonograph sellers that ran from 1905 to 1928, short fictional stories featuring phonographs were included among sales reports and other relevant information. For example, in the February 1906 issue, a story by Howard Taylor, titled "The Girl He Left behind Him – A Tale of the Philippine War," tells of the failed communications of two young lovers: "The young man in the uniform of a General sits in his tent talking into a phonograph. His face bears the marks of toil and conflict, and his voice muffled inside the recording horn sounds strained and harsh" (54). Although the war interrupted these "letters," they eventually make it back home to his beloved, who raptures over hearing his voice. Other issues featured a recurring series about a young college graduate named Jones who starts a talking machine business (e.g., "He Did Something" [April 1906] and "How Jones Made Good" [May 1906]). In one edition, Jones gains loyal customers in "empty sleeve" Civil War vets by having a young woman make the veterans a complimentary recording of a favorite Civil War song. In each of these stories, fiction becomes a way to imagine potential uses for the phonograph that salesmen can use in their pitches.

In these early encounters between literature and the phonograph, one finds a shifting cultural landscape – one in which inventors, business people, and writers alike were responding to larger trends such as phonetic stenography, linguistic ethnography, and dialect writing. Writers like Twain and Harris participated in the late nineteenth-century imaginary of recorded sound, but in each of these literary examples, one detects a degree of skepticism about the future of the phonograph as a writing machine. Twain finds the phonograph cannot compete with his pen, and Harris skewers the phonograph's fidelity to voices. Writers in the twentieth century, however, tended to be less inhibited by the inscriptive qualities of the "talking machine" as a writing machine. As music became the primary use of recording technology around the turn of the century, and with improvements in recording fidelity, writers began to see the phonograph more broadly as a *sound* recording machine. Authors of modernist fiction like John Dos Passos, whom I discuss in Chapter 1, used their writing to redefine what it means to be phonographic, theorizing how our ears process sonic input and rethinking the ways writing records not just speech, but sound more broadly. During the latter half of the twentieth century, writers and other sound artists, including William S. Burroughs, began to deploy sound technologies like the tape recorder as a means to produce and imagine entirely new sounds.

Studies in Sound

Literature has been theorizing sound and its reproduction since the turn of the twentieth century, but as a field, sound studies has only recently established itself as a coherent scholarly domain. Just ten years ago, there were very few studies devoted to sound and the technologies of its repro-duction beyond those written by music historians.[17] The excellent early studies of the phonograph by media scholars such as Lisa Gitelman, Friedrich Kittler, and Jonathan Sterne helped pave the way for new approaches to studying sound.[18] But the terrain is much different today and a dynamic body of interdisciplinary scholarship has emerged.[19] The confluence of literary modernism and media studies has drawn needed attention to technologies like the gramophone and the radio.[20] But the benefits of this mode of inquiry have been especially fruitful in a field like American studies, where sound and listening have ushered in new ways to access areas of critical study such as race and gender, subjectivity, citizen-ship, geography, and the public sphere.[21] Some of the most robust work to analyze the sonorities of text has emerged from the intersections of African American studies and sound studies.[22] Books like Jennifer Lynn Stoever's *The Sonic Color Line: Race and the Cultural Politics of Listening* (2016) and Alexander Weheliye's *Phonographies: Grooves in Sonic Afro-Modernity* (2005), for example, have offered brilliant elucidations of how race informs the ways we process and understand sound. My own work is indebted to theorists like Stoever and Weheliye, and as the strong presence of African American writers and musicians in this book indicates, any thorough discussion of sound technology's relation to American literature requires a consideration of the ways these technologies mediate issues of race. This book aims to contextualize these conversations within a broader discussion of twentieth- and twenty-first-century American literature, emphasizing the technology of sound recording as a mediator for many nodes of identity and geography.

In a larger sense, *Sound Recording Technology and American Literature, from the Phonograph to the Remix* offers a way to view the twentieth century as a coherent literary period. Scholars currently tend to use 1945 as a dividing line, identifying texts of the interwar period as "modernist" and postwar texts as more closely linked to our contemporary moment. I connect these periods by giving greater attention to mid-century modernist literature (of the 1950s and 1960s) and by privileging sound recording technology as a phenomenon not only central to the work of the specific authors featured in this book but to reading and writing across the century. Twentieth-century American literature is composed of many text-recording hybrids that must be heard as well as read. An understanding of this literature, therefore, requires an expanded sensorium attuned to the experiences of living in a continually modernizing world. The most important intervention that this book makes is to insist that twentieth-century American literature often theorizes listening, offering its readers new ways to hear. In the chapters that follow, I read texts for their resonance because they either imaginatively evoke or consciously pursue a sonic aesthetic that continues to reverberate in our own noisy multimedia present.

Resonant Reading

There have been a number of terms developed to account for the kind of analytical listening that I am interested in. Terms like deep listening (Pauline Oliveros), musical listening (Jean-Luc Nancy), literary listening (Craig Dworkin), and close listening (Charles Bernstein) appear across a range of fields.[23] But attempts to append adjectives to *listening* often fall short because most definitions of listening suggest that it is already an analytical practice. Roland Barthes (with Roland Havas), for example, suggested that "*hearing* is a physiological phenomenon; *listening* is a psychological act" ("Listening" 245). Not unlike the activity of reading, listening can make "what was confused and undifferentiated become distinct and pertinent," according to Barthes (248). And, in at least one regard, listening itself can signify as it creates an "inter-subjective space" – or "an interlocution in which the listener's silence will be as active as the locutor's speech" (252). When listening becomes active, empathetic, and reciprocal in this way, "*listening speaks*" (254). Although Barthes's model of listening is most interested in speech (rather than sound more broadly), his sketches of listening allude to the ways that *all* listening – whether to real sounds or to seemingly silent texts – is a contingent activity.

One attempt to return listening to literacy comes from the poet and critic Charles Bernstein. Closely aligned with the Language poets of the late twentieth century, and a co-founder of PennSound (the online repository of poetry recordings hosted by the University of Pennsylvania), Bernstein has brought critical attention to poetry's performed contexts. In his edited collection *Close Listening: Poetry and the Performed Word* (1998), Bernstein frames close listening as a way to approach poetry that treats "sound as material where sound is neither arbitrary nor secondary but constitutive" (4). This can mean poetry in performance but also poetry that is recorded or performed visually on the page. Whereas much has been made of the *voice* of the poet and of his or her breath in twentieth-century poetry[24] – here I am thinking of Charles Olson in particular – Bernstein attempts to complicate that relationship, marking a critical distinction between orality and aurality:

> By *aurality* I mean to emphasize the sounding of the *writing*, and to make a sharp contrast with *orality* and its emphasis on breath, voice, and speech – an emphasis that tends to valorize speech over writing, voice over sound, listening over hearing, and indeed, orality over aurality. *Aurality* precedes *orality*, just as language precedes speech. Aurality is connected to the body – what the mouth and tongue and vocal chords enact – not the presence of the poet. (13)

The term that Bernstein assigns to this attitude is *a/orality*. The slash both divides and bridges the space between aurality and orality, between the sounded (or heard) and the spoken. In returning "speech back to sound," Bernstein paradoxically suggests that the interpretive possibilities for poetry are greatest when we "stop listening and begin to hear" (18, 22). That is to say, he wants to allow for the sensuality of language to enter back into the equation. Bernstein's a/orality offers a useful point of departure but stops short of defining a methodology for attending to the sonic features of literature across genres, or to the literary features of sound in the phonographic era.

To address this space between reading and listening, I have chosen the term *resonant reading*, rather than close listening, as a way to describe my methodology and recenter reading as a sonic activity.[25] The practice of resonant reading is not a challenge to or critique of close reading, nor is it a shift away from listening itself. By invoking this term, I am not interested in wading into the murky postcritical debates surrounding the disciplinary practice of reading. I will not attempt to reinstantiate surface reading (*a la* Best and Marcus), postcritical reading (Felski), reparative reading (Sedgwick), distant reading (Moretti), or any of the other attempts to redefine the kinds of "reading" literary scholars do. Rather, what I am proposing is a kind of *extended technique* for reading – one in which we blend the strategies of actual listening (whether to speech, to music, or to our acoustic environment) with an ear-oriented approach to reading texts. As in music, extended technique is required when a composer (or writer) experiments with form in such a way that the instrument (our reading eye and listening ear) must be used in a nontraditional way.[26] In this sense, the extended technique of resonant reading requires us as readers to become a bit more like musicians and make "ear training" a part of our practice.[27]

More simply, it is a practice explicitly invoked to deal with literature in the era of sound recording technology.

But what does it mean to call reading practices *resonant*? What is resonance? The *OED* describes resonance as "the reinforcement or prolongation of sound by reflection or by the synchronous vibration of a surrounding space or a neighbouring object." This definition has to do with the nature of sound itself and how it is amplified. Sounds require a medium through which to travel; sounds resonate *in* something or *with* something. In the context of reading, we might think about resonance as requiring synchronous vibration by re-sounding the text. We might also think about the ways text itself creates its own reverberations through repetition or reflected themes. But of course, resonance also has its figurative meaning, such as when we say, "That resonates with me." We find this sense of the term in the second definition: "corresponding or sympathetic response; an instance of this. In later use also: the power or quality of evoking or suggesting images, memories, and emotions; an allusion, connotation, or overtone." This definition of resonance seems somewhat obviously constitutive of the practice of reading, and I find resonance to be a helpful term for imagining how we navigate between sound and text precisely because of its multiple meanings. We can treat resonance as the vibratory possibilities of sound, but we can also view resonance as that intersubjective space between sound and listener, between text and reader.

Among theoretical explorations of sound, listening, and resonance, few have so intently considered the textual qualities of auditory attention as philosopher Jean-Luc Nancy. "To hear a siren, a bird, or a drum is already each time to understand at least the rough outline of a situation, a context if not a text," Nancy explains in his 2007 essay *Listening* (published in French as *À L'écoute*) (6).[28] Like Barthes, Nancy distinguishes between hearing and listening, but for him there is a productive space between these different registers of auditory experience. By reconfiguring sound not as an object or as a symbol but as a sense, Nancy suggests that "to listen is to be straining toward a possible meaning, and consequently one that is not immediately accessible" (6). For Nancy, listening refuses to reside merely in the subject listening or the sonorous object. That in-between quality of hearing and listening is a product of resonance. Playing upon the recursive qualities of all listening and the sympathetic vibrations that the human ear produces in order to transduce sound, Nancy describes resonance by suggesting that all sound "re-emits itself while still actually 'sounding'" (8). These "acoustic otoemissions," as Nancy describes them, are what I regard as the aspects of the ear that are already phonographic (16). We are always listening to our listening, and our listening itself has its own sonorous qualities. There are returns and repetitions implicit in sound and in our attitudes toward listening, as Nancy explains: "All sonorous presence is thus made of a complex of returns [*renvois*] whose binding is the resonance or 'sonance' of sound, an expression that one should hear – hear and listen to – as much from the side of sound itself, or of its emission, as from the side of its reception or its listening: it is precisely from one to the other that it 'sounds'"(16). This edgy, liminal space between sound and listener seems especially pronounced when dealing with textual sound and when reading between recordings and texts. Such an act of reading invites the imagination of sound and the position of listening, even when the sounds themselves are silent. To read is, to some degree, to re-sound.

When listening between texts and recordings, this striving toward resonance as a recursive path becomes even more pronounced. We might even call it *elliptical*, a concept that I discuss in Chapters 2 and 3. As a form of punctuation that expresses what is *not* there – a pause, a break, or even a silence – the ellipsis is one of the ways that writers attempt to account for and overcome the mediated difference and create a space for listening in the text. Because texts do not emit their own vibratory sounds, they call upon readers to re-sound them. This resonance can be internal and imagined, or it can be performative. We can describe resonance in terms of sounds of language there on the page, or of the sounds evoked through description, or through reference. But however one defines resonant reading, it puts demands upon the reader to perform the literary listening.

Across both sound studies and literary studies, the term resonance has become central to defining the broader 'listener function' – a term coined by Veit Erlmann.[29] By tracing the listener function in the history of modern aurality in his book, *Reason and Resonance: A History of Modern Aurality* (2014), Erlmann, an ethnomusicologist, treats listening and listeners as culturally constructed and historically bounded. Erlmann's articulation of the listener function is partly a response to the ways that the humanities have blurred the line between resonance's metaphorical meanings and its acoustic roots. As Erlmann notes in his entry on "Resonance" in *Keywords in Sound*, scholars in the humanities have taken up resonance as "part of the rich metaphorology that seeks to replace the binaries of structuralist thought with a notion of discourse that is diametrically opposed to a distancing and objectifying form of knowledge" (177). In her 1997 essay, "A Theory of Resonance," Wai Chee Dimock explicitly co-opts the sonic phenomena of resonance as an analogy for an approach to textual historicism that is overtly diachronic. More recently, scholars who work at the intersection of literature and sound studies have taken up resonance as a way of reading in the acoustic space. Emily Lordi's *Black Resonance* explores the reciprocal relationship between singers like Billie Holiday and Bessie Smith and writers such as James Baldwin and Richard Wright, pointing to the ways that writers have *performed* their listening for us. "What they hear and what they miss" are her subject matter, and so instead of studying influence, she searches for *resonance* (5). "Resonance," she writes, "connotes reverberation, echo, the sounding again that 're-sound' implies. It names a 'sympathetic response' or vibration between things, an elusive relationship that averts narratives of cause-and-effect but may be more diffuse and wide ranging for that" (Lordi 6). Like Lordi, I am drawn to the sympathetic and relational possibilities of resonance, but resonance can take on different valences, as Julie Beth Napolin has noted in her exploration of the "sinister resonance" of Marlow's voice in Conrad's *Heart of Darkness*, for example.[30] In articulating vibration as a modernist literary aesthetic, Napolin argues that the text brings "attention to the deep materialism of the world, a reality not of void but of sonorous, vibrating relationality" (73). In Napolin's *The Fact of Resonance*, she offers a compelling narrative theory that recenters sound and the relational ethics of who speaks and who hears when reading (5).

Listening and resonance, as framed by some scholars, not only promise new pathways into the critical analysis of sound, music, and the voice, but even seem to promise new ways of empathizing with one another. Sympathetic vibrations become a metaphor for a persistent utopian vision of listening. (Josh Kun's term *audiotopia* makes this connection explicit.) But of course, with listening, as with the other senses, our ears are prone to mislead us; we misunderstand and misinterpret sonic information and hear voices or sounds that are not there. Listening poorly can lead to the misappropriation of sounds and the erasure of rich cultural and historical contexts. Case in point: jazz in the recorded era brought the sound of African American voices into the homes of white Americans, but it also made it easier to appropriate and exploit African American sounds without acknowledging their multilayered origins. Listening has its affordances as well as its limits, but it nevertheless remains an underexplored mode of critical inquiry that contains exciting possibilities for approaching actual sonic materials, as well as for treating expression that aspires toward sound. Resonant reading in particular becomes a way to reinvigorate the ear in textual analysis.

My own conceptualization of resonant reading leaves open these larger senses of resonance in both its sounded and metaphorical contexts. But in terms of praxis, I am mobilizing resonant reading in order to return it to sound and more specifically to its re-sonant roots. As a heterogeneous field of literary texts, different kinds of reading will be required of the works discussed in this book in order to hear them. The friction between writing and recording opened sites of experimentation and new ways of thinking about the role of writing, literature, and the self. This book offers a resonant reading of twentieth-century American literature that amplifies the ways writers attended to the *techne* of sound as an avenue for rearticulating a modern relationship to history, to the voice, to nation, and to noise.

***

Across my book, I use resonant reading to trace three larger thematic strains that one finds in nearly all the literary works I explore: *writing the voice* (or dialect and the limits of re-sounding speech), *recording versus the record* (or sound and historical time), and *intermediality* (or text-recording hybrids). To the extent that resonant reading is a concept that carries a postphonographic sense, these three thematic areas reinforce the idea that American literature came to take on different emphases in the era following the rise of the recorded sound.

If writers of the late nineteenth century like Mark Twain and Joel Chandler Harris were interested in *writing the voice*, as I have shown, their dialect writing was not without its problems. Any attempt to capture accented speech on the page, especially phonetically, invites the reader to imagine, if not sound out, a character's accented speech. The problems here may be obvious given the inevitable limits of any given reader's ability to do so. On the page, read silently, there is perhaps the possibility that one might richly imagine a character's voice – an articulation of difference but not deficiency. However, unlike a phonographic recording, a reader's reproduction must be imperfect and incomplete by definition. Any attempt to re-sound speech (whether imagined or aloud) harbors the potential for a parodic (or worse, minstrel) performance, depending on the identities of the reader and character. The ethical problems of reading dialect writing become especially stark in the classroom, as countless teachers can ruefully attest, when it comes to reading aloud the works of authors like Twain. At best, dialect writing is a record of the writer's own attempts to listen to the contours of the speaking voice, but the reproduction of that voice left to the imagination of the reader leaves room for error and misappropriation.

The question of how to represent vernacular speech in literature – to acknowledge linguistic difference while avoiding parody – is a question that ethnographers and novelists alike confronted in the twentieth century with the phonograph in mind. John Dos Passos, for example, drastically scaled back his phonetic approach to writing the vernacular voices of his characters in his *U.S.A.* trilogy (1930–36). Writers like Zora Neale Hurston, Alan Lomax, and Sidney Bechet (and his editorial collaborators) developed a more flexible approach to transcription shaped by the theories of Hurston and Sterling Brown, which reflected an emphasis on idiom rather than phonetic misspellings. Jack Kerouac, too, struggled with what it really meant to capture a voice on the page as he debated whether word-for-word transcriptions of tape recordings truly represented his mad conversations with Neal Cassady. Even Langston Hughes's poetry of the 1960s came to rely less on writing the sounds of Black vernacular speech. As the fidelity of sound recording technologies improved during the first half of the twentieth century, so too did the fidelity of voices recorded in print. What is more, writers began to ponder what it meant to record sound (and not merely the voice) in their literature.

Thematically, writing voices is but one strand of how writers were imagining the function of sound in their texts, and frequently the presence of sound and recording technology in these literary works coincides with a reconsideration of the temporal register of history. Many of the texts in this study blur the line between *recording* and *the record*. One thinks of Jelly Roll Morton arriving at the Library of Congress to "set the record straight" about the history of jazz – and then literally making recordings on a Presto disc recorder with Alan Lomax. This philosophical-acoustical glitch that allows for the elision of sound recording and the historical record has something to do with the ways that mimetic technologies like the phonograph take sonic events out of time and space and make them repeatable. This capacity of phonographic technology renders sound not time*less* but time*ful* – as is the case when a recorded sound comes to stand in as a record of the times. It is no coincidence that John Dos Passos calls his multimodal, media-saturated *U.S.A.* trilogy a "chronicle." Likewise, the adoption of ethnographic recording and transcription practices by Alan Lomax to write an auto/biography of Jelly Roll Morton demonstrates an emphasis on the transparent, archival imagination of sound recording technology. If writers earlier in the twentieth century treated media technologies like the phonograph as potentially transparent and documentary in nature, writers at mid-century and after, confronted by tape, stereo, and studio engineering, were increasingly self-aware of recording's malleability. Jack Kerouac and William S. Burroughs came to distrust the transparency of tape. Langston Hughes and Amiri Baraka imagined stereophonic futures. And remixers have assumed temporal disjuncture and imaginative sonic spaces as de rigueur; hence the asynchronous narrative of Chuck Palahniuk's *Invisible Monster's Remix* (2012). To the extent that my own resonant readings attempt to re-sound the historical contexts of these works of literature and their media, I do so while acknowledging the limits of pure chronology. Given the tendency of sound recording technology to unsettle temporally bounded thinking, my own work aims at readings that are recursively resonant. We have to play the 1960s back against the 1920s and 1930s when reading Alan Lomax or Langston Hughes; the 1930s against the 1900s when considering John Dos Passos; the 2010s against the 1980s and 1990s with Chuck Palahniuk and Kevin Young. My resonant readings will necessarily reverberate across these chronologies.

A subordinate, but no less important, thread of analysis considers the hybridity of print texts and recordings, and the instability occasioned by *intermediality*. Resonant reading as a methodology is intermedial in the sense that it is conceived as a way to read and listen between the mediums of writing and recording. This practice manifests itself in a few different ways. First, I take this as a way to encounter texts that aspire toward the recorded medium, like parts of Dos Passos's *U.S.A.* and Langston Hughes's *Ask Your Mama*, or like the remixed books of Kevin Young and Chuck Palahniuk. Intermediality is also critical for engaging works that explicitly use recording technology *as a writing technology* (e.g., the works of Lomax, Bechet, Kerouac, Burroughs), and it is a way of "reading" recordings as literature (e.g., Baraka). Rather than understanding literature as a genre of the written word in isolation, these authors understood the written word and the recorded voice to be inextricably linked. We cannot, in other words, understand these texts without appreciating this reciprocal relationship.

Keeping in mind this intermedial relationship between writing and recording is especially important when we consider the history of sound recording technology. The ability to hear one's own voice outside one's body is a relatively recent achievement in human history. Even so, listening to my voice played back on my phone's digital recorder is an entirely different experience than listening to it played back on a tape recorder (or on a wax cylinder, for that matter). And yet, we often treat the advent of recorded sound as a single apocryphal event, generally signified by the appearance of the phonograph. What I am proposing is that we also remain attentive both to how sound recording devices changed over time and to how writers in turn did not merely react, but actively shaped the ways we listen.

On the Lower Frequencies

The prologue to Ralph Ellison's 1952 novel *Invisible Man* has become a regularly anthologized example of a text that incorporates phonographic sound and listening. References to phonographs and popular recordings percolate throughout twentieth-century literature, but in Ellison's prologue, the phonograph and a recording of Louis Armstrong are the central figures through which Ellison endeavors to introduce his concept of invisibility and the complex relationship between race and history. Speaking to the reader from the confines of his basement "hole," Ellison's nameless narrator – a self-proclaimed "thinker-tinker" who compares himself to Thomas Edison – uses sound technology beneath the glow of 1,369 electric light bulbs to plot his eventual reemergence into a world that refuses to see him. While putting a record on his radio-phonograph, the narrator enters a scene of imaginative listening:

> There is a certain acoustical deadness in my hole, and when I have music I want to *feel* its vibration, not only with my ear but with my whole body. I'd like to hear five recordings of Louis Armstrong playing and singing "What Did I Do to Be so Black and Blue" – all at the same time. (8)

The scene has become a touchstone for discussions about literature and sound because it so elegantly depicts the distinctly modern sensation of listening not just to music, but to a recording of music. For what is the voice of the phonograph but the voice of an invisible man?

Evan Eisenberg, author of *The Recording Angel*, has suggested that Louis Armstrong had in fact become synonymous with the phonograph. Recording made it possible for anyone to imitate his gravelly voice, and "any critic could recognize in him the voice of the phonograph, the voice of invisible man" (121). As both Robert O'Meally and Alexander Weheliye have pointed out, the scene is one in which the narrator is probing for a sense of identity in light of his invisibility and locates a potential identity in sound when the visual fails.[31] Armstrong becomes an important figure by whom Ellison introduces the concept of invisibility, and in this example, Ellison suggests the visual element of invisibility (i.e., the metaphoric invisibility of blackness) as well as the sonic – what Jennifer Stoever calls the *sonic color line*.[32] As a recorded sound, Armstrong is invisible in the literal sense: he has no bodily presence and exists only as a technologically reproduced vibration or a disembodied voice. He is a sound taken in through the ear and felt through the body. While listening to Armstrong, the narrator imagines hearing "unheard sounds" and traversing space and time, leading some scholars to suggest that the scene is a parody of the act of listening.[33] Yet Ellison's text here must be understood as a serious investigation into the possibilities of listening. The narrator thus continues:

> Invisibility, let me explain, gives one a slightly different sense of time, you're never quite on the beat. Sometimes you're ahead and sometimes behind. Instead of the swift and imperceptible flowing of time you are aware of its nodes, those points where time stands still or from which it leaps ahead. And you slip into the breaks and look around. That's what you hear vaguely in Louis' music. (8)

Descending, like Dante, into the depths of the music, the narrator begins to describe "hearing not only in time, but in space as well" – he hears the sounds of spirituals, of a Black preacher, and even talks to a former slave (8–9). The narrator's description reframes Black history through the syncopated rhythms of the music; but this scene of travel across time and space is *also* a description of what the invention of the phonograph did to sound. By taking sounds that were once ephemeral and making them repeatable, recording changed the relationship between sound and time by making it possible to fast-forward and leap back, and to play sounds at different speeds and pause them at will.[34]

One of the things we often overlook when reading this scene is that, although Ellison was writing at a mid-century moment when high-fidelity and stereo technologies were in their nascent stages, the scene in which the narrator imagines listening to Louis Armstrong's 1929 recording of "What Did I Do to Be so Black and Blue" hearkens back to an older technology and an early encounter with a popular jazz record. Although portraying a historical moment when phonographic sound was just recently electrically amplified, the allusion to the five radio-phonographs implies the spatial dimension that high-fidelity and stereo would bring. Sound technology was incredibly important to Ellison, who self-identified as an audiophile. As he recalls in "Living with Music," an 1955 essay for *High Fidelity* magazine, he was "obsessed with the idea of reproducing sound with such fidelity that even when using music as a defense behind which I could write, it would reach the unconscious levels of the mind with the least distortion" (11).[35] Ellison was always at the forefront of technological advances in sound; in later years, when tape recording technology became available, Ellison would use it to dictate and then listen back to his writing in order to perfect its rhythms.[36] For Ellison, writing and sound reproduction technologies were intertwined. *Invisible Man* illustrates a strain in American modernism that reveals the extraordinary importance of listening and sound recording technology for how we mediate issues of American cultural identity and for how we detect resonant frequencies amid difference.

Ellison's prologue is a helpful example for conceptualizing resonant reading because it encapsulates many of the ideas and themes that one encounters when examining the broader relationship between literature and sound reproduction technologies: a heightened approach to listening, the paradox that sound is both disembodied and felt within the body, and the ability of the machine to evoke voices of the past while allowing the listener to traverse time and alter its tempo. However, the question remains: *what* are we supposed to hear when we read this passage? Are we meant to hear what the invisible man hears? Are we supposed to play Louis Armstrong's record? Are we meant to allow our bodies to resonate in the absent space of his? Is that even possible? Or are we merely supposed to try to *hear* his voice and imagine its cadences? When I teach this text, I try to find ways to incorporate all of these elements – through reading aloud, playing recordings, and encouraging students to listen for echoes of the prologue elsewhere in the novel. But even for the narrator, this is a scene of imaginative listening. I like to think of Ellison's narrator as a stand-in for the resonant reader who would listen to texts because, inevitably, the reader can imagine more sounds than the ear can hear.

Tracks

The invention of the phonograph raised philosophical and acoustical questions for writers at the turn of the twentieth century. What role were writers to play in recording the voice when the phonograph could both record *and* reproduce it at any time and any place? What other kinds of sounds could texts reproduce? Over the course of five chapters, I investigate how writers variously responded to developments in sound recording technology and advanced new frameworks for listening. Writers were clearly fascinated by the novelty of phonographic sounds, but few captured the ways that phonography changed the relationship between listening and literature. Perhaps no writer was more attuned to the shape-shifting nature of sound recording technology than John Dos Passos, whose attraction to modern mass media inflected his early theatrical writing and shaped the form of his multimodal novel trilogy *U.S.A.* (1930, 1934, 1936). By the mid-1920s, where my first chapter begins, the phonograph was no longer new and was, in fact, threatened with obsolescence by the emergence of the radio. Nearly fifty years had passed since Edison had etched his voice into tinfoil, and the proliferation of cheap Victrolas and gramophones had transformed recording technology into the literal furniture of everyday American life. And yet, at the same moment that radio began to encroach on the consumer market for phonographs, rapid changes were taking place in sound reproduction – including the introduction of the condenser microphone and electrical recording – that were reshaping the ways people would hear recorded sound. As I show, Dos Passos's innovation was to make use of readers' ears as highly tuned instruments for listening. But today these novels require a recuperative act of resonant reading to resurface the sonic logic of Dos Passos's noisy prose.

Since the early years of the phonograph's invention, writers imagined dictating their stories to the recording device. However, some of the earliest practitioners to use recording for transcription purposes were ethnographers (rather than novelists), and the first self-proclaimed "recorded book" was an as-told-to autobiography written by folklorist Alan Lomax from his recorded interviews with jazz musician Jelly Roll Morton. Given the increasingly important role that music, especially jazz, played in the American literary soundscape, my second chapter explores two instances of jazz autobiography: Alan Lomax's *Mister Jelly Roll: The Fortunes of Jelly Roll Morton, New Orleans Creole and "Inventor of Jazz"* (1950) and Sidney Bechet's *Treat It Gentle* (1960). I investigate the Library of Congress recordings of Jelly Roll Morton and Sidney Bechet's archives at Tulane University and the Bibliothèque Nationale de France to raise questions about what it means to write a "recorded book." Through my analysis, I also reveal the critical intervention of Zora Neale Hurston in shaping the practices of transcription so that the voices represented on the page adhere to the "laws of sound." Although the texts incorporate transcriptions of recorded interviews, these books are not oral histories in a strict sense, but rather *aural* histories that require readers to think critically about the sonic identities of musicians who themselves experimented with recording technology to create some of the most groundbreaking records of the era. While the tendency has been to read Lomax and Bechet's books in the context of popular jazz autobiography, I argue that the avant-garde nature of their transcription practices warrant their consideration alongside more canonical works of modernist prose.

Of the various developments in recording technology, perhaps none proved so intriguing to writers as audiotape. My next chapter investigates the use of tape recording as a mode of composition for late-modernists Jack Kerouac and William S. Burroughs. For Kerouac, the impulse was toward improvisatory transcription, but for Burroughs tape was an integral part of his notorious "cut-up method." I focus on the emergence of commercially available tape recording technologies in the 1950s and 1960s, which enabled amateurs to record as well as edit, loop, and manipulate recordings in other imaginative ways. I look most closely at Kerouac's *Visions of Cody* (written 1951–52, published 1972) and Burroughs's *The Ticket That Exploded* (1962, 1967). In both books, tapes play a key role within the plot; but they were also employed in the construction of the texts. Although Kerouac initially envisioned using a tape recorder as a way to capture word-for-word his rapturous conversations with Neal Cassady, his opinion of the technology changed while transcribing the tapes for *Visions of Cody* and in the process he developed his method of spontaneous prose. Burroughs from the outset distrusted recording as a transparent technology and experimented with subversive techniques for producing previously unheard of sounds. As friends and collaborators with largely different approaches to tape, Kerouac and Burroughs demonstrate how the transformation of agency from consumer to producer of recordings shifted the ways writers imagined their literary projects.

In Chapter 4, I consider how poets reconfigured the long-play stereo album and challenged the spatial limits of the printed book. In particular, I turn to Langston Hughes's LP book, *Ask Your Mama: 12 Moods for Jazz* (1961), and Amiri Baraka's poetry album, *It's Nation Time* (1972), recorded for Motown's Black Forum label, in order to discuss how the stereo LP opened new Black sonic spaces at a contentious moment in history. While many poets made recordings during the 1960s, what distinguishes these works is their ongoing dialogue with the specificities of stereo sound, the LP, and sound in its spatial dimensions. Part of what is radical about a stereophonic poetic is the way that it opens a space within a space – one that sits neither inside nor outside history. For Hughes, stereo's dual channels manifest on the page as two channels of poetry. For Baraka, the vinyl LP offers a new space in which to project a Pan-African nation. Although one work is in print and the other in vinyl, in both instances we find Hughes and Baraka invoking stereo's ability to create previously unimagined auditory spaces in the service of Black radical thought.

More fully articulating the stakes of the project as a whole, the fifth and final chapter reads contemporary remix culture against the long history of literary engagement with technologies of sound. While the literary remixes of poet Kevin Young (*To Repel Ghosts: The Remix* [2005]) and novelist Chuck Palahniuk (*Invisible Monsters Remix* [2012]) serve as case studies of the ways writers have adapted the practice of remix to the medium of print, the scope of this chapter is more wide-ranging, investigating remix as a cross-disciplinary aesthetic mode. I explore the origins of remix in the dance hall, but also in the cut-up techniques of William S. Burroughs; I examine how remix inflects more traditional literary publications, but also its impact on digital spaces for iterative writing (such as fan fiction). The literary implications of remix are still in a nebulous state of formation, but, as this chapter reveals, remix's inherently textual bent has been embedded in the practice since the beginning. If contemporary critics like to compare remix and mashup to modernism's collage aesthetics, it is because modernist and avant-garde textual practices have been implicated by sound recording technology all along.

In the Postscript, I turn to Anne Washburn's 2012 *Mr. Burns: A Post-Electric Play*. Set in a postapocalyptic near-future after the electrical grid has collapsed, *Mr. Burns* offers a meditation on the persistence of storytelling in a postdigital age. Although the premise is simple, even comical – a band of survivors try to recall and restage episodes of the *The Simpsons* – the play's remix of the detritus of contemporary popular culture offers a more serious appraisal of the digital era and the nature of art. However, my own reading reveals surprising ironies about even the most digitally resistant genre – theater – and the embeddedness of sound recording in present-day writing practices. The questions posited about the relationships between new and old media, and between sound recording, writing, and performance, are ones that reverberate across this book.

Many of the works discussed in these chapters are the less-known works of canonical authors, or texts that have fallen to the side of American literary history. In that sense, perhaps my readings might sit like alternate takes on the rerelease, or like the tracks that never made it on the album. What I aim to show is that sound recording is an unacknowledged practice that marked the careers of writers whose voices are thought to have shaped the American twentieth century and laid the foundation for our twenty-first-century multimedia aesthetic practices. The lineage between these texts is often surprising, and my own path through them is circuitous, looping, recursive. I fast-forward and rewind the chronology. Like Ellison's invisible man, I "slip into the breaks and look around." By attending to the sonic contours of literature, resonant reading wants to put the scratches and skips back in – not as nostalgic effects, but as part of the register, the timbre, and the tone of history, literary and otherwise.

CHAPTER I

Ears Taut to Hear
John Dos Passos Records America

He heard our voice and recorded it, and we play it now for our solemn contemplation.
    E. L. Doctorow's "Introduction" to John Dos Passos's *U.S.A.*

As early as 1937, John Dos Passos had started thinking about the possibility of recording excerpts from his novel trilogy *U.S.A.* After publishing the first three volumes individually as *The 42nd Parallel* (1930), *1919* (1932), and *The Big Money* (1936), Dos Passos was negotiating with Harcourt Brace to release the trilogy as a single volume, but, like many writers in the 1930s, he worried about slumping book sales. Despite receiving critical acclaim and popular success – even landing on the August 10, 1936, cover of *Time* magazine – Dos Passos found that book sales had tapered considerably since the 1920s. In his correspondence with his literary agent, Bernice Baumgarten at Brandt and Brandt, Dos Passos expressed dismay that *1919* and *The Big Money* (published by Harcourt) never did as well as *The 42nd Parallel* (published by Harpers). That diminished sales had anything to do with the ongoing economic depression never seemed to cross his mind; he felt that the books simply needed better promotion. In a letter to Bernice dated October 13, 1937, he wrote, "I think that something must be done to get the contents of the book into people's heads – I mean the heads of people who haven't read it." In a follow-up letter from November 6, 1937, he asked whether C. A. Pearce of Harcourt would "want to make a phonograph record of one of the pieces in *U.S.A.*?"[1]

The idea of a promotional record was certainly novel, and even Dos Passos seemed a little tentative about its uses. "Maybe he [Pearce] could use it on a radio book hour," he suggested. At the time, the idea of adapting literature for the radio was gaining popularity – just a year earlier, for example, CBS had launched its Columbia Workshop (featuring Orson Welles), the radio program famous for its panic-inducing 1938 broadcast of *War of the Worlds*. For Dos Passos, who disliked book tours and often turned down radio interviews, the possibility of making a record of his noisy novel seemed like a natural way to "get into the heads" of new audiences – if they could only *hear* it, they would understand it. Since Dos Passos had first begun work on his novel trilogy in the late 1920s, the technological soundscape had undergone a radical transformation as talking pictures replaced silent films, microphones and loudspeakers amplified voices, radios entered homes, and phonographic recording had gone electric. His novels, which chronicle the first three decades of the twentieth century, are particularly attuned to the rhythms of the modern world and the ways technologies of sound were shaping new practices of listening; it seemed only logical that the novel itself could be recorded. Although Harcourt and Brace never made the promo record, perhaps the record would have been redundant: the novels were already phonographic.

Dos Passos's interest in recording was not unique; the phonograph was a regular feature in modernist literature. By the mid-1920s, more than half of Americans had a phonograph in their homes, and recorded sound had become part of the clamor of everyday life.[2] It was no surprise that phonographs began to appear in the pages of poetry and novels. Readers of Gertrude Stein thought she sounded like a broken record. Jean Cocteau wrote an avant-garde play featuring phonographs as narrators, James Joyce's *Ulysses* is filled with the sounds of phonographs, and Hart Crane is known to have composed his poetry while listening to records.[3] But the most frequent manifestation of the phonograph within literary modernism is the sound of the disembodied voice. To be phonographic, it was assumed, had to do with capturing the sound of the voice and abstracting it from the body.[4] We think of the sourceless voices of T. S. Eliot's *The Waste Land* (1922), with its allusions to the ghostly voices of the dead, the typist who "smoothes her hair with automatic hand, / And puts a record on the gramophone," and the phonographic rhythms of "that Shakespeherian Rag."

In modernist fiction, the phonograph (or "talking machine") is often shorthand for the modern sensation of dissociation or inauthentic speech. In F. Scott Fitzgerald's 1920 short story "Head and Shoulders," Horace Tarbox, the stiff academic prodigy, has a hollow and mechanical voice: "When he talked you forgot he had a body at all. It was like hearing a phonograph record by a singer who had been dead a long time" (312). In Eugene O'Neill's *The Hairy Ape* (1922), the men who work the stokehole of the ocean liner speak monotonously with a "brazen metallic quality as if their throats were phonograph horns" (101). William Faulkner, known for his attentiveness to the expressive qualities of voices, uses the phonograph as an analogy in *Light in August* (1932) for the "dead," ghost-like voices of Joe Christmas's cruel grandparents. After speaking of his past misdeeds in the third person, Doc Hines abruptly stops speaking: "His voice ceases; his tone does not drop at all. His voice just stops, exactly like when the needle is lifted from a phonograph record by the hand of someone who is not listening to the record" (371). Even Edith Wharton in her 1898 short story "The Pelican" waxed that the aging Mrs. Amyot's "voice had the same confidential inflections, but was like a voice reproduced by a gramophone: the real woman seemed far away" (82). In each of these examples, we find the phonograph as a modern symbol of dissociation, detachment, and alienation of the voice from the body.

Almost as quickly as the phonograph entered the popular imagination at the turn of the twentieth century, stereotypes about the machine's tinny sound, its mechanical glitches, and its dead voice emerged. Early theorists of phonographic technology, such as Theodor Adorno, echoed common anxieties about the machine's ability to displace voices from their bodies and even to resurrect the voices of the dead by recording them for posterity. Friedrich Kittler would later explore the trope of death and phonography at length in his essay "Gramophone," noting the ways advertisements and literature perpetuated the idea that sound recordings could "immortalize" speech and evoke the utterances of the departed (51–73). Many of these associations between dead voices and the phonograph were holdovers from the Victorian era.[5] And yet, as early accounts of the machine attest, it was not at first clear that the phonograph could *speak* at all. Adorno's complaint that "the expression 'mechanical music' is hardly appropriate to talking machines" suggests that even in 1927, the optimal uses of the phonograph were still in flux ("The Curves of the Needle" 50); in fact, the demonstrations and tone tests of phonographs inaugurated by Edison and Victor continued into the 1920s, revealing the ongoing perception that listeners must be taught to hear the new technology.

The tendency to refer to the *dead* voices of the phonograph is, however, not only evidence of how listeners perceived the phenomenological changes brought about by recording technology (at first a "talking machine" rather than a music player); in the era of acoustical recording, prior to the emergence of the microphone and electrical recording in the mid-1920s, the sound itself was frequently *dead*, dull as a result of equipment that lacked the sensitivity to capture the sounds of voices with much fidelity. In the acoustic era, performers would speak, sing, and play into the mouths of enormous funnel-like horns – often shouting and projecting at full volume – in order to move the stylus tracing their vibrations in wax, only to find that their voices still sounded flat and tinny when replayed. Only exceptionally powerful voices, like that of opera tenor Enrico Caruso, broke through with much fidelity. The introduction of microphones and electrical recording technology radically changed the kinds of sounds that could be registered in shellac. Voices were not merely recorded; they were amplified. Many writers of the period recognized the phenomenological shift occasioned by the invention of recorded sound, but most failed to notice the profound developments occasioned by the later emergence of electrical recording. Few were as attentive to the changing technological soundscape of modernity as John Dos Passos. The rhythmic structures and phonographic soundscapes of *U.S.A.* would influence a number of writers, including Alan Lomax, William S. Burroughs, E. L. Doctorow, and especially John Steinbeck, whose journals and correspondence indicate that he credited *U.S.A.* with inspiring the structure of *The Grapes of Wrath* (1938), with its interchapters and rhythmic impulses.[6]

At the time Dos Passos began writing the *U.S.A.* trilogy in late 1927, technologies of sound reproduction and sound recording were undergoing a period of rapid development, and listening (to music on the phonograph and speeches on the radio) acquired new cultural currency. Attuned to this evolving sonic environment, Dos Passos, who had become known for his ability to capture the sounds of voices in his early writings, began to develop new experimental techniques that would enable him to represent listening on the page. In other words, he does not merely capture American voices but demonstrates the ways listening ears shade the voice, mishear it, and misinterpret it. He exaggerates the ways our ears must strain to hear the semblance of our own voices in those of others over the rising noise of music and machines. Through moments of listening, Dos Passos restructures the modern novel along resonant lines.

Modeling Literary Listening: Ears *Taught* to Hear

In the opening prose poem of his *U.S.A.* trilogy, John Dos Passos depicts a young man walking through a city "with greedy eyes, greedy ears taut to hear, by himself, alone" (xiii).[7] The passage buzzes with the swift pulse of urban imagery and nameless faces in the street, but as these images scatter, Dos Passos insists,

> Only the ears busy to catch the speech are not alone; the ears are caught tight, linked tight by the tendrils of phrased words, the turn of a joke, the

singsong fade of a story, the gruff fall of a sentence; linking tendrils of speech twine through the city blocks, spread over pavements, grow out along broad parked avenues, speed with the trucks leaving on their long night runs over roaring highways, whisper down sandy byroads past wornout farms. (Dos Passos, *42nd Parallel* xiv)

Across America, from Allentown to San Diego, the young man wanders, but finds he is less alone "in his mother's words telling about longago, in his father's telling about when I was a boy, in the kidding stories of uncles, in the lies kids told at school, in the hired man's yarns, the tall tales the doughboys told after taps" – that is to say, in the stories told by regular people. The narrator insists that, in the face of this vast geography, "it was speech that clung to the ears, the link that tingled in the blood; U.S.A." (xiv). The rhythmic depiction of the solitary young man with his "greedy ears taut to hear" frames the trilogy and creates a model for the kind of listening that *U.S.A.* requires of its readers. "Only the ears" have the power to forge connections, not simply between the characters, but across the various multimodal sections of his book: the character narratives, the Newsreels, the Camera Eye, and historical biographies. The pun between ears *taut* to hear and ears *taught* to hear underpins the kind of work the ear can do when reading for abstract meaning and connection. In approaching a novel as lengthy and with as many characters and storylines as *U.S.A.*, one must develop resonant reading strategies. The metonymic use of the ear stands in for practices of listening that allow readers to link the disparate narratives of the novel. As a kind of corollary to the disembodied voice, the surreal disembodied ears are linked together as though along a vine or a piece of twine; they are "caught tight, linked tight." On the one hand, Dos Passos is working through the connections that are created by repetitions of speech sounds and imagining the difficulties of deciphering sonic connections amid the noise of the city.[8] But on the other hand, these disembodied ears evoke the dissected cadaver ears that Alexander Graham Bell used in his early telephone experiments.[9] Like Bell, Dos Passos also dissects the ear – placing pressure on its mechanical function to sympathetically vibrate – in order to suggest relationships between imagined communities of a disparate people with a disparate history.[10]

As the prologue continues, the tendrils linking the ears spread out over the streets and avenues, alongside trucks and planes, and eventually from coast to coast. For Dos Passos, the listening ear makes sense of the broad expanse of a nation because America is made up of the voices of its people, but only when there are ears to hear them. However, one might also notice that while Dos Passos emphasizes speech, he does not mention the words themselves; instead, he describes the undifferentiated speech sounds and the sensuous, almost tactile qualities of the "gruff" voices, the "sing-song fade." Although the invocation of voice and speech is almost certainly meant in a larger political, democratic sense, his appeal to speech here is also about its vibratory sound and the extent to which the sounds of voices themselves matter. As E. L. Doctorow has said of Dos Passos, "he heard our voice and recorded it, and we play it now for our solemn contemplation" (xi).

Dos Passos's experimental, synesthetic approaches to representing sound on the page not only reflect the rapidly evolving technology that marked his era; they offer readers new ways to hear text. While readers have long been mesmerized by the voices in his works, Dos Passos was not merely interested in a realist mode of dialect writing – a mode that had characterized an earlier generation of American literature – nor was he interested in the clichés that made phonographic sounds synonymous with the voices of the dead. In *U.S.A.*, there is a more expansive approach to listening at a moment when electrified sounds were becoming mainstream. His writing, to the extent that he inscribes sound, does not imitate the microphone – it *is* a microphone, amplifying and recording sounds. His attention to sounds and rhythms as *structural* takes advantage of the ways resonant readers after the phonograph understood sound in its repeatable, amplified contexts.

Early reviews of *U.S.A.* seemed especially attuned to the sonic qualities of the text. Upton Sinclair referred to the "jazz effects" (Maine *Critical Heritage* 88); V. S. Pritchett of *Spectator* thought of *42nd Parallel* as "making noise. Sometimes it is amusing noise and alive; often monotonous" (93); Mary Ross of the *New York Herald Tribune Books* described *1919* in terms of a complex symphony, with each instrument playing its own part separately. D. H. Lawrence explicitly invoked the phonograph when describing the style Dos Passos first developed in *Manhattan Transfer*: "if you set a blank record revolving to receive all the sounds, and a film-camera going to photograph all the motions of a scattered group of individuals, at the points where they meet and touch in New York, you would more or less get Mr. Dos Passos' method" (75). Not only are Lawrence's remarks revealing of the affinity between Dos Passos's all-encompassing style and the new technologies but they are indicative of a particular moment in the technology's history when sound and film were not yet synchronized. The first so-called talking picture, *The Jazz Singer* (1927), was released the same year that Dos Passos began writing *The 42nd Parallel*. Lawrence's comment also reveals the attitude toward the technology as an objective record, which was common at the time. Prior to this point, the technology of film and phonograph isolated the senses from one another, and, in *U.S.A.*, Dos Passos writes in distinct modes, such as Newsreel and Camera Eye. But try as he might to segregate the senses and attach them to their related media, even the most visual sections are permeated by sounds of voices, music, machinery, and noise that echo across the sections. On a structural scale, *U.S.A.* presents an asynchronous novel that encourages the ear to make the connections.

U.S.A. places immense pressure on the traditional novel form, making Dos Passos a modernist innovator whose style is more clearly aligned with the formal experimentation of a poet like William Carlos Williams than with the novelistic prose of his friends Ernest Hemingway and F. Scott Fitzgerald. Eschewing a traditional narrative arc or a single narrator, the novels instead weave back and forth between the more realist narratives of individual characters, the brief biographical sketches of historical figures that take the form of prose-poems, the collage of Newsreel headlines and popular song lyrics, and the autobiographical stream-of-consciousness Camera Eye sections. The primary bulk of the novels follows the individual lives of several fictional characters at the beginning of the twentieth century (just prior to and following World War I) whose lives overlap in tangential and serendipitous ways. They come from various walks of life, including the working-class socialist Mac, the ambitious secretary Janey, and the wealthy public relations mogul J. W. Moorehouse. These fictional figures are recognizably modern, and their occupations reflect the changing socioeconomic scene; they are innovators in aviation, Hollywood starlets, revolutionary labor organizers, and interior decorators. As their stories unfold and intersect, some stories are conveyed multiple times from different points of view, all against the backdrop of the noisy mass media, history, and subjective experience. Readers often note the unique idiomatic voices of Dos Passos's characters and their use of slang, but Dos Passos is not what we would call a dialect writer in the sense that Mark Twain or Joel Chandler Harris were in the late nineteenth century. Even in the Camera Eye sections, which would seem to evoke the realm of the visual, Dos Passos offers arresting audible portraits of how his generation encountered technologically mediated sounds in the era *after* the phonograph's rise to popularity.

To the critics of his generation, Dos Passos represented a certain kind of promise for an ambitious, socially conscious, formally innovative American prose. Jean-Paul Sartre famously called him "the greatest writer of our time" and praised Dos Passos for making the reader a "reluctant accomplice" who must play the role of the chorus (Sartre 80). In his 1942 review of Dos Passos's writing, Alfred Kazin argues that Dos Passos is the "first of the American technological novelists" and praises him for his ability to wield machine age rhythms in his prose (4). These sonic and rhythmic qualities are part of what set Dos Passos apart from his lost-generation colleagues. According to Kazin, "politics and technology" are Dos Passos's domain, and he rejoices in the "slangy rhythms" that Dos Passos had earlier used in *Three Soldiers* but takes to new heights in *U.S.A.* (11). However, as Kazin is careful to distinguish, Dos Passos is not merely someone who captures slangy speech but a stylist in sound and its structural forces:

> The brilliance of the structure lies therefore not so much in its external surface design as in its internal one, in the manifold rhythms of the narrative. Each of the various narrative sections has its dominant musical mode, as it were; each of the characters is encased in his characteristic prose.... That smell, the clatter of the presses, the political arguments, the muddy streets and saloons, give the tone of Mac's life from the first as his life – Wobbly, tramp, working stiff – sounds the emergence of labor as a dominant force in the new century. (15)

For Kazin, to read the novel is to hear "the clatter." That rhythm is so often invoked to describe Dos Passos's artistry is telling, for these are not simply the literal rhythms of music or the sentences – the structure of the novel itself is also *rhythmic*, rather than more conventionally *narrative*. As Kazin describes it, "everything that lives in the book is wound up on the spool of that style; from the fragments of popular songs in the Newsreel and the clean verse structure of the 'Biographies' down to the pounding beat of the narrative, the book seems to be propelled by one dynamic rhythm" (17). Kazin likens the novel's mechanical rhythms to a conveyor belt, but perhaps we might also think of those rhythms as the drive belt of the phonograph, pulling the reader along its spiral groove.

The multiplicity of rhythms that Kazin describes, which operate at the musical, the structural, and the social levels of the novel, bears some resemblance to Marxist philosopher Henri Lefebvre's concept of rhythmanalysis. In an attempt to understand the polyrhythmia of the sensible world, Lefebvre asked, "But what does a midge perceive whose body has almost nothing in common with ours, and whose wings beat to the rhythm of a thousand times per second? This insect makes us hear a high-pitched sound, we perceive a threatening little winged cloud that seeks our blood. In short, rhythms escape logic, and nevertheless contain a logic, a possible calculus of numbers and numerical relations" (10). In other words, temporal scale and perspective matter when it comes to the rhythms of history and society. Dos Passos, it would seem, was uniquely attuned to the polyrhythmia of twentieth-century life – the individual rhythm played against those larger, louder rhythms of institutions, media, and history. He hears the midge *and* the man – the footstep and the jackhammer. But for Dos Passos, the rhythms of the novel are never entirely derivative of the social and historical rhythms. There is, occasionally, room for improvisation. In more recent scholarship, rhythm has also become an important framework for thinking about how large-scale narrative structures behave. Caroline Levine, for example, has used rhythm as one of the key features of formal analysis; "from the repetitions of industrial labor to the enduring patterns of intuitions of over time," she says, "all these have corollaries in literature and literary studies" (21). But for Levine, who is careful to distinguish her methods from a Marxist mode of reading, aesthetic or literary forms are not merely the epiphenomena of political forms but overlap and interpenetrate one another (14). As one of these formal structures, rhythms, she offers, "reveal opposing affordances: on the one hand, they can produce communal solidarity and bodily pleasure; on the other, they can operate as powerful means of control and subjugation" (49). One can find these opposing qualities of rhythm across Dos Passos's trilogy. As a chronicle, *U.S.A.* is bound by temporal rhythms, and yet Dos Passos determinedly interrupts the forward march of time via an asynchronous narrative. A resonant reading of Dos Passos's *U.S.A.*, attuned to its polyrhythmic sounds and structure, begins to reveal how technologies of recorded sound in the era of amplification were disrupting the temporal and historical frameworks of modernity.

From the Acoustic Era to the Electric Era

U.S.A. chronicles a period marked by two advances in recording technology that would shape the technological-acoustical landscape. The first is the shift in format from cylinders to discs – a shift that took place between roughly 1894–1912 – which also fundamentally altered the way the phonograph was used, marketed, and understood. The second major transition during this period was from acoustical to electrical recordings starting in 1925. Although Thomas Edison had invented his tinfoil phonograph in 1877, it was not until Emile Berliner's 1895 gramophone (with its flat, shellac discs) that records and record players became popular devices for home entertainment and music.[11] Instead of recording in the bottom of the groove, Berliner's gramophone recorded in the sides of the groove, a process that allowed Berliner to increase the volume of playback. By using a chemical process, Berliner was also able to make a negative copy of the gramophone's recording and could thereby stamp an infinite number of copies (Morton 34). But while Berliner's gramophone was louder and more musical, it still struggled to record the voice. As Berliner's disc gramophone (whose patents were purchased and marketed to great effect by Victor Talking Machine) rose to prominence, listeners lost the ability to record their own voices, in contrast to Edison's cylinders, which initially allowed users to both record and playback.[12] Instead, Berliner stressed the possibility of using the gramophone both for the mass production of music and for mass communication. Friedrich Kittler has argued that "Berliner's gramophone is to the history of music what Edison's phonograph is to the history of literature," and other media theorists, such as David Suisman, have credited Berliner's innovation as the birth of the modern music industry (Kittler 59; Suisman 51). And yet, as the prevalence and popularity of spoken-word recordings would suggest, the transition from talking machine to music machine did not happen overnight – the first two decades of sound recording's commercial popularity remained provisional and listeners continued to call phonographs and gramophones "talking machines" into the 1920s.

The shift from acoustical to electrical recordings led to greater fidelity and enabled amplification. Voices, no longer dead or far away, could *croon* – they could sound like they were being whispered directly in your ear. Electrical microphones made possible the careers of singers like Bing Crosby and Billie Holiday; they captured the nuanced sound of instruments like the saxophone.[13] The shades and contours of sounds just below human audibility could be amplified, and the interior was made exterior through amplification and loudspeakers. Writing about the recent past with an ear toward the future, Dos Passos modeled amplification as a structural tool to turn up the volume on certain kinds of voices and certain kinds of sounds.

There were a number of benefits to the electrical recordings that employed microphones that made them superior to acoustical recordings, which had relied on proximity to a large horn. The recordings sounded better, louder, and they were easier on performers. Unlike the acoustical horn that relied on directionality, "the condenser microphone picked up virtually all sounds indiscriminately," which meant that recording engineers were able to get richer sounds with more room-tone, but they also had to adjust the acoustics of the studio space to account for this new sensitivity (Horning 43).[14] Bell Labs had started developing the technologies that would form the basis of electrical recording in 1919 while studying speech and hearing in an attempt to improve telephone transmissions (Milner 58). In many ways, the development of the microphone and emergence of electrical recording in the mid-1920s was driven by the confluence of several technological developments, including radio, loudspeakers, and telephones. Although many saw the emergence of radio as the death of the phonograph, the profitable merger of Victor and RCA (Radio Corporation of America) in 1929 illustrates the way the two were actually becoming complementary industries.

In her history of the recording studio and early sound technology, Susan Schmidt Horning argues that "electrifying the studio became the most revolutionary improvement in sound recording to date and the first step in transforming recording from the art of capturing sound to the engineering of an illusion" (33). This philosophical-acoustical shift may not have initially registered with listeners like Dos Passos, and yet the ways that Dos Passos manipulates and even engineers the sound of his text reflect and, at times, anticipate the changing sounds and listening habits initiated by the electric era. Although *U.S.A.* chronicles the era when the phonograph first became a popular musical commodity, Dos Passos was writing at a moment when the nuanced sounds of electrified crooning brought a new sense of interiority to vocal styles.

An Evolving Dialect

In his early writings, Dos Passos's renderings of working-class voices and modern slang were part of what first captured the attention of readers in popular works such as *Three Soldiers* (1921). While regionalist dialect writers of the late nineteenth century had focused on the voices of rural and southern Americans, Dos Passos turned his attention to urban, working-class environments, and to the newly formed linguistic patterns of the immigrant groups one found in Northern cities. In fact, Dos Passos had become so known for this characteristic of his writing that a 1922 theater review praising Eugene O'Neill for his portrayal of working-class voices in *The Hairy Ape* compared O'Neill's stokehole idiom to Dos Passos's *Three Soldiers*.[15] But while Dos Passos's vivid portrayal of dialects was the mainstay of his early writings, the kinds of sounds recorded and presented in *U.S.A.* reflect an evolving approach to representing not only voices but a variety of sounds on the page.[16]

Dos Passos's approach to writing the sounds of voices in prose reflects the changing ways that voices were recorded, from the early spoken-word recordings made in the acoustic era to voices recorded with microphones in the electric era. On acoustic-era recordings, voices were notoriously hard to hear, and that very *un*intelligibility became fodder for the popular humorous spoken-word albums of the first two decades of the twentieth century. In the Library of Congress's large archive of digitized recordings of Victor records from 1900 to 1925 that make up their "National Jukebox," the number of records categorized as "Spoken Word" (including mono-logues, speeches, comedies, and other recitations) and "Ethnic Characterizations" rivals the number of music recordings. Quite often, these recorded performances play up the humorous possibilities of the recorded medium and sound technologies. Actors exaggerate the musical qualities of the thick Irish brogues of police officers or the off-kilter cadences of Yiddish accents. Mishearing and repetition are all part of the humor of these early records. Ralph Bingham's 1915 minstrel recording "Mrs. Rastus at the Telephone" caricatures the voice of an African American woman on the telephone in ways that echo Joel Chandler Harris's "A Queer Experience with the Phonograph" (1892) featuring Uncle Remus, registering the ways the new technology obscured Black speech. Another recording by the popular Avon Comedy Four called "Hungarian Restaurant Scene" (1916) finds humor in the familiar urban scene of a cross-cultural exchange in a crowded restaurant. Between the patron's Yiddish accent and the noise of the restaurant, the waiter struggles to take the order. Because recordings were themselves difficult to hear, the humor lies in the exaggerated intonation, the facts of *not* hearing, the mixing of sight and sound – for example, in a moment of exasperation, one of the actors exclaims, "What, are you blind? I just told you!" These early recordings of ethnic stereotypes and caricatures are obviously offensive to today's ears – a fact emphasized by the Library of Congress's inclusion of a disclaimer with most of these recordings – yet as documents of a radically changing sonic and linguistic landscape, they are evidence of the stakes of listening across media and across cultures.[17]

Voices of the "other" provided entertainment and novelty for listeners from many backgrounds, but not all of these recordings were humorous. One of the most popular recordings was a recitation of Paul Laurence Dunbar's poem "When Malindy Sings" (Victor 1909), a "Negro Dialect Recitation" by J. A. Myers, who was one of the Fisk Jubilee Singers. Again, what makes this poem so suitable for recording is that the subject of the poem is what Malindy's voice sounds like; it is a defense of the Black voice and of blues and gospel traditions in the face of Western music at the same time that it distances the reader/listener from Malindy's voice through third-person descriptions.[18] Part of what makes these recordings fascinating to listen to more than a hundred years later is the way they thematize the challenges of *listening*. Recordings like the ones I have referenced here draw attention to the ways Americans struggled to communicate – struggled to really hear one another – but voices mediated through accents also call attention to another kind of meditation: through the phonograph.[19]

Dos Passos was particularly attuned to the ways voices and listening mediated relationships among multiethnic groups of working-class people and, in particular, among soldiers during World War I. In *Three Soldiers,* the cadences and characteristics of speech are central to his characterizations. This effect is perhaps most pronounced in the speech patterns of the big-talking Fuselli, an Italian American soldier from San Francisco. Relaying a story about a jealous girlfriend at home, Fuselli's speech is rich in vernacular phrasing and diction:

> "Well, it's like this," said Fuselli. "You have to cross the ferry to Oakland. My aunt . . . ye know I ain't got a mother, so I always live at my aunt's. . . . My aunt an' her sister-in-law an' Mabe . . . Mabe's my girl . . . they all came over on the ferry-boat, 'spite of my tellin' 'em I didn't want 'em. An' Mabe said she was mad at me, 'cause she'd seen the letter I wrote to Georgine Slater. She was a toughie, lived in our street, I used to write mash notes to. An' I kep' tellin' Mabe I'd done it juss for the hell of it, an' that I didn't mean nawthin' by it. An' Mabe said she wouldn't never forgive me, an' then I said maybe I'd be killed an' she'd never see me again. An' then we all began to bawl. Gawd! it was a mess." (15).

Marking every dropped consonant and noting every varied pronunciation, Dos Passos meticulously and phonetically transcribes the *sound* of Fuselli's speech. By contrast, a character like Andrews, a Harvard graduate, sounds positively genteel. Voices and their accents underline the ethnic and class diversity of enlisted soldiers during World War I and of American cities in the wake of its largest immigration boom. The very sounds of the voices articulate difference, but Dos Passos's strategies in representing these voices (with misspellings, dropped consonants, etc.) do not stray far from his earlier dialect writing predecessors.

Between writing *Three Soldiers* and *U.S.A.,* however, Dos Passos started to adapt his approach to writing voices. In *U.S.A.* there are many more characters from different walks of life, and giving individualized voices to even the most mundane characters is one of the central ways that Dos Passos insists upon their agency and worth.[20] Joshua L. Miller describes

U.S.A. as "bursting at the seams with vernacular and multilingual voices" (160).[21] But by comparison to those in *Three Soldiers*, the accents of characters in *U.S.A.*, like the Irish-American Mac (from Chicago) and the sailor Joe Williams (from Baltimore), are noticeably subdued, even as their sonic markers remain important to their characterization. Rather than transcribe the phonetic pronunciation of Mac's every word, Dos Passos represents his thoughts and speech with idiomatic phrases and the repetition of signature mantras. For example, the phrase "Anyway, it was a job" is one Mac repeats to himself continually while working jobs he knows can lead to no good (*42nd Parallel* 28). Joe trades "Yare" for yes, but otherwise Dos Passos uses dialect very sparingly, preferring instead to bring forward Joe's unique voice through his idiomatic word choices. On a trip back to Baltimore to visit his sister Janey, for instance, he remarks that "he still had more'n fifty iron men, quite a roll of lettuce for a guy like him" (*1919* 43). In the archival manuscript drafts of the *U.S.A.* trilogy, one can see evidence of Dos Passos's meticulous attention to a tempered approach to dialect and voicing. In one of the "Joe" sections from *1919*, he had initially notated the speech of a Polish man awaiting release from customs with heavy phonetic spellings, writing "de" for "the" and "deir" for "their" (among other things), but later he restrained the phonetic transcription, limiting his focus to the way the character swaps his v's and w's.[22] The choice to restrain his phonetic spellings in this way highlights the central conflict of the scene, where border control agents detain the man, thinking he is German because of his accent. This slight adjustment allows the reader to be in on the confusion without muddying the legibility of the Polish man's speech. In these various examples, we find that each character develops an individualized *sound* made recognizable through repetition and idiom rather than merely through a phonetic attempt at an accent. Although the change is subtle, we might think about this new approach to the voice as improved *fidelity*. Their voices, no longer obscured by the misspellings that slow the reader's eye, are amplified so that the reader may better hear them. In *U.S.A.*, Dos Passos, not content to merely render voices, places them within the context of their larger soundscapes.

Loudspeakers and Microphones: Amplifying the Voice

The amplifying of some voices and the silencing of others is clearly one of the central philosophical concerns at the heart of *U.S.A.* – a novel that explicitly lacks a central, heroic protagonist, actively resists any kind of bildungsroman plotline, and makes the "speech of the people" one of its central unifying figures. Socialism is one of the driving political forces portrayed in the novel, but the novel itself privileges the sovereignty of individuals, even in a world where larger social forces are shaping the trajectories of the characters' lives. For Dos Passos, concerns about individuality and voice are intimately tied to developments in sound technology, namely, microphones and loudspeakers.

Figure 1.1 *Political Convention*, a watercolor illustration by John Dos Passos

In an article covering the Republican Convention for *The New Republic* on June 29, 1932, Dos Passos included an entire section, subtitled "Spotlights and Microphones," attending to the ways the new technologies were shaping politics. Although the talking picture of Herbert Hoover at the convention was "a flop," he remarked that, "Kidding aside, we do not appreciate yet how enormously the whole technique and machinery of politics has been changed by the mechanics of communication. The architecture of stadiums, of klieg lights, radio and the imminent danger of fairly perfected television are as important a factor in future political life as committees, votes, resolutions, theories, vested interests. Even in this Republican Convention ... a couple of things happened to prove the powers of the technicians who tune the loudspeakers and handle the lights" (179).[23] In a watercolor illustration Dos Passos appears to have made around this same time titled "Political Convention," he depicts the blurry mass of the crowd washed out by spotlights and politicians overshadowed by the massive horns of the "NBC" loudspeakers that dominate the frame (Figure 1.1).[24] In both the illustration and the description in *The New Republic*, there is a kind of muted skepticism of the ways technology enables certain figures and certain voices to overshadow individuals and ideas. Of course, Dos Passos's concerns about technologized politics were not unfounded. A year later in 1933, when Hitler would come to power in Germany, the Third Reich mobilized the radio and prerecorded messages broadcasted publicly over loudspeakers to disseminate Hitler's speeches and other Nazi propaganda.

Worries that the voices of everyday people might literally be drowned out by the volume of sound technologies had been on Dos Passos's mind since at least 1925 when he wrote his first full-length play, *The Garbage Man: A Parade with Shouting* (previously titled, *The Moon Is a Gong*). The experimental play, which debuted at Harvard before moving to the Cherry Lane Theater in New York, blended elements of expressionism and Broadway. Superficially, the play is a boy-girl love story about Tom and Jane accompanied by a jazz band and dance numbers, but beneath the surface is a more existential plot about the passage of time, the inevitability of death (symbolized by a garbage man), and the overbearing noise of modern, industrial life. In an early draft of the play, the list of characters even included "six phonographs" and "The Radiophone" among the players.[25] As the action of the play reaches its apex and Tom and Jane attempt to reconcile, they are faced with the cacophony of a parade, a band playing, people dancing to phonograph records, and the "Voice of the Radio" expressing platitudes praising "prosperity" and criticizing foreigners. In this climactic moment, Tom shouts into the din: "Voice of the machine, voice of the machine, I defy you" (151).[26] In the context of a performance, Tom's proclamation is purposefully melodramatic and no doubt would have been barely audible above the racket made by noise-emitting machines onstage. But on the page, Dos Passos must find other strategies to dramatize the philosophical and acoustical problems of amplification. In writing *U.S.A.*, Dos Passos sought ways to *perform* on the page the kinds of tensions between voices and technology that move beyond the more simplistic phonetic dialect writing of earlier works like *Three Soldiers*. Like a studio engineer adjusting the levels, Dos Passos mixes the voices of ordinary characters alongside biographical sketches of famous figures, news headlines, street sounds, war machinery, and popular songs. In a democratic move, he levels and flattens certain voices while bringing others forward, allowing the "speech of the people" to ring through above the din.

Although reviewers of *U.S.A.* like Kazin were just as likely to comment on the sounds of Dos Passos's texts, much of the scholarship about the *U.S.A.* trilogy has tended to focus on Dos Passos's invocation of visual technologies like film and photography. However, such scholarly works have a difficult time reconciling the aural qualities of what purports to be visual.[27] In *Camera Works,* Michael North aptly notes "the suspicion that it [*U.S.A.*] is not nearly so visual as it claims to be," yet he forcefully asserts the visual lens of Dos Passos's subjectivity in the Camera Eye sections (143). North explains that the discontinuity of the lives in *U.S.A.* "is a feature not merely of their having been lived under industrialism but also of their having been lived in a field of vision delimited by the camera" (150). Stephen Hock also remarks upon the strangely aural qualities of the Camera Eye, but, like North, subjugates the aural in *U.S.A.* to the assertion of a subjective camera angle that narrows the line of vision.[28] Dos Passos himself remarked that while the rest of his novel aims "at total objectivity," he felt he could only do so by distilling his "subjective feelings" into the autobiographical Camera Eye sections (*Prose* 247). However, part of the confusion of the audio and the visual in the Camera Eye arises from the fact that hearing, not vision, is traditionally recognized as the interior, subjective sense. To achieve the subjective interiority he seeks in the Camera Eye, he paradoxically turns to the listening ear.

The Camera Eye interludes are written in a stream-of-consciousness style with few capital letters and light punctuation that is meant to immerse the reader in sensory descriptions drawn from Dos Passos's own life. But in spite of the visual title, early in the first novel of the trilogy, *42nd Parallel,* Dos Passos depicts a youthful encounter with the phonograph, linking it to the heightened aural qualities of his writing. Dos Passos recounts listening to a gramophone during a visit with a family friend:

> and here was Mr. Garnet come to tea and he took a gramophone out of the black box and put a cylinder on the gramophone and they pushed back the tea-things off the corner of the table   Be careful not to drop it now they scratch rather heasy   Why a hordinary sewin' needle would do maam but I ave special needles
>
> and we got to talking about Hadmiral Togo and the Banyan and how the Roosians drank so much vodka and killed all those poor fisherlads in the North Sea and he wound it up very carefully so as not to break the spring and the needle went rasp rasp   Yes I was a bluejacket myself miboy from the time I was a little shayver not much bigger'n you rose to be bosun's mite on the first British hironclad the *Warrior* and I can dance a ornpipe yet maam   and he had a mariner's compass in red and blue on the back of his hand and his nails looked black and thick as he fumbled with the needle and

the needle went rasp rasp and far away a band played and out of a grindy
noise in the little black horn came *God Save the King* and the little dogs
howled. (*42nd Parallel* 43)

Despite the fact that Dos Passos mistakenly calls a phonograph a gramophone (gramophones use discs, not cylinders), his attention to the specificity of the technology captures the disorienting experience of hearing
sounds abstracted from their source. The sounds emitted by the recording
are markedly mechanical and the needle rasps twice as it settles into the
groove. Through the ears of a child, the spatial orientation of the sound is
skewed. The band plays "far away," and the song, "God Save the King,"

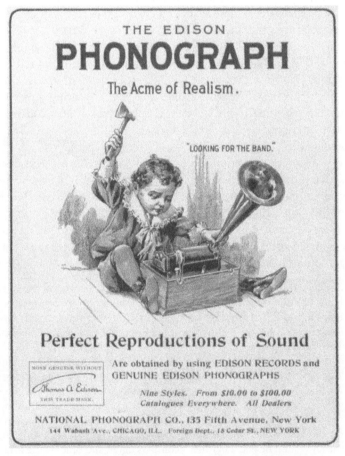

Figure 1.2 The Edison Phonograph, "Looking for the Band," 1901

emerges from a "grindy noise in the little black horn." Dos Passos, the boy-listener, does not distinguish between the mechanical sounds emitted by the phonograph and its music; his ear must work to situate the sounds spatially in relation to the horn and synthesize their coexistence. But such a process of simultaneous synthesis and articulation is disorienting, and the boy-listener's experience is not unlike this early advertisement for Edison's Phonograph where a little boy is "looking for the band" and ready to break open the machine to find it:

The rasps, the grinds, and the band are the product of the phonograph, but at this moment in the history of the technology, such noises had not become naturalized into the practice of listening to the music. But as this early encounter with the phonograph reveals, the kind of listening for which we are now conditioned is not a natural but a cultivated practice.

This particular passage accentuates the difficulties of listening to an early phonograph, but it also gives the reader a kind of acoustical portrait of listening more generally. By removing the punctuation breaks between Mr. Garnet's accented speech, Dos Passos models the undifferentiated manner in which ears receive sonic information. Filtered through the ears of young Dos Passos, Mr. Garnet's speech is not only accented, but amputated, illustrating how the act of listening selects, mediates, and arranges sound. In this regard, Dos Passos's writing is phonographic in the sense that he records all sounds in an undifferentiated manner regardless of origin.[29] The phonetic transcription of Mr. Garnet's accent with words like "ornpipe" and "miboy" is reminiscent of earlier dialect writing techniques, but also helps to situate Mr. Garnet's speech geographically. Thus, it is important that the song "God Save the Queen" come from a faraway place, like Mr. Garnet and his British drawl. The passage alerts the reader to the complex negotiating between hearing and listening during which the sound itself comes to inform an audible geography.

In other places in the trilogy, Dos Passos attends to the ways speech is already phonographic. A later Camera Eye (34) in *1919* finds Dos Passos in a WWI hospital attending to wounded soldiers. In pain and in shock, there is an automatic quality to the soldier's speech that is both alarming and disorienting:

> his voice was three thousand miles away   all the time he kept wanting to get up outa bed   his cheeks were bright pink and the choky breathing   No kid you better lay there quiet we dont want you catching more cold that's why they sent me down to stay with you to keep you from getting up outa bed [. . .]

all the time he kept trying to get up outa bed   Kiddo you better lay
there   quiet his voice was in Minnesota but dontjaunerstandafellersgottogetup   I   got   a   date   animportantengagementtoseeabout those
lots ought nevertohavestayedinbedsolate I'll lose my deposit   For chissake
dont you think I'm broke enough as it is? (*1919* 135)

If records were notable for separating sounds from their source, in this scene
Dos Passos records the voice as already separated from its body, "three
thousand miles away" in Minnesota. Like the band in Mr. Garnet's phonograph, the sound of the soldier's voice and its source have been divided across
space (as well as time). In complicating the relationship of voices to the bodies
that produce them, he also remarks upon the other phonographic qualities of
the body. Later in this same scene, we find that the ears too can act mechanically when agitated by the sounds of war, and after an air-raid, he finds his ears
ringing long after the noisy disturbance has ended: "they've cut off their
motors   the little drums in my ears sure that's why they call em drums"
(136). It is a jump cut of a realization, but one that reveals how the eardrum's
sympathetic vibrations can produce a ringing or drumming after a high level of
sonic input – here again, the sound and the source are disconnected.

As the section continues, the sounds of speech and the sound effects
of mortar blasts run together into a seamless cacophony. Only through
resonant reading can the reader synthesize the complex harmonies created
by the sound-sense of run-on words within the context of the scene. Text
such as "dontjaunerstandafellersgottogetup" resists the eye's expectations,
placing pressure upon the reader's ear to decipher meaning. This treatment
of language, which bears some resemblance to the elision of words in e.e.
cummings's poetry, differs from phonetic dialect writing. In this instance,
the reader must sort through the undifferentiated onslaught of sounds and
speech as it hits the ear. And yet, in context, the coherence of the feverish
soldier's words is secondary to the fact that his words are senseless utterances. The repetition of phrases, such as "I gotadate," make the young man
sound like a broken record, repeating the memory of times past. In *Three
Soldiers*, Dos Passos had made this connection between the broken bodies
of soldiers and broken records more explicit. In the midst of trench
warfare, the musically minded protagonist John Andrews hears a soldier
singing "There's a girl in the heart of Maryland," but as the smell of
carbolic and blood fills the air, "the song of the man beside him rose to
a tuneless shriek, like a phonograph running down" (195).[30]

These references to the broken phonograph are not only indicative of
the temperamental operation of early phonographs, but to their connection to the sounds of wartime. Mechanical and repetitive, the bodies of war

and bodies of industrial labor are themselves subject to the mechanical breakdowns of the machinery they support. Because of the acoustic-era phonograph's connection to the voice, the running down and silencing of the voice (and especially the singing voice) become metaphors for the ways individuals are silenced within the larger machinery of industrialized capitalism. Although phonographs too are products of capitalist markets that were fast turning music into an industry, their frequent personification as having *mouths* and *ears* humanized them. While the time period that Dos Passos chronicles in these sections roughly corresponds to WWI and the pre-electric, pre-microphone era, his strategies for recording voices, which seem to amplify them over the deafening noises of war, might be said to also reflect the ways that microphones made it possible to amplify the nuances of voices and other kinds of sounds. Microphones, like microscopes, were meant to take that which is small and make it large – and just as microscopes enable the scientific eye to see things that were previously invisible to the naked eye, so too (at least it was thought) might microphones make audible that which was previously inaudible.

"Come On and Hear!" *U.S.A.*'s Noisy Prose

Of the various sonic elements of *U.S.A.*, the most recognizable feature is undoubtedly the presence of popular songs running throughout the trilogy, most notably in the Newsreel sections. Although Dos Passos had made strategic use of popular music in *Manhattan Transfer* and even in *Three Soldiers*, in *U.S.A.* songs function as structural devices. Collaging headlines from actual newspapers such as the *Chicago Tribune* and the *New York World* with the lyrics from a vast array of popular songs – from patriotic war songs and tin pan alley tunes to ragtime, blues, and African American spirituals – Dos Passos made several assumptions about his readers: that they would be able to recognize these songs, that the songs had acquired some kind of cultural cache, and that readers would know the songs well enough to "play" the melodies in their heads and fill in the missing lyrics.[31] In interviews, Dos Passos remarked that the "Newsreels were intended to give the clamor, the sound of daily life" (*Nonfictional Prose* 283). But Donald Pizer has asserted that the effect of all this "noise" is to show how essentially meaningless it is – that it is just empty "nonsense" (*Critical Study* 84).[32] However, the notion that the songs in *U.S.A.* are merely part of the "clamor" may have been an important reason to include them; not because they are nonsense, but because they were increasingly part of how Americans made sense of their

noisy lives.[33] The songs help to situate the various narrative lines historically, but they are also a crucial aspect of Dos Passos's attempts to engage
readers' ears and express the strong cultural power that popular songs had
acquired.

Throughout his life, Dos Passos was an avid record collector, and he
even left an extensive collection of LPs to the University of Virginia
Libraries along with his papers.[34] His memoir includes wistful early memories of listening to records with his father. Recalling the summer of 1912
and the years when his father and mother were finally married, he describes
his father improvising a tap dance to *Pinafore* on a yachting trip on the
Potomac: "We had a Victor talking machine aboard, one of those with
a big horn the fox terrier used to listen to so raptly in the ads: 'His Master's
Voice'" (*The Best Times* 20). References to phonograph records also litter
Dos Passos journals and letters from WWI, along with recollected song
lyrics and descriptions of war sounds – enthralled by his sonic landscape,
his writing records not only music, but the sounds of laughter, airplanes,
footsteps, and marching.[35] Correspondence from the 1920s and 30s reveals
that Dos Passos frequently traded and received phonograph records from
his friends Gerald and Sara Murphy, wealthy expats living in France who
were part of the social circle that included Fitzgerald, Hemingway, Picasso,
and others (Trombold 290). In a letter from March 9, 1933, Murphy, in his
characteristic jocular tone, wrote "I am forwarding also a mess of records
for which I should prefer not to be held responsible. Should you not like
them, just stand on the corner of Commercial and hand one to each passer-
by until they are disposed of."[36] Through his friendship with the Murphys,
Dos Passos would also have the good fortune to meet Cole Porter at the
Murphys' villa in Cap d'Antibes in summer 1923 (Carr 197).[37] Several songs
by Porter would make their way into various sections of *U.S.A.*, including
"I'm in Love Again" (1925) and "Fifty Million Frenchmen Can't Be
Wrong" (1927).[38] When it came to incorporating samples of popular
songs into the text of *U.S.A.*, Dos Passos appears to have attended to the
process with meticulous skill. In the manuscripts of the trilogy, one finds
that Dos Passos quite literally cut-and-pasted together strips of paper with
headlines and popular songs, often adding and rearranging the placement
of the songs up to the final edits, even adjusting the spelling of lyrics to
more accurately capture the way they are sung.[39] But the question remains:
what are readers supposed to *hear* when they encounter these fragments of
lyrics?

In order to activate his reader's ear, Dos Passos literally calls the reader to
"*Come on and hear*" in a rather clever appropriation of lyrics from

"Alexander's Ragtime Band" in Newsreel II.[40] Taken on their own, the lyrics to Irving Berlin's famous 1911 song are not especially complex. They are highly repetitive and offer a meta-commentary on how great the band is (*"It is the best / It is the best / It is the best band in the land"* [*42nd Parallel* 18]). And although the song is already repetitive, Dos Passos exaggerates the almost mechanically repetitive lyrics to the point that a "listener" might assume that the record was broken. He repeats "Come on and hear" an extra time, skips forward to another part of the song, and then repeats an earlier section:

> *Come on and hear*
> *Come on and hear*
> *Come on and hear*
> In his address to the Michigan state Legislature the retiring governor, Hazen S. Pingree, said in part: I make the prediction that unless those in charge and in whose hands legislation is reposed do not change the present system of inequality, there will be a bloody revolution in less than a quarter of a century in this great country of ours.
>
> CARNEGIE TALKS OF HIS EPITAPH
>
> *Alexander's Ragtime Band*
> *It is the best*
> *It is the best*
> the luncheon which was served in the physical laboratory was replete with novel features. A miniature blastfurnace four feet high was on the banquet table and a narrow gauge railroad forty feet long ran round the edge of the table. [. . .]
>
> *It is the best band in the land* (17–18)

Only a selection of the lyrics appears in the text, spliced between news headlines and stories of politicians and industry moguls, and underpinned by signs of labor unrest; but if the lyrics as quoted by Dos Passos seem nonsensical, they are not much improved upon by listening to the entire tune. And yet, "Alexander's Ragtime Band" was not only one of the most popular songs of the period, it also provided inspiration to budding songwriters such as George Gershwin, setting the standard for American songs that would follow.[41] The highly repetitive qualities of the lyrics, the incorporation of pseudo–African American patterns of speech ("that's just the bestest band what am, ma honey lamb"), the brief quote of Stephen Foster's "Swanee River" ("and if you care to hear that Swanee River played in ragtime"), and the quote of a bugle call point to the fact that the song is already a kind of collage or pastiche that benefits from certain practices of listening that were developing during this period of incessant musical exposure. Dos Passos intuitively understood that he didn't need to include the entire lyric for the song to be heard. He assumes the reader will be able to fill in the blank spaces.[42]

Dos Passos uses the songs in the Newsreels to different effects. "Alexander's Ragtime Band" reflexively reminds readers to listen at an early moment in the trilogy, but Dos Passos gestures directly toward the recorded medium when he chooses to transcribe the lyrics of songs as though sung by a particular performer. In Newsreel XLV from *The Big Money*, he cuts between W. C. Handy's "St. Louis Blues," ads for Ford cars, and headlines heralding murders, holdups, and gang violence; but rather than simply quote Handy's lyrics, he attempts to evoke the song as sung by Bessie Smith. Borrowing inflections from both her 1925 recording and 1929 film version, the song drops and adds d's and incorporates unusual contractions: "*'Twarn't for powder and for storebought hair / De man I love would not gone nowhere*" (*The Big Money* 14). Although Dos Passos does not reference Bessie Smith by name, his transcription does not merely try to capture how a blues singer would phrase the lyric but seems to spark the memory of a particular recording. The effect of "playing" the Bessie Smith recording in one's head is that Dos Passos resituates the phonographic replay within the body and draws upon the way in which the body was already its own sound reproduction technology. The implication of having the reader "play" Bessie Smith's "St. Louis Blues" in the head rather than simply on a phonograph is that her voice becomes reembodied within the reader's ear.[43] That Dos Passos should choose to emulate the recorded performances of Bessie Smith reflects a larger affinity between modern writers and what Emily Lordi describes as Bessie Smith's "vivid lyricism" – that is, the incredibly evocative way that she sings.[44] For writers from Langston Hughes and Richard Wright to August Wilson and countless others, the blues of Bessie Smith – and in particular, her records – embodied a lyrical and spiritual connection to a resonant African American cultural history. Dos Passos's veiled transcription of Smith's lyricism in *The Big Money* also represents the broader ways African American culture was increasingly shaping American expression at large and being appropriated by white listeners – a fact which becomes clear at other moments when Dos Passos turns to the blues in his Newsreels.

At other places in the text, songs travel between the Newsreels and the character narratives as Dos Passos mobilizes the lyrics to catalyze moments of tension. One such case is Dos Passos's repeated use of the "Hesitation

Blues" – a song that reappears across American literature of the period, as we will see in later chapters. As a traditional blues, the "Hesitation Blues" (also known as the "Hesitating Blues") has been performed and recorded by numerous artists since the early twentieth century, including a well-known version by Louis Armstrong. Although the refrain stays the same across versions, nearly every artist who has recorded the blues has offered their own variation on the lyrics. Most versions allude to a thinly veiled attempt by a lover to consummate his relationship with a young woman; however, because of their plasticity, the lyrics also speak more generally to delayed gratification and longing – a theme Dos Passos takes up in his own use of the lyrics. In Newsreel XLVII, the juxtaposition of the "Hesitation Blues" with a list of want-ads creates a moment of irony as ads heralding "opportunity" are undercut by the plaintive, "*Oh tell me how long / I'll have to wait*" (*The Big Money* 23). The Newsreel comes at a moment in the novel when Charley Anderson has returned from the war and is faced with the prospect of being a newspaper boy. Charley eventually works his way into the airplane manufacturing business, but the juxtaposition at this moment in the text highlights the lost-generation dilemma: soldiers return from the war with no sense of purpose except to make money, but the only jobs advertised are for errand boys and clerks. In this instance, the lyrics are meant to be deeply ironic. When the song recurs nearly four hundred pages later in the narrative of Richard Ellsworth Savage ("Dick"), it is whispered in his ear by a Black transgender character named Gloria in a Harlem nightclub, Small's Paradise. Dick started his narrative as an aspiring young poet at Harvard, but after returning from the war he becomes the protégé of the public relations pioneer J. W. Moorehouse – a job he finds meaningless and empty even though he excels at it. For Dick, Gloria's insinuating "Do I get it now ... or must I he ... esitate" speaks to a different kind of opportunity – an opportunity to break from the conformity of the role he has assumed in society (*The Big Money* 414). The lyrics themselves hesitate on the page and are broken by ellipses, but seizing upon the moment, Dick brings Gloria home with him. When he wakes the next morning, it becomes clear that he has been beaten up and robbed by Gloria, who had seized upon *her* opportunity (414). In this scene, the blues lyrics mediate the complexities of interracial relationships in 1920s Harlem as greater numbers of white jazz fans visited the neighborhood. However, on the structural level of the novel, as the lyrics repeat and resonate across character narratives and the Newsreels, the "Hesitation Blues" help to contextualize a historical moment and link together two narratives that otherwise do not intersect. It is a reading that rewards ears taut to hear.

As time passes in the novels, Dos Passos's characters become more adept at reading sounds (musical and otherwise), and *U.S.A.* expects its readers to become better at hearing the resonance between certain kinds of sounds as well. The blast of bombs and shrapnel in one section resonates with the "shrilly clattering" riveters in another. But sounds are just as easily recast to reflect the shifting mood of characters. Dick, the former poet and PR man, has a special knack for reading sounds. On a bad day in the office, the riveters of a neighboring skyscraper ring "inside his head like a dentist's drill," but just a few pages later when Dick's prospects have changed, he describes the riveters as "music to our ears, they make us sing like canaries in a thunderstorm. They mean business" (*Big Money* 384, 397). These resonant associations of the riveters were ones that Dos Passos carefully added into the margins of his manuscript drafts of this section, weaving sound across the drafts.[45] After a while, all sounds have the potential to become musical in this way, but it is how they are listened to that matters.

* * *

Although the *U.S.A.* promo record that Dos Passos had imagined in 1937 was never made, more than thirty years later in 1968 Caedmon Audio – the label that arguably birthed the modern audio book – released a 3-LP boxed-set recording of excerpts from *The 42nd Parallel*.[46] The record features Dos Passos himself reading the opening prose poem and Camera Eye sections with the actor Rip Torn reading Mac. Additional cast members perform rather lively renditions of the Newsreels, singing the song lyrics and even recreating the hiss and pop of phonograph records made in the acoustic era when the records themselves are unavailable for sampling.[47] The sound effects, which also include the background clatter of typewriters, attempt to capture the technologized soundscape of the early years of the twentieth century and point to a kind of media nostalgia. By 1968 such sounds would have been recognizably old fashioned, and while the Caedmon album does an admirable job in adapting the novel to the LP, the reading voices sound tired. Dos Passos's voice in particular, though energized and breathless, is no longer that of the young man pacing the city streets; it bears the wet, ragged edge of a man in his seventies trying to recapture the vigor of youth. In the liner notes for the album, Gerald W. Johnson seems to acknowledge the ways Dos Passos remained both ahead and behind the times, his experimental form "consigned to the ash-can years before McLuhan upset the ash-can itself." In this regard, even the Caedmon album struggles to fully replicate the experience of reading the multimodal *U.S.A.* because Dos Passos's modernist approach to sound plays so heavily upon the resonances that only a reader could imagine. If *U.S.A.* has been experiencing something of a small renaissance of attention, maybe it has something to do with our own technological moment.[48] Even now, streaming audio gives contemporary readers access to sonic contexts that had – for a while, anyway – faded into near silence. To read *U.S.A.* today requires something of a recuperative act, but it is one that digital-age readers are increasingly equipped to do.

CHAPTER 2

Ethnographic Transcription
and the Jazz Auto/Biography
Alan Lomax, Jelly Roll Morton, Zora Neale Hurston,
and Sidney Bechet

"The amplifier was hot. The needle was tracing a quiet spiral on the spinning acetate. 'Mister Morton,' I said, 'how about the beginning? Tell about where you were born and how you got started and why ... and maybe keep playing piano while you talk'" (Lomax, *Mister Jelly Roll* xix). So it was that a young Alan Lomax embarked upon the now-famous recording session of Jelly Roll Morton at the Library of Congress in 1938. Sitting on the floor with a Presto Portable Disc Recorder at his side, the twenty-three-year-old Lomax (1915–2002) would gather over one hundred tracks of Ferdinand "Jelly Roll" Morton LeMenthe (1885–1941) as he told the story of his life while accompanying himself on the piano.[1] The recordings were arguably the first of their kind and laid the groundwork for the field of oral history.[2] Lomax later referred to the recordings as an "autobiography" of Morton, and yet the fact that they turned out to be so was almost purely by accident. Lomax had invited Morton to the Library of Congress to record a few folk songs, but as Morton played, he began to speak about how jazz emerged in New Orleans. Lomax recalled, "As I listened to it, I realized that this man spoke the English language in a more beautiful way than anybody I'd ever heard" (qtd. in Szwed 123). Seizing the opportunity, Lomax took a bottle of whisky from his office and a stack of acetate-plated discs and urged Morton to start at the beginning. However, Morton needed little plying. He had come to the Library of Congress with the express intent of setting the record straight about jazz.[3] As Morton viewed it, he had not received his due as one of the originators of the music, and although he had been one of the most popular recording artists of the 1920s, he had fallen on hard times. The records he made with Lomax are considered foundational documents of jazz history, and ten years later Lomax would use the recordings to write what he referred to as "the first altogether recorded book": *Mister Jelly Roll: The Fortunes of Jelly Roll Morton, New Orleans Creole and "Inventor of Jazz"* (1949) (xvi).

But what does it mean to write an "altogether recorded book"? Was Lomax merely talking about transcription? David Bolter and Richard Grusin have termed the tendency of one medium to refashion and imitate older media forms *remediation*; however, remediation fails to account for the reciprocal relationship between a new medium and the older one that adapts it. Why was a book necessary when we could simply listen to the recordings? Lomax's desire to invent a new term to describe the hybrid genre that is neither biography nor autobiography and straddles two media suggests that we must find innovative ways of thinking about such a text. *Mister Jelly Roll* may have been the first popular book to use recordings and transcripts in the writing process so extensively, but it was not the last. Lomax's book would inspire numerous other writers (including Jack Kerouac) and became a model for many books, especially jazz autobiographies such as the poetic *Treat It Gentle* (1960) by clarinetist and saxophonist Sidney Bechet (1897–1959). Both *Mister Jelly Roll* and *Treat It Gentle* incorporate transcriptions of recorded interviews – a practice rooted in ethnography – and yet these books are not simply oral histories told by jazz originators but rather *aural* histories that require readers to listen and think critically about the sonic identities of musicians who themselves used recording technology in experimental ways.

Jazz autobiographies are usually placed in the context of the history of jazz music rather than the history of American literature. Yet their radically experimental approaches to writing as well as their sonic rhetoric invite us to consider them alongside modernist and African American literature. They might also prompt us to reconsider the literary avant-garde impulses of jazz itself. After all, Alan Lomax's model for transcribing the voice came from Zora Neale Hurston. Meanwhile, Bechet, who lived in Harlem during its Renaissance, drew upon Black folk traditions in crafting his narrative. However, periodizing these autobiographies is complicated. On the one hand, they chronicle the era that parallels interwar modernism and the New Negro Movement; on the other hand, they were published in the 1950s and 1960s. Given their publication dates, it might make sense to think of them alongside Ralph Ellison's *Invisible Man* and in the context of the civil rights era and the Cold War. We might think of them as critical precursors to other as-told-to autobiographies of the era, such as Alex Haley's *The Autobiography of Malcolm X* (1965). Better still, I find we must consider *Mister Jelly Roll* and *Treat It Gentle* in relation to both of these moments – as works of literature read in the 1950s and 1960s, but with an ear toward the decades preceding.

The desire of jazz musicians like Morton and Bechet to tell their life stories starting in the late 1930s was partly a product of the particular moment in jazz's development. When Lomax recorded Morton, the histories of jazz were just beginning to be told, but more often than not these histories were told by white critics and bandleaders and focused on distinguishing jazz styles during a period of transition between Dixieland, swing, and bebop.[4] Perhaps most egregious of these was the bandleader Paul Whiteman's "What Is This Thing Called Jazz?" from the June 1939 issue of *The Rotarian*, which casually glossed over the music's African American roots and named George Gershwin as the most important figure in jazz (34). By the 1940s, the jazz scene had changed significantly as commercially successful white bands were threatening to erase the music's complex roots, and even Alan Lomax had been skeptical of jazz's commercialism. Although the emergence of bebop in the late 1930s and early 1940s offered resistance to what many perceived as the whitewashing of the music, for players like Morton and Bechet, who remained committed to the older New Orleans styles, it seemed like the music (and their claim to the avant-garde) was being taken away from them; as Bechet put it, "These people don't seem to know it's more than a memory thing. They don't seem to know it's happening right there where they're listening to it" (*Treat It Gentle* 2). It is not surprising that autobiographies of jazz musicians began to appear not long after these first histories, including Louis Armstrong's *Swing That Music* (1936) and *Satchmo: My Life in New Orleans* (1954), W. C. Handy's *Father of the Blues* (1941), and Mezz Mezzrow's *Really the Blues* (1946). Autobiography gave musicians some semblance of control over the narratives surrounding their music, but, as Daniel Stein writes in "The Performance of Jazz Autobiography," many of these texts "invent elusive autobiographical personas" (174). In the case of autobiographies that used recordings in the process of writing, those personae inhabit an intermedial zone between sonic and textual presence.

Like Jelly Roll Morton, Sidney Bechet was a New Orleans Creole who felt that he needed to correct the record (both literally and figuratively) and tell the story of the music's origins. Although Morton liked to claim the title "inventor of jazz," the story of jazz's early years is intertwined with a number of New Orleans players, including Sidney Bechet and, of course, the younger Louis Armstrong. Morton, along with Bechet, invented many of the sounds that we now associate with jazz; he wrote dozens of standards, developed masterful arrangements, and possessed a nimble and powerful style of piano playing that distinguished him from his contemporaries. Bechet was noted for his "hot" improvisational solos, which rivaled Louis

Armstrong's, and helped to transform the way the music was played. Moreover, Bechet possessed a truly unique tone, and his fast, wide vibrato makes his recordings instantly recognizable. For pioneering jazz musicians like Morton and Bechet, the possibility of using recordings to "write" a book was a natural outgrowth of their other artistic pursuits because recordings had been central to their musical output and fame. Morton and Bechet were also key innovators in popular recording – a fact that is sometimes obscured by official histories told by recording studios. As musicians with vast discographies, their public identities were intertwined with their music and the particularities of their individual sounds; using recordings to write their autobiographies promised a much closer relationship to their sonic identities.

Reviews of the books at the time of their publication advertise the musical-sonic qualities of the texts and the authenticity of the voices therein. A *Chicago Daily Tribune* review of *Mister Jelly Roll* remarked, "Lomax has woven a narrative symphony that will endear him to hot waxheads, and wax hot-heads alike; this is the diskophile's dream book" (Savage H4). Of *Treat It Gentle*, the *New York Times* said, "Sidney Bechet played his clarinet and soprano saxophone with a soaring lyrical passion, and he produced an intense, full-bodied music uniquely his own. Some of this same lyricism, a projection of this same inner vision, appears in his autobiography, 'Treat It Gentle'" (Wilson BR3). The review goes on to praise the editors for preserving Bechet's speech, "for he can make words sing with that vividness and excitement that was so much a part of his great talent." Reviews like these imply that the voices contained within recorded books promise a higher degree of authenticity because of the fidelity to the musician's *sound*, but few questioned what happened in the space between the recording, the transcription, and the editing of these books.

The complexity of how an "altogether recorded book" comes into being and the role of editors and recording devices in the process has been largely unexplored. The process varies from subject to subject, and the degree of collaboration is not always explicit. In the introduction to *Good Morning Blues* (1986) – an autobiography that also employed tape transcripts – Count Basie compared his co-writer Albert Murray to a staff arranger or even an accompanist, stating: "He comps for me pretty much as I have always done for my soloists. . . . And of course, we have also done quite a bit of four-handed piano playing, just like Bennie Moten himself and I used to do, sometimes with two separate pianos and sometimes on the same keyboard" (xii). As Basie's shifting metaphors suggest, there are varying degrees to which an editor-collaborator takes a hand in the writing process;

but whereas a later autobiography like Basie's fully acknowledges and celebrates its complex, dual-voiced (or four-handed) authorship, the same cannot be said for the first books that experimented with the genre. Those who have written about *Mister Jelly Roll* and *Treat It Gentle* tend to accept the authenticity of the musician's "voice" without question in part because these texts are generally only studied in the context of jazz history or by eager fans.[5] Given the guiding mentorship Lomax received from Zora Neale Hurston regarding ethnography, recording, and writing the voice, as well as jazz's role in the modernist imagination, these texts deserve greater attention. By exploring the intermediality of these understudied texts and situating them within traditions of ethnographic recording, I aim to bring them into a broader discussion of modernism's engagement with sound reproduction technology.

Transcription and "The Laws of Sound": Zora Neale Hurston and Alan Lomax, 1935

Recording as a tool for transcription, while in use since the 1890s, remained a relatively underutilized method among those wishing to write the testimony of folk voices until the early 1930s.[6] The first ethnographers to employ the phonograph tended to focus on the romantic documentation of so-called primitive and exotic cultures. Jesse Walter Fewkes, who made cylinder recordings of the Passamaquoddy Indians in the 1890s, like others of his generation used phonographic technology for the preservation of languages of nonliterate peoples, who were presumed to offer a window to the past even as their cultures were being compromised by modernization and de-population.[7] The cult of preservation is tarnished with ironies. Despite the scientific promise of phonograph recordings as tools of preservation, the early wax cylinders were used primarily for the purposes of transcription and treated almost like scratch paper. As Erika Brady points out in *A Spiral Way: How the Phonograph Changed Ethnography,* the "derived" text and *not* the recordings were the basis of descriptive and analytical work and "particular performances were important only insofar as they could be used to reconstruct a paradigm for song, story, narrative, or myth in a given culture"; it was therefore assumed by most ethnographers that one would need to "improve" the material (62, 63). The narrative value was prized above all, and the presence of the machine and even of the ethnographer was made invisible in most of the ethnographic work done between the 1890s and the 1930s, despite widespread use. Franz Boas, the "father of anthropology," advocated the use of the recording machine, which fit well with his mandate for the study of folklore, or what he called "people['s] records of themselves in their own words" (Brady 66). Boas, like others of his era, tended to treat phonographic recordings as transparent. But implicit trust in the scientific objectivity of the machine and the transcriber belie the fact that both recordings and transcriptions contain, according to Brady, "a full measure of characteristics resulting from subjective motivations, conscious and unconscious, of collector and performer" (7). In other words, not only does the machine affect the performance that is recorded, but the transcription is merely the record of one person's listening. To this day, practices of field recording and transcription continue to be under theorized, despite widespread use across a range of social science fields.[8]

Quite early in his career, Alan Lomax sensed that the transcription of voices required something more than simply writing down the words spoken on a recording. As anyone who has ever used a dictation machine knows, transcribing speech to text can be a tedious process, as listening and typing fall in and out of sync with one another. Even with recent advances in dictation and transcription software, it is a difficult and time-consuming task. Cases in which the speech is muffled, unintelligible, or spoken too quickly require one to deduce words from the context and to make a best guess.[9] Transcription also necessitates decisions about whether to codify redundancies, pronunciation, and nonverbal utterances (such as coughs, laughs, or pauses), not to mention the problem of punctuation. As such, transcription always involves a question of representation.[10] How to represent folk voices – and in particular, Black voices – was a problem for Lomax in his early work as he traveled the South with his father John Lomax, recording cowboys and folksingers in the early 1930s. The Lomaxes made their first recording expedition in 1932 with a cylinder phonograph borrowed from none other than Thomas Edison's widow. The success of these recordings prompted the Library of Congress to promise a small amount of funding to the Lomaxes to outfit a Model A Ford with an office Ediphone (better suited to recording voices) (see Figure 2.1). As they passed through Baton Rouge, they were able to purchase a vastly improved recording system that included a 315-pound disc-cutting recorder as well as amps, microphones, mixing equipment, and recordable discs. But recording discs and capturing the voice on the page were markedly different activities.

In his quest for better models of transcribing the voice, Lomax was "dazzled" by the phonetic transcriptions of Zora Neale Hurston, whom he believed had "the editorial style necessary to transmit the whole plangent sound of Black folks' speech onto the page then confused by

Figure 2.1 John and Alan Lomax's mobile recording studio, 1930s

mistransliteration or the redundancies that no eye can accept" (qtd. in Szwed 79). Although Hurston, who had trained under anthropologist Franz Boas while at Barnard College, did not initially use recordings in her fieldwork, when Alan Lomax came across her 1931 article "Hoodoo in America" in the *Journal of American Folklore*, he found the intellectual and literary mentor he had been searching for. At the time of their meeting, Lomax, who was only about twenty years old, was in the middle of helping his father transcribe recordings of the songs of blues singer and twelve-string-guitar player Huddie Ledbetter (aka "Lead Belly"), whose collaboration would prove to be one of the most fruitful and controversial of their careers. In his attempt to write a brief character study of Lead Belly for *Negro Folk Songs as Sung by Lead Belly* (1936), Alan Lomax tried to capture something of Lead Belly's characteristic speech by writing in dialect, but he also recognized that doing so could be perceived as patronizing. He needed a better model. According to Lomax's biographer, John Szwed, "Hurston represented to Alan what was possible for an intellectual of a certain type, and pointed the way toward how he, too, might come to write in a deeply personal and expressive style and still be an ethnographer and folklorist true to his subject" (Szwed 78). Eager to work with Hurston, Lomax invited Hurston (along with New York University English Professor Mary Elizabeth Barnicle) to accompany him on a recording trip through the Southeast to collect folksongs.

The trip made during the summer of 1935 under the auspices of the Library of Congress's new Folklore division was a catalyst for Lomax's career, and Hurston's mentorship gave Lomax access to innovative approaches to cultural anthropology. Hurston, Barnicle and Lomax made a strange trio: Lomax was just twenty, Hurston and Barnicle were in their forties, and yet Alan was officially in charge (Szwed 77–86). The trip, which has elements of an adventure story, complete with romantic intrigue and a run-in with the law, allowed Alan to break from his father's influence. Hurston introduced Lomax to Black communities (including her native Eatonville, Florida) in ways that had previously eluded him, but he also gave Hurston coveted access to recording equipment to supplement her own work. Among their recordings of singers and musicians was the first recorded interview with a former slave, which they made on St. Simons Island, Georgia. Lomax would also make several recordings of Hurston singing and speaking. It was during this trip and his later trip to Haiti that Lomax would solidify his commitment to collecting folksongs and helping the voices of the masses reach Washington, DC. It was also during this time that Hurston was finalizing her groundbreaking work of autoethnography *Mules and Men,* published in October 1935.

Letters from the time illuminate the critical mentorship role that Hurston began to play for Lomax at a point when he was coming into his own. In a letter to his father on July 1, 1935, he remarked, "I have worked harder and learned more in the past two weeks than I have ever done since I have been in the field" (*Letters* 7). In another more detailed report from August 3 sent to Oliver Strunk, the chief of the Music Division of the Library of Congress, he described Hurston as "probably the best informed person today on Western Negro folk-lore" and praised her ability to act as guide among African American communities – as Lomax put it, "she has been almost entirely responsible for the great success of our trip" (8–9). The feelings of admiration appeared to have been mutual, for in a letter from Hurston to John Lomax from August 30, 1935, she praised Alan's work ("I deserve no thanks if I have been helpful to Allan [*sic*] in any way. He is such a lovely person that anybody would want to do all that they could to please him. He will go a long way") but also revealed her firm, albeit subtle, commitment to making Lomax a more responsible ethnographer: "I carefully insisted that he see further than the surface of things. There has been too much loose talk and conclusions arrived at without sufficient proof. So I tried to make him do and see clearly so that no one can come after him and refute him."[11] Although Hurston would leave the southern expedition early due to a falling out with Mary Elizabeth Barnicle, she and Lomax would meet again a year later to record in Haiti, where Hurston had a Guggenheim Fellowship to support her research.

Hurston's interest in continued collaboration with Lomax seemed to center on his access to recording technology, which would continue to play a role in her own work.[12] Writing on June 7, 1936, from Kingston, Jamaica, Hurston told Lomax, "There is plenty for your machine to do," and outlined not only the kinds of musical materials he will want to record but also how he ought to *frame* his research:

> You will please have the Library in your letters of introduction, ask permission for you to record some songs and not use the general term folk-lore or magic practices. [^If the letters are not specific they may think you're another sensation seller.] Seabrook and those who have followed him have disgusted the Haitian government with voodoo hunters. You do not need it with the great wealth of material at hand. The music is certainly worthwhile. I hope that your father and the Library will trust my judgment in this matter.

Here, one can witness the extent to which Hurston was helping to shape Lomax's research agenda, as well as the ways Hurston was subtly pushing Lomax to rethink the underlying racial biases of his previous work. By urging him to frame his work as a music *recording* project, he could avoid reinforcing stereotypes of the exotic made by previous white folklore hunters. In letters Alan would later write to Haitian government officials, he emphasized the "scientific" aspects of his recordings for the "archive" at the Library of Congress (Lomax, *Letters* 27).

This strange genealogy by which ethnography comes to the recorded book is not without problems, and Lomax like Hurston would occasionally receive criticism for his portrayal of folk voices. Richard Wright in particular accused Hurston of propagating minstrel stereotypes, and others considered her ethnographic methodologies unorthodox.[13] As we now know, one of her early manuscripts, which relied heavily on a vernacular diction – *Barracoon: The Last Black Cargo* (2018) – was rejected by Viking Press in 1931 because Hurston refused their request to rewrite it "in language rather than dialect" (xxii). As editor Deborah Plant argues, "the dialect was a vital and authenticating feature of the narrative" (xxii). But even though her phonetic transcription is notable for its sonic qualities, Hurston's writing is not strictly phonographic. Rather, her writing reflects her interpretation as a participant-observer. Lori Ann Garner has noted that in *Mules and Men* (a 1935 collection of folklore from Hurston's hometown of Eatonville, Florida) "her depiction [of voices] is necessarily selective and her writing becomes an artistic construction of speech, a form of performance in itself" (222). Hurston had already published various works of fiction when she produced her first collection of folklore, and critics have remarked upon how Hurston borrowed stories from her fiction for *Mules and Men*. The phonetically transcribed tales are linked together by a first-person narrative account of her various encounters, written in conventional English (which she jokingly called "Barnardese"), and conversations with Eatonville's storytellers, in which Hurston slips into the dialect used by her subjects. For example, Hurston explains in the introduction to *Mules and Men*, "It was only when I was off in college, away from my native surroundings, that I could see myself like somebody else and stand off and look at my garment. Then I had to have the spy-glass of Anthropology to look through at that" (9); but several pages later, as she is entering Eatonville and narrating her encounters with the storytellers, she switches voices: "Calvin, Ah sure am glad that you got here. Ah'm crazy to hear about John and dat frog" (14). The shifts elegantly represent the code-switching required to be a participant in the culture she studied. The result is a blend of literature and ethnography rather than a strict anthropological study, but at the time Hurston was criticized for breaking the rules of serious ethnography. For Hurston, it was about adhering to the "laws of sound" – getting the right sound *and* the right context, because these stories were not isolated events but part of a larger performative culture.[14] By including herself (and others) in the narrative as listening subjects, she preserves the cultural context and implicitly acknowledges the role of the listener-transcriber in translating these oral stories to the page. To Lomax, Hurston's combination of personal narrative with the voices of ethnographic subjects made for much better reading and a more useful access to culture. He would later model this style in *Mister Jelly Roll*.

One of the ways the phonograph and later tape recorders changed approaches to American writing had to do with the ethics of dialect writing. As we saw in the previous chapter, twentieth-century writers like John Dos Passos had begun to temper the elaborate phonetic spellings used by nineteenth-century writers like Mark Twain, Joel Chandler Harris, and Charles Chesnutt to capture the particularities of regional speech. Phonetic approaches to dialect – especially in depicting African

American speech – came under increased scrutiny. Jennifer Stoever has argued that even Chesnutt's use of dialect revealed the racist undertones of the "listening ear" of white readers by including the frame of white listeners in stories such as "The Goophered Grapevine."[15] Hurston and Lomax would continue to find themselves at the center of an ongoing debate about the representation of Black voices as a result of their participation collecting slave narratives for the WPA Federal Writer's Project in the 1930s. Under the direction of Sterling Brown, collectors were encouraged to adopt an idiomatic (rather than phonetic) approach to transcription. Brown praised Zora Neale Hurston's writing as an example but cautioned writers against writing "ah" for "I" and "poe" for "poor," and so on (Brown, *Slave's Narrative* 38). Instead, Brown suggested "simplicity in recording the dialect" in order to keep readers' attention, adding that "truth to the idiom is more important, I believe, than truth to pronunciation" (37). For example, phrases that give a local flavor such as "durin' of de war" were considered acceptable, but various pronunciations of "master" (such as marsa, massa, etc.) were not. Brown's directive is indicative of the politically charged ideas surrounding representations of Black voices. Although many Black writers, including Sterling Brown, felt that misspellings and the overtly incorrect grammar of literary dialect demeaned ex-slaves and their stories, as Henry Louis Gates, Jr. and Charles T. Davis acknowledge, in the longer tradition of slave narrative, the sense of presence evoked by the Black voice was crucial to the genre of Black life writing: "The very *face* of the race, representations of whose features were common in all sorts of writing about blacks at that time, was contingent upon the recording of the black *voice*. Voice presupposes a face but also seems to have been thought to determine the contours of the black face" (*The Slave's Narrative* xxvi). However, given the correlation between literacy and political rights in African American history, there was a sense of unease surrounding representations of speech that suggested a lack of sophistication or education. Lomax was thus driven to negotiate the line between these conflicting impulses in his transcriptions: to effect greater transparency, to translate sound to the page, and to create works of literature.

Mister Jelly Roll and the Library of Congress Recordings

> A folksong in a book is like a photograph of a bird in flight.
> Charles Seeger[16]

Alan Lomax is typically characterized as a pioneer of ethnomusicology, but he was also deeply invested in literature and believed that the recording machine would lead to new kinds of writing, reinvigorating what he called "the kind of epicene prose that had taken possession of everybody." In a *New York Times* interview from 1950, he argued that writing had reached a "dead end" and claimed that he was "interested in doing for language what recording was doing for music" by employing recordings in the writing process. When pressed by the interviewer, "How would recording the people and then writing out of the recordings liberate us from the dead-end?" Lomax responded:

> The ordinary people are alive and have kept alive truth and beauty. Even Jelly Roll – his is the story of corruption and yet it has a terrific optimistic kind of bounce. Shakespeare really reported. He had a golden ear. Anyone less good ought to look at himself three times and say, "Hadn't I really better use a recording machine?" (Breit BR7)

The actual technique of transcription to which Lomax alludes is somewhat shrouded by the high ideals that drove it. Coming into the heady and prosperous 1950s after a long stint working with the Federal Writers Project at the end of the Great Depression, Lomax was charged with a populist patriotism and declared: "I believe this is the beginning of a technique which will make novel writing and biography a profoundly democratic thing." Clearly part of the democratic "truth and beauty" of which he speaks has to do with the *sound* of the voice, but Lomax says little about the difficulties and complexities of transcribing sounds to text aside from his admission that the process required "a lot" of editing. The resulting book is a combination of edited transcriptions of Jelly Roll Morton's speech as well as "Interlude" chapters in which Lomax provides historical context and additional biographical information that draws upon research and interviews with other New Orleans jazz musicians.

The challenges of transcription that surface in *Mister Jelly Roll* illuminate the tension between a desire for "authenticity" or "truth" and what Van Wyck Brooks called a "usable past," and resonate with contemporary questions about archival practice.[17] In *Archive Stories* (2006), Antoinette Burton frames the relationship between archives and history by suggesting that, "history is not merely a project of fact-retrieval . . . but also a set of complex processes of selection, interpretation, and even creative invention" (8). To the extent that acts of transcription in the era of recordings always involve an encounter with an archive (and in Lomax's case, the creation of one), Burton's assessment reminds us to consider the interpretive strategies not only of those who write recorded books but also of those who established the archives. Alan Lomax is a particularly complicated figure, in this regard. Lomax is certainly guilty of what Derrida called "archive fever" as he crossed the globe making and collecting recordings of as many sounds as one could imagine, and tracking his findings using his controversial theory of cantometrics. But in his collecting, Lomax was also committed to making his collections available and useful to as many people as possible, whether through books, his radio show, or the posthumously digitized Global Jukebox.[18] Although Lomax has been criticized (sometimes rightfully so) for his use of others' voices, he was not unaware of the problem.[19] *Mister Jelly Roll* uniquely illustrates the complexities of such an endeavor.

The transformation of the Library of Congress recordings of Jelly Roll Morton into a book did not initially motivate the recording sessions. In fact, more than a decade lapsed between the time Lomax recorded Morton and the publication of *Mister Jelly Roll* in 1950, during which Morton passed away and a limited number of the recordings were released as a box set by Circle Records in 1947. It is worth asking whether a book was necessary since we can easily listen to the recordings of Lomax's interviews with Morton. There are in fact a number of recorded jazz autobiographies that have no correlating book such as *Coleman Hawkins: A Documentary*, made in 1956 for Riverside.[20] *Mister Jelly Roll*, however, is not simply a direct transcription of the Library of Congress recordings but rather a multimodal text that resists generic classification; combining first- and third-person narration, it is what might be called *auto/biography*.[21] Rather than a cohesive biographical narrative, the book is a wrangling of disparate parts, and it bears resemblance to the multimodal writing of John Dos Passos, who (along with John Steinbeck) was one of the models the publishers suggested to Lomax when writing his book.[22] Through the mobilization of an elliptical method of transcription, Lomax seeks both to supplement and extend what is heard on the recordings. At its core, *Mister Jelly Roll* is Morton's story, but it is also a record of the experience of recording.

It was just three years after Lomax's trip with Hurston that he would encounter Jelly Roll Morton in Washington, DC, and bring him to the Library of Congress to record. Lomax was initially skeptical of recording Morton because he thought of jazz as part of the commercialization of culture that was killing folk life in America. However, Morton proved to be a gateway into a different understanding of jazz as an African American folk music that emerged from the unique cultural mixing of New Orleans. For Morton's part, he hoped to retune the ears of those who, like Lomax, could not hear the richness of jazz, for as Morton put it, "A lot of people have a wrong conception of jazz. Somehow it got into the dictionary that jazz was considered a lot of blatant noises and discordant tones, something that would be even harmful to the ears" (Lomax, *Mister Jelly* 81). Recording – and specifically phonographic recording – offered the possibility of a permanent engraving of speech, and outside the constraints of the commercial recording studio, Morton could renarrate the meaning of his music for the historical record. For African Americans, whose voices had been both functionally and figuratively suppressed, recording at the Library of Congress in Washington, DC, was an important symbolic action. When Morton arrived at the Library, he was dressed in his best suit and approached the building with the gravity one carries when going to court.

At the time Morton met Lomax, he was down on his luck and playing in an unremarkable Washington, DC, club. The state of affairs was a far cry from the height of his career in the 1910s and 1920s when Morton had been one of the most successful and in-demand players. Having risen from the Storyville sporting houses of New Orleans, the Creole musician had a hustler's bravado, but what set Morton apart was his sound. When he reached Chicago in the 1920s, he signed a recording contract with Victor and gained representation with MCA.[23] The recordings he made with the Red Hot Peppers were among the most popular and influential of the period and helped to establish Jelly Roll Morton as one of the biggest names in jazz. With songs like "Black Bottom Stomp" and "Doctor Jazz," his "hot" sound became his hallmark on his records and in dance halls. Due to consumers' repeated listening to popular records, jazz musicians like Morton and Bechet were able to establish sonic identities marked by their unique style of playing. Although musicians were often skeptical of the recording industry and its influence on the music, recordings allowed them to tell one kind of story through the music that later enabled a more direct kind of testimony.

The intertwined nature of the music and the autobiography must have become clear to Lomax from the moment Jelly Roll started playing. Asking Morton if he knew the song "Alabama Bound" as a test of his folksong knowledge, Morton happily obliged, sat down at the piano, and sang a version of the song that impressed even Lomax. While playing "Alabama Bound," Morton began talking over the introduction. "It came out of nowhere, the fact that he decided to do that," said Lomax (123). Telling the story of losing a piano contest and leaving New Orleans establishes why Morton went out on the road, playing pool in honky-tonks, ending up in Mobile. As Morton explained, "The frequent saying was any place you was going why you was supposed to be bound for that place. So in fact it was Alabama Bound and when I got there I wrote this tune . . ." which he proceeds to sing (*my transcription*, Disc 1, Track 1, The Complete Library of Congress Recordings: Jelly Roll Morton).[24] Listening to "Alabama Bound," we find that talking, playing, and singing are part of the same performance for Morton. Establishing convincing narratives of authorship and authenticity around tunes such as "Alabama Bound" and "King Porter Stomp" helped Morton to legitimate his claims to ownership and to effect a kind of copyright on the songs that the legal system was not successfully protecting.

During the recording session, the stories unfolded a-chronologically, and it was unclear where they might lead; but as a whole, the Library of Congress Recordings constituted an improvised autobiography – a substantial work that could stand on its own. Stretching over eight hours and 128 tracks, the recordings consist of Morton accompanying himself on piano while talking, demonstrating different styles, and performing songs that had a significant role in both his life story and in New Orleans jazz history – he was a master of the recording studio (see Figure 2.2). Yet the four-and-a-half minute tracks are more like loosely related vignettes. Morton's storytelling is shaped by associative thought and memory, and the occasional prod by Lomax. He remembers different details at different times, and his vision of New Orleans and the beginnings of jazz is built piece by piece; the whole picture emerges from the assembled fragments. Like a song, themes and motifs recur, both musically and verbally. In addition to the overlapping beginnings and endings of tracks necessitated by the four-minute limitations of the discs, there is a substantial amount of repetition and recursion as Morton retells and revises certain stories. Everyday speech is filled with these kinds of repetitions and returns, and indeed, our ability to comprehend speech is predicated on the emphasis of repeated information. To a listener, these returns in Morton's story are not jarring so much as they are rhythmic and important to our ability to link various aspects of the narrative, which do not flow so neatly. The resonance between the music and stories is forged by the ear. However, the fragmented and overlapping nature of the four-minute tracks does not directly translate to the page, where the reading eye is more accustomed to a linear narrative. For Lomax, the challenge in bringing Morton's story to the page was in defining a mode of transcription that preserved Morton's unique voice and sonic identity, while adhering to the more standard conventions of autobiography.

One of the first things a reader notices when beginning *Mister Jelly Roll* is that the book opens with an ellipsis. These three little dots start every chapter in which Morton is speaking in the first person; they are one of the

Figure 2.2 Jelly Roll Morton at RCA Studios, 1939

ways Lomax indicates that this is a "Morton" chapter rather than an "Interlude" narrated from Lomax's perspective. Jelly Roll begins: ". . . As I can understand, my folks were in the city of New Orleans long before the Louisiana Purchase, and all my folks came directly from the shores of France, that is across the world in the other world, and they landed in the New World years ago" (*Mister Jelly Roll* 3). Beginning in this way, the ellipsis creates the feeling of *in medias res*. An ellipsis typically represents the omission of words in a sentence. It points to an absence in the text and suggests that Morton's story was already in progress. As alluded to earlier, the recording "Jelly Roll's Background" (Disc 1, Track 5) is not the first track that Morton and Lomax recorded; this track begins with a few chords on the piano, followed by Morton asking Lomax: "Ready?" – an interesting role reversal of interviewer and subject. Lomax proceeds to ask him to start at the beginning and Morton replies: "Well, I'll tell ya. As I can understand

[. . .]." The ellipsis at the start of the chapter accounts for the actual omission of the meta-dialogue and the music at the beginning of the track, but it also creates a more general sense of omission, loss, and inability to fully express Morton's voice. The ellipses at the beginning of these chapters also point to that other dimension of Morton's speech that cannot be expressed on the page: his tone, pacing, and manner. Piecing together the narrative sentence by sentence, the ellipses may also serve as a blanket statement of omission, for Lomax's patchwork transcription style is characterized by his deletion of repeated phrases, superfluous information, and other verbal tics.

Describing *Mister Jelly Roll* as elliptical encompasses both punctuation and a narrative mode. Not only is the narrative characterized by ellipses as a way of accounting for the auditory loss and the actual omission of words, but the ellipsis may also account for Jelly Roll Morton's elliptical oratory style, which is circumlocutory and repetitive. Perhaps because Morton had told his stories so many times before, he repeats certain tales in the course of the Library of Congress recordings more than once. In moving from recording to text, Lomax compresses these multiple tellings into a single story for the sake of narrative cohesion. An example of this occurs in Morton's story about the lice-ridden St. Charles Avenue Millionaires. In order to better illustrate how Lomax constructs this passage as a composite, I have placed the text side by side with my transcript of the two versions Jelly Roll tells:

From *Mister Jelly Roll*
[. . .] and many times you would see
St. Charles millionaires right in those
honky-tonks. Called themselves
slumming, I guess, but they was there just
the same, nudging elbows with all the big
bums – the longshoremen and the illiterate
screwmens from down on the river.
[. . .]So in those days in honky-tonks the
St. Charles millionaires would bump up
against the fellows that was on the levee,
some of whom didn't bathe more than
once in six months and, I'll go so far as to
say, were even lousy. They would reach up
in their collars, when they saw anyone that
was dressed up, get one of these educated
louses and throw it on that person when his
back was turned. Then maybe a St. Charles

**From the Library of Congress
Recordings** (my transcription)
*"New Orleans was a Free and Easy Place"
(Disc 1, Track 13):*
Many times you would see some of that
St. Charles Avenue bunch right in one
of those honky-tonks. They was
around, they call themselves slummin'
I guess but they were there just the
same. Nudgin elbows with all the big
bums. And I would go so far to say that
some of them were even lousy. [*Here,
he's talking about the millionaires*] You
would meet many times with some of
those fellows that was on the levee such
as the inferior long shoremans [*pause*]
what is it? Long shoremans, is that
right? And screwmans, and many

Avenue millionaire would be in the same situation they were – lousy – and didn't know how they got to be that way. It was a funny situation. And away in the dark there would always be an old broke-down piano and somebody playing the blues and singing something like this . . .
I'm a levee man,
I'm a levee man (65)

I would doubt [*pause*] they were very unclean [*pause*] some of them was even lousy, I believe. I've known many cases where they'd take a louse and throw it on another guy that was dressed up to get him in the same fix they were in [*Alan laughs*]. Oh, it was funny situation. [*Alan asks if he remembers what they used to sing, and then Morton sings "Levee Man*] (0:30–1:24)
The other instance of the story occurs on "Honky Tonk Blues" (Disc 3, Track 16)
And the men I have personally seen some of 'em that was actually lousy. They would reach up maybe in their collar if they seen a decent person coming and formed a dislike for 'em and get one of those educated louses I guess and positively throw onto the person when his back was turned. There was a many that became lousy and didn't know how they got to be lousy. (3:10–3:37)

As these passages show, at the level of the phrase and of the sentence, Lomax provides a nearly direct transcription from the recording. But at the level of the paragraph, Lomax stitches together the disparate pieces in order to make chronological or narrative sense – it is a *rhapsody* in the Greek sense of stitching together song.[25] He reorders phrases and compresses longer ones as he eliminates those "redundancies that no eye can accept" (in the manner of Hurston). While Lomax preserves much of Morton's phrasing and maintains the rhythmic patterns of his syntax, his desire to create readable sentences must account for the differences between the practices of reading and listening. In forgoing phonetic transcription, Lomax's approach reflects the influence of Sterling Brown, but in reshaping Morton's speech, Lomax demonstrates a residual tendency to "improve" the material (as early ethnographers and folklorists did) in order to reconstruct a paradigmatic tale.

Lomax also uses ellipses to indicate the absence of the accompanying music, a feature that distinguishes the book from the recordings. Without the accompanying piano, the voice transcribed in *Mister Jelly Roll* is like listening to a singer *a cappella*. In this passage, the ellipsis leads the reader into a brief citation of the "levee man" lyrics which Morton sings on the recorded track "New Orleans was a Free and Easy Place" (Disc 1, Track 13). In order to create a sense of the missing music, Lomax paradoxically adds a visual description of the honky tonk scene, with its "old broke-down piano" and blues singer. This description situates the reader spatially within a scene of performance in order to arouse listening. However, in doing so, Lomax puts words in Morton's mouth in order to create a cohesive storyline. As evidenced by this example, Lomax erases his own presence from the transcript and turns the interview into a monologue in the "Morton" chapters, but in doing so, he must find other ways to account for this lost presence of the interlocutor and listener, which he does by adding the description of the performance.

In addition to the spaces left by the ellipses, Lomax alludes to and makes space for the missing recordings through footnotes and other supplementary paratextual materials. When writing about the famed piano player Tony Jackson, Lomax notes that "Jelly, after thirty years, not only recalled the names of these bygone musicians but remembered their music, and as he named them one after another, he paused to play a selection in their various styles" (54). In another footnote, Lomax clarifies the pronunciation of Morton's nickname and famous song, "Wining Boy": "*Wining* (pronounced with a long ī) is the term Jelly preferred to *winding* [which] also means rotating the hips in dancing or sexual intercourse" (59). Some references to omissions are precisely because of the explicit nature of the songs Morton sang for Lomax that, as he put it, "would burn the pages they were printed on" (60). This is to say nothing of the seventy-three pages of appended materials that include an annotated discography, a list of compositions, and transcriptions of several of the songs Morton played on the Library of Congress sessions. Footnotes and supplementary materials such as these, which point the reader to the "source" recordings, make bold the limitations of the book while providing a feast for serious audiophiles. Because a large selection of the Library of Congress sessions were released in 1947 on 78 records (and later LPs) as *The Saga of Mr. Jelly Lord* by Circle,[26] and many of Jelly Roll's Victor recordings had also been rereleased, it was quite possible for fans to read *and* listen side by side. The possibility – indeed, aspiration – of supplementary reading and listening is evident in the references to the recordings in the book, as well as the marketing materials that framed the album released by Circle, which treated each disc as a book chapter. In this way, the book and the recordings have a supplementary relationship to one another. Although the text and recordings can easily stand alone, the inter-medial aspirations express themselves as aesthetic gestures of gaps, "ghostly listeners," and phantom sounds. In this space between the text and the recordings, Lomax urges listening for the full range of signifying that Morton's testimony embodies, and Morton himself becomes a kind of recording body who "brought his old friends vividly alive" by recreating their piano styles (290). In the Prelude to the book, Lomax introduces a listening frame in order to model listening for his readers, as well as to suggest a new avenue for accessing the past through sound. Lomax describes how, "As the legend grew and flowered over the keyboard of that congressional grand piano, the back seats of the hall filled with ghostly listeners – figures dressed in Mardi Gras costumes, fancy prostitutes in their plumes and diamonds, tough sports from Rampart Street" and many others (xx). Like early frame tales such as the *Arabian Nights*, these ghostly listeners resituate readers in relation to an aural text. What strikes me about these scenes is that Lomax insists that the ghosts are listeners who emerge from, or are implied by, the recordings of Morton's music and speech. Usually the relationship between sound and listener is inverted; the audience listens *to* music, the music does not produce listeners. It is a subtle move, but the insistence on a performance that generates its own audience – a kind of self-contained performance and listening – parallels phonographic technologies like the Presto that both listen (i.e., record) and playback.

Listening, as an act of reckoning, and performing as an act of listening, takes shape in *Mister Jelly Roll*, and in its pages and on the acetate records: "New Orleans and her boy, Jelly, were getting their hearing at the bar of history itself" (290). Repositioning the "altogether recorded book" as not merely biography or literature but as a *hearing* in the juridical sense raises the ethical threshold of what sound can mean, the role listening can play, and the place of jazz within America's cultural history. The ghostly listeners alluded to in the Prelude and the Coda thus perform a number of roles and become a kind of jury of peers. Giving voice to these various Creole and African American characters who enter Morton's story is part of the underlying political thrust made by Lomax in which Black voices evoke presence that must be produced by resonant reading.

One of the ways Lomax does this is through the use of synesthetic-aural imagery, which neither serves to approximate the voice nor transcribe it, but rather to reinscribe Morton with an abstract sense of sonic identity. Unlike onomatopoeia, meter, rhyme, alternative spelling, or other poetic methods of infusing language with sound, synesthetic-aural imagery turns on adjective, uneasy metaphor, and simile. Pushing at the edges of this limited literary-sonic toolbox, Lomax attempts to describe that affective quality of Jelly Roll's voice:

> . . . a gravel voice melting at the edges, not talking, but spinning out a life in something close to song . . . each sentence almost like a stanza of a slow blues

. . each stanza flowing out of the last like the eddies of a big sleepy Southern river where the power hides below a quiet brown surface . . (xx)

Although in most places, Lomax uses three-dot ellipses, here he experiments with two-dot ellipses, as though to indicate a different length of pause or to insert space without implying absence.[27] It may be surprising that the appellation "gravel voice" was not widely recognized until the early 1940s.[28] It was a slang term meant to evoke the granular quality of gravel, so to say that a voice is gravelly is to simply say that it has a *grain* (as Roland Barthes might say).[29] The term is also used synonymously with *husky*, which refers to the sounds produced by dry cornhusks (here, the outer layer of a grain) rattled by wind. In both instances, the comparisons rely on recognizable references to the natural world. If you pull your hand through gravel, for instance, the friction of the individual stones or grains as they rub against each other create a distinctive sound; a recognizable whispery quality. Evan Eisenberg points out the strange symbiosis between the phonograph and sonic identification: "Music would now imitate records, especially [Louis] Armstrong's. Anyone could imitate his ballooning cheeks and gravelly voice, and any critic could recognize in him the voice of the phonograph, the voice of the invisible man" (121). Eisenberg's nod to Ellison's novel reinforces that book's insistently vocal quality. The emergence of gravelly voice as a term in the 1940s acknowledges a struggle with new ways to characterize the sounds that became such a part of everyday life through sound technology.

Given the roots of such terms in the natural world, the transition Lomax makes between Morton's "gravel voice" and the eddy of a river seems less jarring as we think about the gravelly riverbed. In this sense, Lomax is attempting to describe the *literal* grain of the voice, that is, the way that a voice is shaped by its geography and sense of place. What begins as an attempt to characterize Morton's voice quickly slips into a reference to the music and then quite suddenly transitions to a highly visual portrayal of the geography. The ever-morphing metaphor makes Morton into the mouthpiece of New Orleans and the Mississippi Delta, and the compressed description conflates his sound with a mythic geography that simultaneously allows Lomax to make a legend of the recording experience itself, as Morton spins the legend of New Orleans onto the disc. Lomax even strangely collapses the image of the phonograph with southern African Americans: "Something came along where the Mississippi Delta washes its muddy foot in the blue Gulf, something that bullies us, enchants us, pursues us out of the Black throats of a thousand music boxes. This something was jazz" (xxi). Lomax's description of Jelly Roll Morton's voice as *gravel* is an attempt to give his voice a geographic and technological marking, but it is also an indirect way of marking his voice as Black.[30] The descriptions are evocative in their way and help to contextualize Jelly Roll's world, but it would be more accurate to say that they only help us to understand how Lomax *hears* Morton. The compressed image of the phonograph's black throat illustrates how the sound of Morton's voice and the sound of the recording have become inseparable for Lomax – he can only represent the experience of *recording* Morton. While the book continues to point to the recordings to compensate for the loss of sound on the page, there are also elements that writing (through metaphor or figurative imagery) is better equipped to represent than the recordings alone. This is the condition of the "altogether recorded book" as it hovers in an intermedial zone.[31]

Sidney Bechet and the Tape Recorder

In the process of interviewing Sidney Bechet for *Mister Jelly Roll*, Lomax realized it was impossible to tell Morton's story without including his as well.[32] Less abrasive and self-promoting than Morton, Bechet was considered the golden boy of New Orleans; although not nearly as famous as his younger contemporary Louis Armstrong, Bechet is credited as one of the pioneers who brought the hot sound to jazz solos, first on clarinet and later on soprano saxophone. Like Morton, Bechet did not stay long in New Orleans, setting out on the road in 1916 and spending extended amounts of time in Chicago, London, New York, and Paris (which he would make his permanent home after 1950). His brother Leonard Bechet, a dentist by trade and erstwhile trombone player, made nearly two hours of recorded interviews with Lomax in 1949, and through these stories Sidney Bechet appears in *Mister Jelly Roll*. Sidney Bechet had also met Alan Lomax on several occasions while playing on his various radio shows in the 1940s.[33] The use of recordings in the writing process of his own autobiography and the desire to infuse the text with Bechet's sound are a direct nod to *Mister Jelly Roll*, and *Treat It Gentle* serves as a key link between the first "altogether recorded book" and the various kinds of as-told-to books that materialized thereafter.

There are a few important differences between Morton and Bechet's books, most significantly that *Treat It Gentle* calls itself an "autobiography" (*Mister Jelly Roll* was officially a "biography") and lacks the interludes and other mediating texts that we find in *Mister Jelly Roll*. Even though it was transcribed and pieced together by editors, it is narrated entirely in Bechet's first-person voice. While Lomax did not begin the process of writing *Mister Jelly Roll* until after Morton's death, the recorded interviews of Bechet were always made with the express purpose of writing a book, and Bechet thought of himself not only as a musician but as a writer. Differences at the institutional level (commercial publishing vs. Library of Congress) greatly shaped the interview and transcription process, making for a complicated editorial history; *Treat It Gentle* went through three editors and two publishers before reaching print, and most of the recordings used in writing the book have gone missing or were recorded over. When I began this project, I was hopeful that I would be able to locate the taped interviews used to write *Treat It Gentle* in order to give them the hearing they deserve; mostly, I was met with silence.[34] Sifting through the catalogs of disparate archives, the only tapes I located amount to a little over two hours of interviews made in Paris in 1957 by the book's final editor, Desmond Flower of Cassell & Company Ltd., which are held at Tulane's Hogan Jazz Archive. These interviews, which offer a rare sample of Bechet's unique voice, were taken after a substantial amount of the manuscript had been drafted and served primarily to fill in gaps and bring the story up to date from where it left off around 1936. The Foreword to *Treat It Gentle* by Flower offers a few clues about the multiple hands at work and the use of recordings, crediting Joan Reid, Bechet's secretary, for "getting a very considerable amount of material on to tape" (v). However, Reid played a conflicting role, transcribing the first draft but also waging legal battles for authorial credit that halted initial attempts to publish the book. We now know that *Treat It Gentle* may never have come to print without the guiding hand of Bechet's manager and champion in Paris, Charles Delaunay (founder of *Le Jazz Hot* magazine), a fact made evident by the extensive collection of letters and other Bechet materials recently located within Delaunay's collection at the Bibliothèque Nationale de France in Paris.

As the letters between Delaunay, Bechet, and his publishers indicate, the bulk of the tapes were made by Joan Reid with additional tapes made by the poet and editor John Ciardi, and there were most likely tapes made by Bechet himself.[35] Yet, the unknown location of these tapes, if they still exist, presents something of a problem for those who wish to understand how Bechet's so-called recorded book came to be. The mystery of the tapes may be a casualty of the medium itself. If the poor quality of the existing tapes made by Flower is any indication, those who worked on Bechet's book treated the tape recordings like scratch paper – just another way of making disposable notes – and for this reason, the attitude toward tape and transcription is much like that of the early ethnographers who treated the text as primary. Indeed, had the Hogan Archive not digitally remastered their tapes a few years ago, listening to Bechet would have been nearly impossible, for the original tapes have such poor, muddled sound quality as to almost be unlistenable.

But even with Flower's additional interviews and chapters, the story was never quite finished. Bechet had more to say but illness left him without a voice for the last months of his life; Delaunay had tried to coax him into writing more of his story, but Bechet insisted upon using his tape recorder. In a letter from April 8, 1959, Delaunay lamented, "I have tried in vain several times to get from Sidney the few things he wanted to change in the manuscript [...]. The thing is that Sidney wanted to answer himself and record it. But since September he never recovered his voice. And now I am getting convinced that Sidney will never recover not only his voice but his health."[36] When I interviewed Sidney's son, Daniel, in Paris on October 2, 2012, I asked him about his father's tape recorder, to which Daniel remarked, "He had two! A big one and a little one." In fact, Bechet used the tape recorder for the dictation of his stories as well as to compose music. Since Bechet never learned to read music, in his later years he composed at the piano with the tape recorder at his side, playing and sometimes singing too. "He had so many melodies and concepts inside him," Daniel remarked, and "if he had the opportunity to translate a different way, he might have." While Daniel still has a few of these tapes of his father's composing, the interviews for *Treat It Gentle* are not among them. Were these tapes locatable, they might comprise a rather extensive collection – one that could rival the interviews of Morton made at the Library of Congress.[37] Even without the recordings, the impulse to hear the poetry of Bechet's playing (Lomax called Bechet the "poet of jazz") in the pages of his book by his devoted fans says something of the need to always be listening for Bechet.

Whereas Morton's interviews with Lomax were highly performative, Bechet's demeanor on the recordings with Desmond Flower reflects a writerly bent, and these recordings do not include accompanying or interceding music. Instead, Bechet self-consciously refers to his "book" throughout his interviews with Flower. Time and again, he tells Flower, "as I've said in my book ..." as a way to curtail the interview and limit his responses, but in doing so, he reveals his disposition toward the recording-as-writing, as well as his knowledge of the existing transcript (which he is said to have read and approved before his death). In such instances, Bechet often stops and starts the tape, and it is clear from the conversation on the beginning of the tape that Bechet is the one in charge of the recording (Flower asks if the machine is working and if he is speaking loud enough). But despite Bechet's assertive presence during the recording sessions and investment in text, his words were held captive for several years as his various publishers and editors sorted out legal disputes over authorship.[38] And yet, Bechet's hyperawareness of the "book" – versus the recorded narrative – hints at his acute sense of the media and their differences.

That Bechet thought of himself as a writer has been made more evident by my archival research at the Bibliothèque Nationale de France, which revealed that Bechet's writerly pursuits extended to short fictional works meant for either stage or screen. Among his papers in the Charles Delaunay collection are two short unpublished manuscripts; the first, a stage play or screenplay titled "Wildflower (or, The Story of Frankie and Johnny)," was written around 1952 and is a retelling of the popular song "Frankie and Johnny." Bechet did not seem to know what form "Wildflower" ought to take – a ballet, a film, or a book – and the eleven-page manuscript reads more like a sketch than a full-fledged play, focusing on the colorful story of Nelly Blay, a blues singer who leads Johnny astray, but it hints at the shape of Bechet's style as he improvises and dramatizes the popular standard. A few years later, around 1955, Bechet put together a second treatment for a film or a novel – an untitled four-page story about a jazz musician, King Joe, a singer named Lilli Tiger, and King Joe's long-lost son.[39] As the story of an older musician living in Paris reminiscing about a love affair from twenty years prior, it reads as vaguely autobiographical. Bechet, it would seem, treated the events and scenes from his life like standards over which to improvise.

Treat It Gentle, as published, is narrated in Bechet's first-person voice, but in the initial manuscript, Joan Reid included her own editorial commentary. John Ciardi, the second editor, and Twayne found her "purple prose" distracting and eliminated it to form the uninterrupted first-person narrative we now know (Cifelli 154). This rather harried publication history raises questions about the voice of the text and the relationship of Bechet to his interviewers and editors. The narrative voice is further complicated by the fact that interviewees like Bechet and Morton tend to adjust their manner of speaking both as a result of the presence of the recording machine and in accordance with the identity of the interviewer. For example, there are moments on the tapes when Bechet adopts Desmond Flower's posh British accent or performs Fats Waller's Harlem drawl. The different voices assumed by Bechet destabilize the notion that Bechet has one "authentic" voice and make the possibility of conveying this aspect of his speech even more problematic.[40] The relationship between interviewer and subject influences how and what stories are told, but in the tradition of ethnographic recording and transcription, texts derived from recordings tend to erase or obscure the presence of the interviewer. The decision of whether to include the interviewer or not – that is, to establish a listening frame – illustrates the ongoing tension between the renewed sense of aurality in these recorded books and the traditions of print.

Analysis of Desmond Flower's transcription style reveals the challenges of wrangling a chronological narrative from a multitude of vignettes. Since Flower interviewed Bechet after a significant portion of the manuscript for the book had been completed, his additions to the book are interspersed throughout the text. Like Lomax, Flower preserves idiomatic expressions and sentence-level syntactical choices while eliminating redundancies. Whereas Lomax did a good deal of editing to coax Morton's stories into cohesive paragraphs, Desmond Flower stays more faithful to Bechet's meandering patterns of speech, and his transcriptions frequently run for several paragraphs with scarcely any embellishments or additions. However, moments that in the interview have a certain element of drama or emotional pull sometimes fall flat in the transcription, which seems unable to capture the tone or the important role of the interviewer in extracting a story. For example, I have included a side-by-side comparison of Bechet's account of his brother Leonard's death in *Treat It Gentle* and my own transcription of the tape made by Desmond Flower:

In *Treat It Gentle*:	**On Tape** 071 (10:27–12:38) *(my transcription)*:
But I came back to Paris, and it was around this time that my brother Leonard died. I said how he used to come up from New Orleans to see me, and after I came to Europe we kept corresponding together. I wanted him to come to Europe, and I was always on to him about it but he never made up his mind. Then about two or three o'clock one morning, I received a telephone call to tell me my brother Leonard, he was dead; and that was the end of him, poor fellow. Leonard, he never made up his mind. He never just wanted to play trombone,	SB: I was fixin to have him come and live with me, but he got ill, and I went to Chicago to work, and my brother he got alright. And that was around '48, so he made two visits to Chicago and in '49 as I came to Europe, you know, and we kept corresponding together, you know, and I wanted him to come to Europe. And a few years later I received a telephone call bout two, three 'clock in the morning to tell me my brother Leonard had died. [*long pause*] That was the end of him, poor fellow. [*slowly, belabored*] DF: He died in New Orleans?

and it was a sort of hobby for him, you see. But in later years we had a feeling that he really wanted to leave the dentistry alone and just play Jazz music. That was his intention, but I guess, time caught up with him, and he had to leave us. He died right there in the hospital in New Orleans. He was around twelve or fifteen years older than me, and he was the member of my family who had always been nearest to me – right from the days when he started the Silver Bells Band – and whom I loved best. (196–97)

SB: Yes, he died in the hospital.
DF: Was he still practicing as a dentist?
SB: Oh yes he was still practicing and playing too. He never made up his mind. He never wanted to just play trombone like that, it was a sort of hobby for him, you see, but later years he had a feeling that he really wanted to just leave the dentistry alone and play jazz music. That was his intention. But I guess time caught up with him. He had to leave us.
DF: He was a year or two older?
SB: No, he was much more [*pause*] between fifteen and twelve round [*pause*] oh yes
DF: And he was the member of the family you were fondest of?
SB: Oh yes. Yes.
[*mumbles – unintelligible*]
I think we better wind it up [*tape cuts out*][41]

Even my transcription does not quite capture the sighs and slowing pace of Bechet's story as he approaches the phone call. We lose the belabored way in which Flower carefully attempts to draw out details and the seeming insufficiency of questions like "He died in New Orleans?" The emotion seems to overwhelm Bechet at Flower's last question, and quickly thereafter Bechet half mumbles, "I think we better wind it up," signifying the end of a place where speech is possible. The tape cuts out; the book simply moves on to the next paragraph and the narrative chronology continues.

Flower's transcription can at times feel stiff and err on the side of literary cohesion; like Lomax, Bechet and his editors recognize the limits of translatability between the medium of the recorded voice and the written word. A self-consciousness about the media infiltrates the tone in other parts of Bechet's story that were written prior to Flower's intervention as well. Talking about learning the blues in prison, Bechet begins to quote a few of the lyrics he heard but then recognizes how poor a rendering this will be when his interview is transcribed:

> The man prays to the Lord to hear his cry
> And the Lord says, 'Go down Angel, that man's got
> no right to die.'

Well, it would be easy for me to tell you some lyrics, make up other ones, just fill it in and fake it for you. But that won't do – that's not the way I'd want. You got to hear it for yourself, you got to *feel* that singing, and I got no way to make that possible for you in a book way. But what you've got to realize is this blues, it had a memory to it; it was like I was talking to one of these people come to hear us play. (107)

This moment of meta-discourse encapsulates several of the conundrums one faces in moving between sound recording and text – and particularly music and text. By including a few lyrics and simultaneously acknowledging the impossibility of representing the blues on the page, Bechet creates a paradox that calls out for resonant reading. The use of the second-person imperative "You" indicates the residual presence of the interviewer to whom Bechet told the story and reaches out toward the reader holding the book. For Bechet, the experience requires more than simply hearing the blues, and he insists that the reader must *feel* the memories within the blues. Pointing to the void in order to fill it may seem a similar strategy to the ellipses Lomax uses in *Mister Jelly Roll*, but whereas Lomax points to the absence of music in order to reference the recordings, *Treat It Gentle* accounts for the absence by suggesting a more ambiguous idea of listening. The sense that one must *feel* the memory of the blues extends the idea of what sound can mean and implies that even a recording would be insufficient to convey the depth of sound that Bechet experienced in prison. This same impulse also allows him to bring the memory of his grandfather, a slave, into the story as an audible memory. For Bechet, listening (or hearing "for yourself") is always at the heart of the resonant critical practice he is imagining, even as he is quite consciously "writing" a book. That Bechet claims that there is no way for him to put the blues "in a book way," rather than simply saying there is no way to *write* the blues, seems deliberate here, for it focuses the attention on the medium rather than the method. On the one hand, he is referring to the way that the lyrics capture only a part of the blues, but he is also talking about the ever-evolving, shape-shifting nature of the blues as a living thing. Thus, Bechet's idea of listening is always expansive, rather than purely referential, as it works along the "edge" of meaning, as Jean-Luc Nancy might put it.[42]

Of course, this edgy quality is also one of the hallmarks of Bechet's sound with its wide vibrato, and these moments of self-reflexivity and hesitation, which cause him to stop himself short and unsettle the narrative, could be said to parallel certain aspects of Bechet's playing. The distinctive quality of Bechet's fast, warbling vibrato can also be a bit unsettling. After all, one of the ways to think of vibrato is as a refusal to settle on a single note in favor of a pulsation between pitches. John Chilton has gone so far as to say that the intensity and width of Bechet's vibrato, which nods to the stylings of the great operatic tenors, was the "biggest obstacle to his achieving universal acclaim," "touching a nerve" with certain listeners and creating an "aural hardship" (291, 46). Paradoxically, the vibrato is also what makes Bechet's sound recognizable and palpable on recordings and brings it closer to a vocal grain; the unsettling quality and the underlying desire to unseat inflects the writing.

Part of Bechet's ambiguity about the capacity of language to relate his autobiography is the sense that the music already contains the narrative: "I wouldn't tell all this in a story about the music, except all I been telling, it's part of the music" (201). For Bechet, the line between musician and author is forever blurred, but he occasionally checks himself and expresses insecurity about his role as a writer. In another self-conscious turn, he cuts himself short and says: "But I don't want to get away from my story. There's so much books and speeches made about it, there's not much use talking about it all. I just play my music" (40). This evasion erupts in a moment when Bechet begins to talk more directly about racial tensions and the subjugation of Black people during slavery. The dismissal, "I just play music," may hint at a feeling of unease, not just with the literary role Bechet has assumed in telling this story but with the political role it inevitably implies. Bechet is far more comfortable *playing* the sounds of his enslaved grandfather, Omar, than he is trying to explain the institution of slavery. But rather than undermine Bechet's authorial voice, the appeals to music strategically allow him to reassert sound's capacity for meaning: "The music, it's my whole story," he says (218). Of course, the book itself tacitly refutes this assertion. If the music were the whole story, or if the recordings could serve as their own history, writing a book would be unnecessary. As Bechet's approach to writing suggests, he can hear the story and its sound, but he struggles to find the right medium in which to express his ideas. Music alone is often not enough.

Bechet's insistence that readers must hear, listen, and feel sounds pervades his book. Nowhere is this clearer than in the story Bechet tells about his grandfather Omar – an ill-fated escaped slave, who was also one of the most famous drummers of Congo Square. Omar loses an arm before suffering an untimely death at the hand of his beloved's jealous master, but even during his exile in the bayou with a lynch mob at his heels, he was able to communicate with his people through rhythm and song. Many, including Bryan Wagner and Bechet's biographer John Chilton, have disputed the historical facts of Bechet's account of Omar, which closely echoes the famous tale of Bras-Coupé made legendary by George Washington Cable. (Bechet did not have a slave grandfather named Omar.) Wagner has argued that the figure of Bras-Coupé, with his amputated arm and limited history, created a space in which writers have been able to intervene, fictionalize, and reify legend into autobiography and history.[43] But Bechet's fictionalizing does not reduce the story's fundamental truth. The story of Omar may divulge more about Bechet's musical genealogy than his actual blood lineage. For Americans who are the descendants of African slaves, the issue of genealogy is exceedingly complex: laws prohibiting slaves from attaining literacy prevented them from keeping written records; as captives wrested from their homeland, slaves were forced to give up their native languages and to take the names of their masters – all factors that have impeded genealogical study. In a story about the music's origins (Bechet's original title for the book was: *Where Did It Come From?*), this kind of genealogy is perhaps more important, and the Omar or Bras-Coupé figure's actual amputated limb makes space for the kind of phantom limb of Black musical history that Bechet is trying to conjure.

As a drummer in Congo Square, Omar is "like a piece of rhythm," one that reappears throughout Bechet's music as well as throughout his book (44). Bechet and the editors treat Omar like a refrain that ties various vignettes together, for as Bechet goes on to say, "As an idea, the way he [Omar] played his horns, the way he beat on his drums, he was still a background music" (44). The impulse to treat Omar as a "rhythm" or "background music" emphasizes Omar's position within the musical genealogy and frames him as a sonic character. For if Omar is a piece of rhythm, it would follow that he can be *played*, and even improvised. In one such flight of fancy, Bechet uses the Omar story to explain the relationship between the music, memory, and Africa. Talking about the drum, he says:

> That was how the Negro communicated when he was back in Africa. He had no house, he had no telegraph, no newspaper. But he had a drum, and he had a rhythm he could speak into the drum, and he could send it out through all the air to the rest of his people, and he could bring them to him. And when he got to the South, when he was a slave, just before he was waking, before the sun rode out in the sky, when there was just that morning silence over the fields with maybe a few birds in it – then, at that time, he was back there again, in Africa. Part of him was always there, standing still with his head turned to hear it, listening to someone from a distance, hearing something that was kind of a promise, even then. . . .
> And when he awoke and remembered where he was – that chant, that memory, got mixed up in a kind of melody that had a crying inside itself " (7; ellipsis Bechet's)

The idea that a slave in America could *hear* back to Africa – as though the drum were already a broadcast technology – in a moment of silence, emphasizes Bechet's assertion that the blues has "a memory to it." In this way, listening is both an internalized and externalized activity and requires one to enter a meditative, dreamlike state – listening across time and space in unconventional ways. Like the ghostly listeners in *Mister Jelly Roll*, the image of the listening slave is a product of the music, standing in tension with the sounds of the drums and participating in a complex doubling, resonating at once in Africa and America. The scene also resonates with folk representations of High John de Conquer – a shape-shifting, hope-bringing folk hero and slave who Zora Neale Hurston described as "a whisper, a will to hope, a wish to find something worthy of laughter and song" who had "come from Africa. He came walking on the waves of sound. Then he took on flesh after he got here" (*Folklore* 450, 451).[44] To make these sounds more present, Bechet infuses the writing with the kinds of rhythms he is talking about. The repetitive, rhythmic structure of this passage, with its short phrases, carries the markers of oral speech, which, in the words of Walter Ong, is "additive rather than subordinative," and helps us feel that Bechet is speaking to us (36). On the page, this overflowing feeling of 'and' also creates a rhythmic pulse meant to resonate with the drums, drawing us closer to the sounds of the music. In this way, inflections of a poetic orality in the text create a sound that is closer to singing, a sound that buds into the aural realm. Strings of short, paratactic sentences build upon one another with a mounting sense of rhythmic addition, like the drums that call and respond to one another: "First one drum, then another one answering it. Then a lot of drums. Then a voice, one voice. And then a refrain, a lot of voices joining and coming into each other. And all of it having to be heard" (8). In these moments, the music was "being born right inside itself" as Bechet recreates the rhythms in the text (8). Through his poetics, he can point toward those rhythms and try to get the reader to "turn to hear it" and listen in the distance for a *memory* of sound, if not the sound itself. Like Jean-Luc Nancy's *renvoi* or return, these resonant textual performances are less about sound as an object than about adopting a particular attitude to, toward, and in the direction of listening. This reformulation of sound and radical representation of listening offers a model for readers, who could not possibly be expected to reproduce particular sounds.

The line between the music, talking, and writing is never so neatly drawn for Bechet. According to him, "The music gives you its own understanding of itself. But first, you have to like it; you have to be wanting to hear it" (204). The notion of listening as a radically democratic tool is noted by Alan Lomax as well as Roland Barthes; and by Bechet's logic, hearing is more than simply the ear's ability to transduce vibrations into sound. Hearing and listening – and we might say, resonant reading – represent a spectrum of empathy, understanding, and even access to an unrecorded history.

Morton and Bechet in the Studio

Bechet's contributions to the sound of jazz are remarkable enough that we tend to forget that he was also experimental in the recording studio (see Figure 2.3).[45] One of the more illuminating aspects of *Treat It Gentle* is that, in addition to offering new approaches to listening, Bechet spends time reflecting upon the recorded medium, its limitations and its possibilities. Given the undeniably important role that recordings played in the spread of jazz from a regional music to a popular national (and international) form, it is hard for us to imagine a time when musicians actually turned down the chance to record. But Bechet, like Morton and many of their contemporaries, had initially approached recording with a degree of

Figure 2.3 Sidney Bechet plays at Jelly Roll Morton's last Victor recording session, September 14, 1939

skepticism. Bechet struggles to explain, for instance, why Freddie Keppard turned down the chance to record with Victor in New York in 1915, which would have made Keppard's band the first to make a jazz record.[46] "Freddie just didn't care to, that was all," said Bechet (112). Players like Keppard worried that recording would encourage imitators who would "steal" the music, but Bechet's analysis of the recorded medium takes a more nuanced approach:

> You hear a record, you know – you don't see all that stamping and face-making; you just hear the music. And that's the same of today; you take someone that's grinning and stomping and moving around the stand where the *music* should be going – for the moment you're lost from the music, you're so busy watching him fool around. But you get his same record and try to listen to the music then, and there's no music there. (83–84)

This reflection on the acousmatic nature of recordings – a concept Pierre Schaeffer uses to describe the way we hear sounds separated from their source – comes after Bechet's attempt to discuss the differences between the legendary cornet player Buddy Bolden, whom Bechet calls a great showman, and Manuel Perez, who Bechet felt was a superior player. Of course, the irony of this example is that Buddy Bolden never recorded – a fact that is still considered one of the great tragedies in jazz history (it is also the subject of Michael Ondaatje's novel *Coming Through Slaughter* [1976]). The implication of Bechet's assessment, however, is that Bolden could never have really made a record, even if he had the chance; as a showman, Bolden's music would not have shown up. While one might view this as a deficiency of the recorded medium, Bechet's preference for Perez's "sincere" playing and his belief that "you've got to be the music first" suggest that recordings might also help to separate real musicians from mere entertainers (84).

This is not to say that Bechet idealized the recorded medium. He too was critical of the tendency of the record companies to exploit musicians and put profit before quality.[47] He criticized the proliferation of imitators and denigrated the idea that recordings could be equated with ownership: "You can't own a thing like that unless you understand a lot more about it than just repeating what's written down" (114). As someone who played by ear, Bechet remained skeptical of written scores as well. Yet despite these protests, Bechet was a savvy and successful recording artist, becoming one of the early experimenters with the medium; his aptitude for the technology influenced his commercial recordings as well as his personal and amateur recordings.

Both Morton and Bechet shared a technological acumen with the recorded medium. According to Danny Barker, "Morton did what no other musician dared to do at the time: enter the sanctity of the control room of the recording studios and give advice to the engineers. And for that reason, he said, his RCA records were clearer and better defined than others in his time" (Szwed, "Doctor Jazz" 18). Evan Eisenberg has compared the importance of Morton's recording innovations to those of Sergei Eisenstein in film, arguing that Morton's influence can be felt in recordings by "master builders" from Ellington to Frank Zappa and the Beatles (122). "What is even more remarkable is his construction of dazzling phonographic montages in whole takes, without the aid of tape. . . . Morton's records rely less on the power of his personality than on the power of his constructions: the dazzling succession of riffs, breaks, and bittersweet harmonies is what carries the listener along" (121–22). While Eisenberg's assessment verges on hyperbole, it points to the incredible influence of the sound Morton developed in the recorded medium.

Traces of this aptitude can be heard in the recorded interviews as well: Morton occasionally asks Lomax if there is enough time on the disc to continue with a particular story; Bechet decides when to start and stop the tape and answers Flower's questions about whether he is using the machine properly. For these reasons, we must look at the recorded interviews as true collaborations between interviewer and subject, for both Morton and Bechet approached the task with a sense of purpose and a high degree of what we might call recording literacy. These were not merely oral storytellers passively recorded; these were men who knew how to write in sound.

Bechet's philosophical-acoustical aspirations to write sound in *Treat It Gentle* should be read as an extension of his musical recordings, such as his infamous one-man-band recording of "Sheik of Araby" (1941), which is widely acknowledged as the very first multitrack recording. His approach to sound within his book is less referential than it is aspirational, evoking sounds that never existed or that must be felt. On "Sheik of Araby," Bechet experimented with a primitive kind of overdubbing and achieved what would otherwise be an impossible performance by playing every instrument on the recording. Since tape and multitrack recordings had not yet been invented, he played all six instruments one after the other, overdubbing each instrument by playing along to the previous recording (180).[48] "Sheik of Araby" was so controversial that the American Federation of Musicians forced the studio to pay Bechet seven times over for playing all the instruments as well as the role of band leader, and then they outlawed the practice for many years thereafter, citing it as unethical.[49] Today we

think very little about whether a recording represents an authentic performance because multitracking, autotune, and a number of other digital
technologies make it possible to create recordings that could never exist in
performance. Almost every recorded sound we hear now has been filtered,
processed, chopped-up, looped, spliced, amplified, and rebalanced in every
imaginable way. In making sounds more "perfect" than they could ever be
in performance, our contemporary concerns are less about the absence of
an "original" performance than whether live performances can measure up
to the "original" recording.

There is something uncanny, even unsettling about listening to "Sheik
of Araby," which Bechet seemed to be aware of when reflecting upon the
recording in later years. Bechet chalked this up to difficulties with the
engineer, but as a conversation with Fats Waller revealed, there was a level
of absurdity to the performance from the start:

> The funny part was right after that I met Fats Waller going into the theatre;
> he was playing at the Polo. So he said to me, "Bechet, I'm telling you, boy,
> you certainly did make that one man band record!" And I said, "It would
> have been all right if we would have had a rehearsal before," meaning the
> engineer and myself, you know. But Fats, he laughed and said, "Man, how
> the hell you going to have a rehearsal with yourself?" (180)[50]

Not only does the interchange highlight Bechet's technical understanding
of how recordings are made, but it reflects one of the fundamental differences between recordings and live performances. Waller was right: rehearsing with oneself was not an option. A one-man-band recording is nothing
like playing with a band.[51] But without the tools to engineer the recording
to sound more natural, it just sounds *off*.

Experimental uses of recordings were, in fact, central to Bechet's musical
output. Daniel Bechet has explained that his father composed by recording
himself playing piano and singing. Furthermore, Bechet experimented
with overdubbing on at least one other occasion in 1942 with the help of
John Reid, making an overdubbed "duet" of "Weary Blues" with New
Orleans trumpeter Bunk Johnson. At the time, Bechet was acutely aware
that he might never have the chance to actually record with Bunk – one of
his early collaborators – and that he needed to make some kind of *record* of
their playing together. In the space of the recording, Bechet is able to
bridge both the geographic divide between New Orleans and New York
and the many years since they had last played together. Like the "Sheik
of Araby," the performance could not have existed without recording
technology.

It is tempting to draw an analogy between the one-man-band studio recording and the editorial methods employed to write recorded autobiography: both, in their way, reproduce sonic performances that cannot be linked to a single, originary performance and push acousmatic listening to new limits. Like the one-man-band recording, the narrative voice of the recorded autobiography is a composite; different iterations of the same story are layered and filtered together in order to create the effect of a single narrative. The voice of "Morton" in *Mister Jelly Roll* sounds convincingly like Jelly Roll Morton, even though the book is the result of a complex orchestration of many disparate pieces by Lomax (and likewise for Bechet in *Treat It Gentle*). To the extent that these texts insist upon their sonic qualities and root themselves in recordings of the biographical subject's *real* voice, we might begin to think of Lomax, Flower, et al. as *audio engineers* rather than merely editors. To be sure, there are important differences between editing a book and engineering a record. For one, on a recording, we can still hear each individual instrument clearly articulated while all the tracks are playing at once. The same cannot be said of a book in which the various tales woven together can no longer be seen as component parts; the stitches can only be seen with great effort as one listens to the recordings alongside the text. Books have long been subject to editors who manipulate and rearrange text to create a whole; however, the comparison between editors and engineers is useful for thinking about the ways that these two texts are pushing against the boundaries of their media and incorporating the lessons of commercial recording into the writing process. Likewise, it may be helpful to think of the ways that audio engineers have taken on roles that have more in common with literary editors while forward-thinking musicians such as Bechet (and later Les Paul and others) push the possibilities of the technology forward and work to naturalize sounds that are otherwise unnatural.

***

Though there has been a tendency to talk about recorded jazz auto/ biographies as "oral histories," this term ultimately limits the breadth of sounds that these texts contain. Unlike oral history, the recorded book does not merely collect recordings and transcriptions to sit in archives for further research, nor does the recorded book simply transcribe words spoken on a recording. These are not merely oral but *aural* histories.[52] For when it comes to writing about musicians, sonic identity cannot be inscribed within the voice (and especially the recorded voice) alone. Situated on the cusp of two different media, these books and the recordings on which they rely exist in tension with one another, ever pointing in the direction of the other and asking readers to hear across the mediated divide. Because text is a silent medium, it allows us to consider sound in ways that sound recordings alone cannot. As texts whose silence challenges the very notion of listening, *Mister Jelly Roll* and *Treat It Gentle* show us the degree to which all sounds are constructed. Our listening is no more transparent than the act of transcription that makes recording into text. It requires attention. As Bechet says, "The music gives you its own understanding of itself. But first, you have to like it; you have to be wanting to hear it" (204).

CHAPTER 3

Press Play

Jack Kerouac, William S. Burroughs, and the Tape Recorder

On September 7, 1951, just a few months after completing the scroll of *On the Road* (1957) and a month before beginning work on *Visions of Cody* (written 1951–52, published 1972), Jack Kerouac reported in his journal, "Am reading Lomax's 'Mister Jelly Roll'—great material by an important writer about an American artist who will live ... Jelly Roll Morton (without whom maybe Mamie's Blues wouldn't have survived). In the afternoon, in my fields, I discovered once & for all that I need my wire recorder" (*Unknown Kerouac* 119).[1] That Kerouac made note of his reading was not unusual – he was an avid reader and a noted jazz fan. However, the reference here to Alan Lomax's 1950 book about Jelly Roll Morton is especially interesting because it was, as Lomax described it, the "first altogether recorded book" (xvi). In the journal entries and sketches Kerouac would write over the following month while revising *On the Road* and *Visions of Cody*, he frequently interrupted his own prose mid-sentence: "—but wait till *tape recorder!*" as though his pencil could not keep up with his memory (108). By mid-fall Kerouac was on his way back to San Francisco to see Neal Cassady to make recordings of their conversations. As Neal's wife, Carolyn Cassady, recalled, the tape recorder was "always rolling" during this time, but due to the expense of the new technology, they were constantly recording over their tapes.[2] The tape sessions became immortalized in the book we now know as *Visions of Cody* in the two longest sections titled "Frisco: The Tape" (a direct transcription of Kerouac's conversations with Cassady) and "Imitation of the Tape" (a section that contains fictionalized tape transcripts). But what was it about the tape recorder that captured Kerouac's imagination? What did the tape recorder promise writers that other methods and other technologies did not?

Kerouac's interest in making his own sound recordings found an outlet in 1949 when his friend John Clellon Homes recorded Kerouac along with Allen Ginsberg, William S. Burroughs, and others with an acetate disc recorder. These early records, which are now located among the John Clellon Holmes papers and recordings at Kent State, capture readings and conversation laced over radio music and party sounds. As Phil Ford aptly describes in *Dig: Sound and Music in Hip Culture*, the acetate records "are ambiguous as history and doubtful as aesthetic objects. They are documents of lives but do not tell a tale" (95). While fascinating documents in their own right, little became of these early records. Kerouac's encounters with acetate disc recording did not provoke the same kind of kinetic response that the tape recorder would, but the experience introduced him to the capacity of recording to capture speech and sound in the moment of the event.

One cannot know for certain when Kerouac first used a tape recorder, but his 1951 journals not only make reference to his desire to acquire his own, but includes several allusions to making tape recordings in the back room of Jerry Newman's record store. Among other things, Newman was notorious for making bootleg recordings of live jazz shows in the 1940s and selling these records without paying the artists, and it seems he had a side interest in recording poets as well. In an entry dated September 21, 1951, Kerouac recalls heading "uptown to Jerry Newman's record store, 3-hour conversation with gin & coke in that great backroom (which is the greatest in N.Y.) with Bill Fox and for awhile Barry Ulanov (my visions of a Balzacian N.Y. again & how I wish I owned that backroom and could record the era with tape-recorder as it confidentially tells stories behind the hand—and Jerry wants to make *money* with that machine!)" (*Unknown Kerouac* 128). The following week, Kerouac, drunk on martinis, returns to Newman's backroom where "Jerry plays me my recording of my chapters on jazz in *On the Road* and it is on street loudspeaker, my own writings, my own lonely voice, saying, 'it was a warm mad night in San Francisco in 1949 and me and Neal ... etc.'" (131). The combination of making these recordings in Jerry Newman's backroom and reading Lomax's "recorded book" seems to have inspired Kerouac to imagine uses for a tape recorder with a kind of obsession. Throughout October and into November 1951, the tape recorder appears in his journals: "If I had a portable tape-recorder everything would be okay ... just walk & talk," he wrote on October 13, 1951 (142). Then again on November 13: "I walked around Rockefeller Center today wondering if I could write a N.Y. *Vanity of Duluoz* with a portable tape recorder ... it's almost impossible to capture this ocean in a thimble but I think I could but again I might write (or tell) too much with a machine—Oh phooey. *Scratching his chest, showing his teeth to no mirror*—Shakespeare's soul is now waiting for release from the inanimate object called the moon" (158). What is perhaps most notable here is not that he references a tape recorder, but rather specific uses for it: as a tool for writing on the move. In these journals, Kerouac began to theorize how he would use the recording device for *Visions of Cody* just weeks later in San Francisco during his visit with Neal Cassady. Phil Ford's assessment of Kerouac's recordings takes Kerouac's emphasis on memory at face value. Ford likens *Visions of Cody* to "a memory palace, a storehouse of fugitive things captured and preserved from devouring time and forgetfulness" (90) and refers to the tapes as a vehicle for his nostalgia. While this might certainly be true of Kerouac's early thoughts about recording, Kerouac's accounts of the tape recorder in *Visions of Cody* reveal a more complex and intentionally playful understanding of the nature of the technology and the interface between media, memory, and fiction.

Tape recording occupies a unique place in the history of literary engagement with recording technology in that, unlike the phonograph, it was understood as a sound technology that writers could actually use. In the late nineteenth century, Edison had imagined that phonographic technology might be used for dictation purposes and for recording writers reading their works, but the medium of the wax cylinder and later the gramophone disc were better suited to brief musical recordings. Although early iterations of magnetic recording were first tested in the last decade of the nineteenth century, tape was not widely available to consumers until the early 1950s; however, the timing of this was well met – at least for its literary users. Michael Davidson points out in his essay on tape and poetry that, "With the rise of poetry readings in jazz clubs, coffeehouses, and college auditoriums in the late 1950s, the tape recorder returned a kind of oral aura to poetry at a point where it had been, as [Charles] Olson phrased it, removed from 'producers and reproducer'" (99). The portability of tape technology made it possible to record outside the studio and led to the rise of bootleg culture in both music and poetry. That we now have so many documents of poetry readings from this era archived and available on websites such as PennSound and UbuWeb is largely due to this technological shift. Recording poetry readings (or a jazz concert, for that matter) was about preserving an event – a specific voice in a particular moment in time.

This chapter focuses on the tape recorder experiments of Beat generation writers Jack Kerouac and William S. Burroughs, not because writers using tape technology was unique, but rather because tape recording would soon become embedded in the mid-century literary imagination. Tape was everywhere: from avant-garde literary circles to the popular as well. In

Mark McGurl's ambitious study of postwar fiction, *The Program Era*, he has referred to this particular strain of experimentation in postwar litera- ture as "technomodernism" as a way to register the continuity between the project of modernism and postwar interest in new media technologies (42–43). Within the context of the 1960s experimentalism, the tape recorder sits at the center of works such as John Barth's *Lost in the Fun House: Fiction for Print, Tape, Live Voice* (1968) and Andy Warhol's *A: A Novel* (1968). Writers of the "new journalism" such as Tom Wolfe and Joan Didion used tape recorders, as did notorious gonzo journalist Hunter S. Thompson. As we know, Ralph Ellison also recorded himself reading drafts when working on his second novel so that he could listen to the cadences. Beyond the realm of the avant-garde, the tape recorder as a framing device appears across a wide range of late twentieth-century fictions. *Angle of Repose,* the 1971 Pulitzer Prize–winning novel by Wallace Stegner (scion of Stanford's creative writing program) is primarily narrated as-told-to a tape recorder by its wheel-chair bound historian narrator. Gore Vidal's gender-bending *Myra Breckinridge* (1968) claims certain chapters are narrated to a dictaphone. Echoing the appearance of the phonograph in Dracula, Anne Rice's popular *Interview with the Vampire* (1976) adopts a tape recorder narrator. Margaret Atwood's *The Handmaid's Tale* (1985) claims to be transcribed from "found" tapes. In science fiction, the tape- frame device is particularly popular, appearing in Joanna Russ's *We Who Are About To* (1976) and Samuel Delany's *Triton* (1976), just to name a few. In the theater, Samuel Beckett's *Krapp's Last Tape* (1958) offers a medita- tion on how one converses with the self over time. For some, the tape recorder was a stand-in for a broader archival and documentary aesthetic; for others, it represented a fantastic or futuristic technology made present. Both of these strains are present in the tape recorder novels of Kerouac and Burroughs.

Voice, as a marker of authenticity, is one of the dominant features of postwar American writing. For writers aiming to achieve an authentic first-person narrative voice, the tape recorder became a shorthand for the intimate, the personal, and even the confessional. Mark McGurl suggests that that the platitude "find your voice" stands in for a larger trend toward autopoetics, autoethnography, and self-reflexivity that one finds across literature of the era. The emphasis on voice in particular was part of the larger "phonocentrism" of the era, a central theme of the critical debates of Walter Ong, Marshall McLuhan, and Jacques Derrida, but also the schol- arship of Henry Louis Gates Jr. (230–35). The tape recorder was not merely emblematic of the authentic voice, but a tool of programs like "The Voice

Project," which in 1965 encouraged Stanford freshman to find their voices by tape recording themselves as well as community folklore. "Voice, in this context," McGurl claims, "would come to be understood as a vehicle not only of vivacious human *presence* but also of its affective analogue, *pride*" (257).[3] This sense of the expressive voice was certainly part of what drew Kerouac to the tape recorder, but a very different notion motivated Burroughs. Kerouac's *Visions of Cody* and Burroughs's *The Ticket That Exploded* are useful case studies for thinking about the literary potential of the tape recorder in large part because they illustrate how not just the voice, but sound more broadly works as a signifier. Recording the voice was not the only thing that drew writers to the tape recorder.

The prospect of recording was intriguing to Kerouac as he began to imagine capturing and preserving Neal Cassady's unique speech. However, one of the defining qualities of tape is its mutability.[4] This aspect of tape would soon change Kerouac's ideas about the technology; notably, William S. Burroughs used the tape recorder as part of his cut-up process. I turn to the writings of Jack Kerouac and his friend William S. Burroughs to explore how two innovative prose writers redefined literary uses for the tape recorder, but also to show how their experiments with tape informed their avant-garde literary methods: spontaneous prose for Kerouac, and the cut-up method for Burroughs. In particular, I examine Kerouac's *Visions of Cody* (written 1951–52, published 1972) and Burroughs's *The Ticket That Exploded* (1962, 1967) – two lesser-known books by these well-known authors – as works in which tapes and tape recorders are an integral part of the narrative, as well as tools for the construction of text.

It is not uncommon to link Jack Kerouac and William S. Burroughs given their friendship and connection to the Beat generation. In 1944, long before Kerouac or Burroughs had written the works that would bring them notoriety, they collaborated on a hard-boiled novel detailing Lucien Carr's murder of David Kammerer: *And the Hippos Were Boiled in Their Tanks* (2008). In that novel, Kerouac and Burroughs alternate chapters, performing a kind of interlocution and intercutting between voices that both writers would take to new levels in their later experimental tape recorder novels. The two writers would never again collaborate as directly as they did on *Hippos*, but their friendship was often a catalyzing aspect of their individual literary projects. Burroughs hosted Kerouac in Mexico City in 1952 while he wrote *Doctor Sax* (1959); Kerouac typed much of Burroughs's manuscript for *Naked Lunch* (1959), even giving the work its title, while living with Burroughs in Tangier in 1957. The two remained friends throughout their lives, but their literary projects would diverge significantly.

Visions of Cody and *The Ticket That Exploded* are markedly different kinds of works. The former is autobiographical-fiction that reworks Kerouac's materials from *On the Road*; the latter is science fiction that imagines a viral invasion of Earth by the Nova Mob. *Visions of Cody* is a deeply personal account of the friendship between Jack Duluoz and Cody Pomeray (i.e., Kerouac and Neal Cassady), while *Ticket* is generally impersonal and characterized by disembodied voices. And yet, both writers were invested in the writing *process* and the relationship between technologies of writing and tape in relation to memory. While Kerouac's early trials with tape foreshadowed future uses of the technology, Burroughs's experimental tape practices would link the practices of modernism to the digital multimedia aesthetic practices of the early twenty-first century.

Fast-forward, Rewind: A Brief History of the Tape Recorder

When it comes to tape technology, Jack Kerouac and Neal Cassady were what you might call early adopters. Although Cassady and Kerouac began experimenting with an Ekotape recorder in 1951, it was still a new technology and it would be nearly two years before Philips introduced a tape recorder for general consumers.[5] The reference to a wire recorder in Kerouac's journal entry indicates that he was writing at a time when magnetic recording technology was on the cusp of entering the consumer market. Of course, to say that tape was "new" in 1951 when Kerouac made his recordings is not entirely accurate. Magnetic recording technology that initially used steel wire had been in existence since 1898, and tape was first pioneered in the 1930s, but the genealogy of tape recording technology does not follow a linear path – rather one of loops, forward spurts, and parallel tracks.[6] As long as phonograph discs and record players were popular, there seemed to be little consumer demand for magnetic recordings.

Those who have written the histories of recorded music have a difficult time placing tape technology within the chronology, and often mistakenly treat tapes as merely a stop on the train of technological progress from long-play records to CDs and digital recordings. In reality, magnetic recording technology has served as a kind of parallel recording development that fulfilled other needs and drove other kinds of recording developments, from long-play and multitracking in the music world, to live poetry readings and home recordings, to data memory for early computers. Whereas disc devices like the gramophone were branded as a musical medium for individual consumers, the same was not true for magnetic recording, which was initially developed with commercial and military uses in mind. Tape does not sit easily within narratives about the recording industry, and as a result, histories have treated tape alternately as a revolutionary development and as a commercial failure.[7]

Due to the commercial success of phonographic discs, the development of magnetic recording lay dormant until the 1920s and 1930s.[8] Although a few labs in the United States had experimented with the wire recorder, it was German engineers who would develop the Magnetophon, which used lightweight paper or plastic tape coated with microscopically fine iron powder (Morton 114). The Nazis used tape to prerecord Hitler's propagandistic radio speeches, and tape was also used as a surveillance technology for recording phone calls and other messages. When the US military intercepted and captured German tape technology during World War II, they quickly undertook efforts to reverse engineer tape for their own purposes but did not do so successfully until after the war (Shaney 6). That tape was born out of a military-surveillance culture would not be lost on Burroughs, who saw tape as another method of control.

As a medium for recording, tape had a number of distinct advantages over discs. Unlike a disc, whose finite size limits the length of a recording, tape could be made as long as needed and could hold varying amounts of content and fidelity depending on the speed of recording.[9] Tape also did not have the same problems of diminished fidelity after multiple playbacks and did not scratch or warp. Perhaps the most notable difference between magnetic tape and phonographic recording was that tape could be erased and recorded over a number of times, and because you could cut, splice, and loop tape, you could edit tape in similar ways to film.[10] Early magnetic recording was still technically an analog process, but rather than engrave a solid medium with the sound vibration, it recorded sound as a fluctuation of field strength on tape that has been covered with charged iron particles. Magnetic recording operates on a similar principle to the ways magnets have been used to turn iron fillings into interesting patterns (similar to the popular Wooly Willy toy or the Magna Doodle), but on a microscopic level. In his manual *Fun with Tape* (1967), Joachim Staab describes, "When continuous electrical signals are used in this way to create a magnetic pattern on a moving stream of minute iron particles, the resultant magnetic picture represents a lasting translation of those signals" (Staab 14). To reproduce these signals as sounds, the process is reversed.[11] That Staab uses the word "picture" to describe the magnetic pattern that occurs during this process is no mistake; one could even say that tape turned sound into a picture. The similarities between tape and film, both in their physical appearance and editing possibilities, made it easy to conflate the two media – a fact that becomes apparent in the works of both Kerouac and Burroughs, who both draw together images of reeling tape with reeling film. Tape recording seemed more cinematic. However, this conflation of the audio and the visual extended beyond its appearance or the mechanics of its use. As researchers discovered as early as the 1930s, magnetic recording technology could record more than just sound.

Magnetic recording was developed to capture sound, but it became synonymous with memory more generally. During WWII, while the military was experimenting with the magnetic recording devices for surveillance purposes, it was discovered that magnetic recording could also be adapted to electromagnetic pulses emitted by sources other than voice or music, including radar and oscilloscope images (Morton 108). In other words, magnetic wire or tape could record any electronic data broadly speaking. Magnetic recording was fundamentally important to the development of computers, and as early as 1951, IBM was using magnetic tape for computer data storage.[12] Magnetic recording powered VHS video tapes and floppy disks, and a number of other memory devices. Although it is unlikely that Kerouac – who Allen Ginsberg characterized as the "Great Rememberer" – knew much about IBM computers, it is a convenient coincidence that his own experiments with tape treat the technology as a memory device at precisely the same time that IBM starts using tape in its computers.

Tape had many potential uses, but as a medium for disseminating music, reel-to-reel tapes never gained the kind of widespread popularity afforded to LPs and later compact cassette tapes, CDs, and digital formats such as mp3s. Although the tape recorder companies marketed tape as a way for making "family albums," people still tended to use the device for music playback, and particularly for recording music off the radio (Bijisterveld 26). Evidence of this can be seen in *Visions of Cody*, which ends the tape recorder section not with a conversation between Jack and Cody, but with a recording of a Black revivalist preacher giving a sermon on the radio (246–47). Tape recorder books such as *Fun with Tape* proliferated and explained everything from microphone positioning, to editing styles, tape speeds, and other technical specifications. In *Fun with Tape* (1967), recording a letter is the base-level activity, but it also discusses how to add signature lead-in music, splice the tape, and add additional layers of sound. The tape recorder was not just for preserving memories; popular handbooks suggested that users ought to approach tape creatively and implied the technology could be used to imagine new sounds – or make new memories. The tension between the desire to "record" or to preserve sounds and the desire to *make* new sounds was one of the central problems for Kerouac. Magnetic tape was simultaneously a revolutionary medium for memory (literally in the case of computers), but it also enabled a completely new approach to *making* rather than simply recording new sounds. Kerouac initially wanted to use the tape recorder in order to better record his and Neal Cassady's memories of their travels on the road and of Cassady's early life, but instead they find that remembering is more difficult than they realized and that in the process of remembering, they change it. The tape recorder's so-called perfect memory reveals to them the artificiality of their own.

Part of what makes Kerouac and Burroughs's literary experiments so compelling is that their attitudes toward tape parallel, and in some cases predate, those of its experimental users in music. Musicians had been thinking about the innovative possibilities for recordings at least as early as 1941 when Sidney Bechet made his one-man-band recording (pretape). In 1948, guitarist Les Paul began experimenting with multitrack recordings using an Ampex tape recorder, and Pierre Schaeffer, the experimental composer, coined the term *musique concrète* to describe music composed entirely from a collage of prerecorded sounds. Among the foremost thinkers and experimenters with tape was the composer John Cage, who remarked in his 1957 lecture on "Experimental Music" that people were using tape "not simply to record performances of music but to make a new music that was possible only because of it" (*Silence* 8). By Cage's measure, the tape recorder was becoming an instrument. Thus, with tape, the notion of what it meant to *play* a recording changed rather dramatically because it was no longer a simply matter of *playback*, but what we might call "play" in the broader sense.[13] Playing a tape implied the ability to manipulate a plastic medium. With the tape recorder, the boundary between listener and maker of sound was diminished significantly.

The distinction between sound and music during this period provoked substantial debate, and composers like Cage began rethinking the parameters of sound, music, and silence – especially in relation to technologies like tape. Cage was at first skeptical of the "experimental" moniker but used it as an opportunity to redefine the status of the composer, stating that "What has happened is that I have become a listener and the music has become something to hear" (*Silence* 7). Emphasis on the listener as an active participant in sonic creation was later echoed by pianist and recording artist Glenn Gould who predicted a "new kind of listener" ("Prospects of Recording" 121). For Cage, the tape recorder revolutionized approaches to composition, for "whether one uses tapes or writes for conventional instruments, the present musical situation has changed from what it was before tape came into being" (11). Tape allowed Cage and others to extend traditional modes of composition and notation, and "since so many inches of tape equal so many seconds of time, it has become more and more usual that notation is in space rather than in symbols of quarter, half, and sixteenth notes and so on" (11). Whereas the phonograph had in many ways forced a chasm between music consumers and music makers by creating a class of professional musicians – making the home piano obsolete, and transforming listening into a commodified activity – the tape recorder promised a reversal of this trend by putting the music-making tools back into the hands of listeners. In this regard, the tape recorder democratized sound in ways that were fundamentally subversive.

The implications of tape for music were clear to a composer like Cage, who had begun to think of music more broadly in terms of the "organization of sound," but the implications for writers and literature were a little less clear. Could literature also be considered an organization of sound?[14] Alan Lomax had felt that recording would rejuvenate literary forms and made bold claims for its uses after publishing *Mister Jelly Roll*; however, the tape recorder did not immediately revolutionize writing. Part of the reason for this was that writers were not accustomed to using recording technology in the same way that musicians were. Lomax had framed the relationship between recordings and literature as perfect transcription, but as we saw in Chapter 2, his book revealed the creative editing required in translating sound and speech to the page. Even a forward-thinking writer like Jack Kerouac could, at first, only imagine the use of the tape recorder as a means of recording, memorializing, and transcribing speech. *Visions of Cody* shows how the tape recorder became a catalyst for thinking about the organization of sound in literature in the radical Cagian sense.

"I Can't Get It Down": Jack Kerouac's Auditions of Cody

In 1951, Neal Cassady purchased a Webster Electric Ekotape Tape Recorder with the hope that he and Kerouac would exchange tape-letters while he was in San Francisco and Kerouac in New York.[15] Although Kerouac never made good on his promise to get his own recorder, the lure of Cassady and the Ekotape drew him to San Francisco later that year while he was in the midst of revising *On the Road* and beginning to write the manuscript for what eventually became *Visions of Cody*. The Ekotape, which used coated paper tape, was designed for semiprofessional dictation and recording purposes. A pamphlet advertising the machine states, the

Ekotape was geared toward "educators, professional men and women, and business men who used recorders in their work" and advertisements for the machine featured men in suits recording their meetings – a scene in which Kerouac and Cassady would have been noticeably out of place.[16] But as audiophiles who "understood the power of voices," Kerouac and Cassady could easily imagine creative uses for tape (C. Cassady 125). In reality, the tapes were quite expensive, necessitating constant reuse. Remembering those early years with the tape recorder, Neal's wife Carolyn Cassady lamented, "since we had so little cash and tapes were expensive, we used the same two or three over and over. (I'd rather not think of that loss.)" (193). A number of those recordings became the section of *Visions of Cody* titled "Frisco: The Tape," in which Kerouac indicates how he was forced to type his transcripts along the way. As a result, we can no longer listen to those original tapes that Kerouac used to write the middle section of *Cody*.[17]

Kerouac had hoped the tape recorder would be better than memory for capturing their wild speech, and what appears in "Frisco: The Tape" is a virtually unedited transcript of the 1951 recordings Kerouac and Cassady made over five evenings at Cassady's San Francisco apartment.[18] The tape transcriptions are notated like the dialogue of a play. By necessity, Kerouac had to transcribe the tape almost immediate after use so that it could be used again; however, this practice unintentionally caused the tape sessions and the writing to double-up on one another such that on one evening they are recording reflections of a 1947 trip to visit William S. Burroughs in Texas, and the next evening they are reviewing the transcription of that very story while also taping, creating a moment of metafictional reflection. In the process of narrating the first time they met Burroughs, Cody (Cassady's alias) reflects on the difficulty of remembering:

CODY. [. . .] I was hung up on something else, you know, so I can't remember, say, like for example, I can remember NOW for example, but now that I CAN remember it doesn't do any good, because . . . man . . . I can't get it down. You know . . . I just remember it, I can remember it well, what happened' cause I'm not doing nothing, see?
JACK. You don't have to get it down
CODY. (*demurely downward look*) But I can't remember what happened there, man, except I remember certain things. (123)

In other areas of the transcript, Kerouac inserts parentheticals to indicate nonverbal sounds such as *laughing* or *baby cries*. However, the "*demurely downward look*" is not transcription of a sound; rather, it is a notation of

Kerouac's memory that is invited by the content of the conversation on the problems of memory and the difficulty of recording it or "getting it down." The description is what critic Steven Belletto calls a "metonym for the act of narration" (201).

Were this the only instance of the phrase it might not be especially notable, but it later serves a more important position in the text, one that invites a moment of self-reflexivity about the relationship between writing, recording, and memory. In the very next tape session, Jack and Cody read over the transcription of the previous night's recording session and discuss Kerouac's addition of the phrase.

JACK. Then I remembered this, "demurely downward look"
CODY. I seem to remember that myself
JACK. Although it wasn't really
CODY. No
JACK. It was *my* idea
CODY. Yeah
JACK. About the look you had
CODY. Well yeah . . . it was kind of a —
JACK. But it apparently wasn't . . . what you were really doing . . .
CODY. That's what it really amounts to, though
JACK. Why, because lookit . . . the talk is far way from demure . . .
CODY. Well, the reason for the *demure* is . . . any approach to the words like, as I remember like what I said . . here, ah, "I can't get it down," for example, you know, "I can't get it down"—Well, I approached that very terribly, I was talking you know about something you know, that—it's going on—You know what I'm trying to say? (133)

Cody is forgiving of Jack's narrativizing, but Jack recognizes the extent to which he invented and interpreted the moment. The decision to include this meta-discussion in the text itself shows how quite early in the tape recorder sessions Kerouac realized that there was always more to an experience or story or sound than the tape or its transcription could capture. By rerecording over the previous tape and incorporating the discussion of the previous night's recording, Jack and Cody are not only in dialogue with one another, but with their earlier selves. It is the textual equivalent of overdubbing and echoes the practice that Sidney Bechet initiated in recording "Sheik of Araby" in 1941. Unlike actual overdubbing, however, the two tracks Kerouac negotiates between cannot be heard simultaneously because recording over a single-track tape necessitates erasure; textually they intersplice one another. The reremembering erases and replaces the earlier memory, both building upon it and displacing it.

Cody struggles with the idea that he "can't get it down," but the fact is – as this moment reveals – getting it *down,* whether on tape or in text, is to shape it again. But does the tape recorder in *Cody* record memory, or does it displace it?

Even before Kerouac was able to record, he both fantasized about the tape's abilities and worried that it would cause him to be self-conscious. Similar to the notes in his 1951 journal, in one of the sketches from an earlier section in Part 2, he interrupts his own thought to make a note about getting a tape recorder, but the parenthetical overtakes his narration:

> Last night in the West End Bar was mad, (I can't think fast enough) (*do* need a recorder, *will* buy one at once when the *Adams* hits New York next March then I could keep the most complete record in the world which in itself could be divided into twenty massive and pretty interesting volumes of tapes describing activities everywhere and excitements and thoughts of mad valuable me and it would really have a shape but a crazy big shape yet just as logical as a novel by Proust because I *do* keep harkening back though I might be nervous on the mike and even tell too much). (99)

The *demurely downward look* reveals that Kerouac was right to worry about being self-conscious. Even so, that very self-consciousness of the tape and the recursive action of listening and transcribing (and listening and transcribing again) helped him to unlock the spontaneous, yet multi-layered aspects of tape that infuse the structure of *Cody.* Kerouac could not imagine writing from bed as Proust did, so he imagines taping his experiences as they happen – amassing an enormous tape archive. Tape, he fears, might be too unbounded or too limitless, causing him to tell too much.

Kerouac indicated on a number of occasions that he felt that *Visions of Cody* was his masterpiece ("O my best prose there" [*Selected Letters II* 189]), but it is also arguably his most difficult book. Because Kerouac wrote *Cody* simultaneously with *On the Road* (but after his original scroll), he did not initially consider it a separate text, it is both a reworking of the story of his 1947–50 adventures with Neal Cassady/Dean Moriarty, and a reflection on the present state of their friendship. Unlike the 1957 version of *On the Road,* *Cody* lacks a traditional narrative structure and moves between sketching, transcripts of taped dialogues, and an amalgam of the two. Allen Ginsberg deemed the new text unpublishable and, in a frustrated letter to Carolyn Cassady in June 1952, he complained about the form and organization of what Kerouac was then still calling *On the Road,* and in particular the tape recorder section. Although he found the tape conversations "good reading," Ginsberg complained that they were disorganized: "it just skips back and forth and touches on things momentarily and refers to events nowhere else in the book" (qtd. in C. Cassady 184).[19] Years later, however, once Kerouac had untangled the text of *Cody* from what became *On the Road* (*Visions of Cody* was not published in its complete form until 1972), Ginsberg changed his mind about the book.[20] Scholars have since cited *Cody* as the work in which Kerouac developed his characteristic "spontaneous prose" method of writing."[21]

When talking about Kerouac's brief 1953 manifesto, "Essentials of Spontaneous Prose," most tend to point to Kerouac's conflation between his writing methods and jazz. Sometimes referring to his style as bop-prosody, Kerouac felt jazz to be central to his writing (he was a frequent audience member at Minton's in the early years of bebop), and he had idealized notions of improvisation. However, jazz readings of spontaneous prose sometimes obscure the way he treats sound and speech more generally. Describing the writing procedure, he says, "Time being of the essence in the purity of speech, sketching language is undisturbed flow from the mind of the personal secret idea-words, *blowing* (as per jazz musician) on subject of image" (*Portable Jack Kerouac* 484).[22] Instead of laboring over editing or conventions of punctuation, he favors speed: "No pause to think of proper word but the infantile pileup of scatological buildup words till satisfaction is gained, which will turn out to be a great appending rhythm to a thought and be in accordance with Great Law of timing" (484). As an intermediary text between the scroll version of *On the Road* Kerouac composed in 1951 and the published version of *On the Road* from 1957, *Visions of Cody* incorporates this kind of scatological buildup, and the tape recorder enabled Kerouac to hear and transcribe the repetitive qualities of regular speech. The scatological transcriptive style of the novel anticipates Andy Warhol's approach to *A: A Novel* (1968) – a book that transcribes nearly twenty-four hours of tapes, including all the typos and inconsistencies made by his transcribers.[23]

While there has been scholarly agreement that *Cody* was the work that catalyzed Kerouac's style, many, including Joyce Johnson, have attributed this discovery to the practice of sketching, dismissing the tape transcriptions as a failed experiment, or merely a slice-of-life.[24] Johnson says "'sketching' immediately gave Jack what he needed – the freedom to write his 'interior music' just as it came to him, removing the inhibiting presence in his mind of the editor or reader" (419).[25] But the fact is that, in sketching "like a painter in the street" (as his friend Ed White suggested), Kerouac was bound to recording the exterior world, and could not write and engage in conversation at the same time. Steven Belletto, who writes about the politics of historiography in *Visions of Cody*, argues that the experiment with the tapes "ultimately fails" because Kerouac and Cassady "find themselves conscious of the tape" (200) – a sentiment shared by Ann Charters.[26] And yet, that self-consciousness as transcribed is part of its brilliance because it illustrates the problems with memory more generally. Kerouac himself was ambivalent and, in an interview with Ted Berrigan in 1968 for the *Paris Review*, claimed that he had not used the tape method since writing *Visions of Cody* because "it really doesn't come out right, well, with Neal and with myself, when all written down and with all the *ahs* and the *ohs* and the *ahums* and the fearful fact that the damn thing is turning and you're *forced* not to waste electricity or tape." However, just moments later, Kerouac seemed to reverse his thought: "Then again, I don't know, I might have to resort to that eventually; I'm getting tired and going blind. This question stumps me. At any rate, everybody's doing it, I hear, but I'm still scribbling. McLuhan says we're getting more oral so I guess we'll all learn to talk into the machine better and better" (http://theparisreview.org) . Kerouac acknowledges the uncomfortable gap between written and spoken language, the nonverbal sounds that the tape records, as well as the limitations of the machine itself in an era when tape was still quite expensive. Kerouac acknowledges the awkwardness of the *ohs* and the *ahums*, and yet the original transcripts in Kerouac's papers in the Berg Collection at the New York Public Library show that rather than omit these nonverbal utterances, he actually went back over the manuscript and meticulously penciled them in and moved them to their proper places during his revisions.[27] In fact, these ahs and uhms anticipate a writing voice that embraces "the infantile pileup of scatological buildup words" and their "great appending rhythm to a thought" (485).

In the course of listening and transcribing "Frisco: The Tape," rhythm comes to occupy Jack and Cody's attention, and music and other sounds take a more central role. Scenes of listening – especially to jazz records – become moments for meditation on rhythm and sound and what it means to *play* a record. When Cody puts on Coleman Hawkins's 1937 recording of "Crazy Rhythm," it is not merely as background or soundtrack (as music sometimes is in Kerouac's works), but is a teachable moment wherein Cody aims to narrate a listening that will help Jack "hear" the well-worn record anew.[28] Whereas we tend to think of listening to records as a one-directional activity between the listening subject (who is silent) and the sonic object, the scene here represents a dialogue between Cody and Jack and the record.

CODY. No kidding (*stops music at phonograph*). Now. Pardon me son, I don't want
to—you see I've different things that I've got on MY mind you know what I'm
trying to say to you is, I'm gonna tell you something, although there might be
other things that I'm hungup on, ah—the only reason that I'm playing this
record is 'cause now you're high and you're gonna hear see . . . so now I'm gonna
relax it and listen to it, you're gonna hear the *different* things they play. (MUSIC:
Coleman Hawkins' "Crazy Rhythm") (*and demonstrates ideas with hands*) I don't
choose this record for any reason except that we played it three or four times see,
so, that's why you know—even though it's not really—but listen to the man play
the horn, that's all (*they listen to ensemble beginning work*). Ah man I'm gonna try
to change that needle (*after stopping music and Jack riffs on*). Did you hear that
riff? (*puts music back, on alto solo*) when they begin – listen to here (*off, on
again*)[. . .]
CODY. Now Coleman comes in . . . listen to Coleman. (*Coleman comes in low
toned, fast*) Hee hee hee way down there (*gesturing low at waist*)
JACK. Yeah
CODY. Hear it? (*they laugh and gloat*) See? he keeps blowin. Now here comes
Benny, Benny plays like he did first only he backs off more, listening . . . hear it?
Hear? He's going up, and—he's not rockin, listen. (*they listen*) Hear him coming
down on a riff?
JACK. Yap
CODY. He really got that riff didn't he? (*laughing hungrily*) Staying up there, see,
and here comes Coleman (*low again*)
JACK. Ooo-*hoo*! Hey, yes
CODY. He keeps drivin see?
JACK. Yeah, drivin
CODY. (*laughing ecstatically*) Blows that sonumbitch does. Of course (*changing his
tone*) near the ending he falls apart here. Poor man. (*Jack laughing*) He doesn't—
it's just, you know, record . . . the ending (*Bass-player on record calls to Hawk:* "Go
on, go on.") (*Hawk blows a side complex what's this? riff*) What do you mean
falling apart? (142–43)

When Cody decides to play "Crazy Rhythm," the repeated act of listening
is key. Cody knows the song well enough that he can anticipate certain
moments in the music, and he suggests that no two listenings are alike.
There are a number of parallels between this scene and Ralph Ellison's
prologue to *Invisible Man* as the two attempt to descend into the depths of
the music. High on marijuana, Cody wants to narrate a particular kind of
listening to Jack and help him to *hear*. For Cody, a person who can never
seem to complete a thought and who relies constantly on the good will of
his listeners to fill in his thoughts ("you know what I mean?"), the
recording promises to convey that which he cannot express in words, and
which is inevitably represented by the trailing off of an ellipses or long

dash. Paradoxically, at the very moment he asks Jack to *hear* it, he also wants him to *see*.

In Kerouac's transcription of Cody's narration, the point of reference is forever shifting. Cody keeps saying that he just wants Jack to *hear it*, but it is never clear what "it" is; he cannot help but speak excitedly over the recording, an act that both obscures and illuminates the music. There is a subtle punning between *hear* and here, as Cody tries to anticipate and stay in the moment of the *here* and to simultaneously *hear*. However, the *here* is always passing. ("Hear it? (*they laugh and gloat*) See? he keeps blowin. Now here comes Benny, Benny plays like he did first only he backs off more, listening … hear it? Hear? He's going up, and—he's not rockin, listen. (*they listen*) Hear him coming down on a riff?"). Of course, for the reader, there is nothing to hear; if one tracks down the recording in order to listen alongside the text, one finds that there is an audible contrast between the solo playing of Benny Carter and Hawkins and the fast foxtrot of their Paris counterparts on the recording; their solos sound shockingly modern in contrast to the quick-stepping arrangement.[29] Carter in particular plays a number of notes that in jazz are referred to as "outside" – that is, he plays notes outside the specified chords such as 9ths, sharp-11ths (or flatted-fifths), and 13ths. This outside sound is one of the defining features of bebop – and it was one of the ways Black musicians tried to trademark their sound as jazz was co-opted by white big bands – but the line between outside and inside is always fluctuating and fleeting. For attentive listeners who are nonmusicians, like Jack and Cody, it is easy enough to hear that there is something *off* or *out* about this kind of playing, but it is difficult to pinpoint why.[30] The racial underpinnings of this listening session are worth noting. *"Gesturing low at waist,"* Cody also seems to imply that Coleman Hawkins's sound is synonymous with his manhood – a crass allusion to Black male hypersexuality that a white listener like Cody associates with jazz (142). This moment of racial stereotyping is perhaps no more surprising than the fact that Jack and Cody seemingly never acknowledge jazz as an African American music. Listening to a recording, they are able to borrow the hip aura of blackness without the presence of Black bodies. There are gaps, to be sure, and in moments such as these, Cody's narration trails off and fails to account for what is actually happening in the music. And yet, as a moment when speech fails, one senses that there are similarities between these *outside* musical conversations and Cody's own dialogues with Jack as fraught documents of male friendship.

Although we can no longer listen to the tapes of Kerouac and Cassady's conversations that were used in *Visions of Cody*, listening to the 1949–51

John Clellon Holmes acetate disc recordings that include Kerouac, Holmes, Ginsberg, and possibly Burroughs among others reveal that transcription of various kinds was on their minds. On tracks labeled "riffing," Kerouac and friends perform a cappella vocal versions of their favorite bebop recordings, including Charlie Parker's "Ornithology" and Dizzy Gillespie's "Groovin' High" – a practice that I would argue performs transcription.[31] Whereas we tend to think of transcription as writing down speech, in jazz circles transcription often involves listening to, internalizing, and learning to play (or sing) a melody or solo from a recording; it plays an important role in ear training. These vocal transcriptions point to Kerouac's efforts to embody and playfully perform musical memory, albeit in simplified form.

The moment of listening to "Crazy Rhythm" in the novel, however, is transcription of a different order. Jack and Cody are concerned with constantly being in the *here* of the present moment that Kerouac was initially so intent to capture on tape, but they also open the possibility of listening as a multilayered act that ascends different temporal planes. With each successive tape recording and transcription or relistening session, Kerouac's approach to the tape recorder shifts. If at first he thought the tape recorder would help him to capture the energy and liveness of the present moment, in transcribing the tape as nearly as possible, he is also confronted with the decision of whether to include those moments when a past recording momentarily resurfaces and interpenetrates the text. Such is the nature of the early expensive tapes and the necessity of constant reuse.

The functioning of the Ekotape recorder was such that if you did not fully erase the tape prior to rerecording, remnants of the previous recording might remain in the places where one punches in and out – like a palimpsest. Rather than edit out these left-overs or ghosts of recordings past, Kerouac leaves them in. As technological detritus, these tape-ghosts alert the reader to the materiality of the medium and highlight the multilayered temporality of tape and memory. In one particularly apt example of this phenomena, a past recording of Evelyn reading *Hamlet* intersplices a party break when Cody goes out for wine. The ghostly tape remainders are identified temporally, for instance, New Year's Eve, or *"speaking from last month on unerased tape"* (204). That the moment happens to be an unidentifiable excerpt from a reading of *Hamlet* seems prescient as well, as a play very much concerned with the ghostly presence of disembodied sounds and voices.[32] These moments of inadvertent splicing also anticipate William Burroughs's experiments with tape cut-ups.

Kerouac's transcripts of his tape recorder sessions reveal that his attitude toward the tape recorder and its function was in a state of flux; one can get a better sense of Kerouac's attitude toward the technology when he moves away from it and instead emulates the form of the tape in the final section "Imitation of the Tape" – a section which Justin Thomas Trudeau calls the "countermemory of what came before" (339). The final section of *Cody* is not, however, a rejection of the tape recorder; instead, it illustrates how the tape was not just a tool for recording memory, but was also a medium of experimentation. If we think of the magnetic tape as not just a sound recording device, but as "memory"– as an external device for holding consciousness or thought – then this might help us to understand what Kerouac means by imitation of the "tape." Sound and listening become synonymous with memory technology and cognitive practice, and thus the slippery edge between listening and understanding (i.e., processing). The tape helped Kerouac to negotiate between a desire for the authenticity of the voice and breath, with the struggles of memory, and the desire for his own narrative style. When divorced from the constraints of transcription, Kerouac plays upon the musical rhythms of their exchanges.

Ginsberg called the tape dialogues "ritual" – and here, the dialogues between Jack and Cody assume increasingly incantatory, ritual-like qualities, and seem less invested in the content of the conversation than in the poetry of their sounds.[33]

JACK. Made to wring the meaning, made to roam the void Made to sing demeanors to the meeters of the
CODY. You mean this is the pit of night, the moonsaw?
JACK. The moonsaw's come, the rainy night is milk, red eyes sea,
CODY. Can't decide? Have no bones? Pick up stone? Or stick an own?
JACK. Crick alone, turtle dove alone, moan alone, pose alone.
CODY. Nonsense be, as nonsense was; or nonsense is a trapeze
JACK. Nay a hole beneath it; with a balloon upon the void afloat.
CODY. Van Doren, excellent; New Yorker, extrasmash; Walt Winchell, band start
JACK. Tell me Nones; throw a Flying Scone [. . .]
CODY. [. . .] Shee-it, I could tell you stories make you wish you was daid. I could lay you down a hype make you wish you was dead *and* gone, dead *and* gone.
JACK. I could ripple you a houndspack make you wish I was dead and void
CODY. Dead and voiced; (310–11)

Whereas many of the conversations between Jack and Cody while high in "Frisco: The Tape" rely on Jack to play the listening interlocutor, in the imagined conversations from "Imitation of the Tape," Jack and Cody can jam more equally, "trading bars" so to speak and playing on language sounds, rhymes, and associations the way that jazz musicians play upon the melodic lines of one another during improvisation. The sense of the dialogue is, as Cody points out, nonsense, but they keep coming back to certain motifs and sounds (e.g., "void" and "moan").[34] Without the pressures of the real conversation, Kerouac can artfully represent the degree to which their conversations engage in wordplay; they feel closer to the jazz that drives the rhythms of their speech and their nightly reveries but which did not come across in the transcriptions. In later dialogues, Jack and Cody merely "think" and communicate silently as they jointly narrate their experience, their minds finally becoming one in Kerouac's more holistic "visions" of Cody.

Joyce Johnson has suggested that, in fact, Kerouac needed to hear the tape-recorded conversations with Neal to better understand their relationship; "To separate his self-image from the Neal in his mind" (Johnson 434). Listening to the tapes helped Kerouac to realize that the "Neal" of his visions both was and was not interchangeable with himself, and importantly that the Cody/Dean of his visions was in fact fictionalized. Kerouac would later call *Cody* a "vertical metaphysical study of Cody's character" in contrast to the "horizontal account of travels on the road" (i), wherein the scrolling prose moves from the paper scroll to the spooling tape recorder. In search of a medium that would solve the problems of what Kerouac felt to be an incomplete record of his memory, the tape recorder instead presented him with a malleable medium that offered a new proximity and sound, but also opened the possibilities for how he could imagine Neal/Dean/Cody as a character. Because of the cult following of a novel like *On the Road*, and because of Kerouac's celebrity status as the *voice of his generation*, it can be easy to forget the extent to which Kerouac was actively theorizing what it meant to record the voice in a novel. "Imitation of the Tape" from *Visions of Cody* reflects a new way of thinking about the relationship between memory, recording, and fiction in which the sounds of language assume a more playful role.

The concept of *play* – which I invoke here for both its ludic and mechanical connotations – may be a more useful framework for understanding how Kerouac, and later Burroughs, would understand the function of tape technology. To *play* a tape does not simply mean to listen to the sounds it records and repeats, but to play *with* those sounds in the Cagian sense of potentially creating new sounds. In "Imitation of the Tape," Kerouac bends tape conceptually to imagine conversations that never took place, but that nevertheless have the sonic immediacy of sounds recorded live. This approach to language is akin to the "organization of sound" that Cage writes of. While this playful approach to tape sounds is mostly aspirational in Kerouac's writing, Burroughs would go on to actually manipulate magnetic tape.

William S. Burroughs Cuts the Tape

Sound can act as a painkiller. To date we do not have music suffi-
ciently powerful to act as a practical weapon.
William S. Burroughs, The Western Lands

What we see is determined to a large extent by what we hear.
William S. Burroughs, The Ticket That Exploded

Shortly after Kerouac finished his tape sessions with Neal Cassady in San Francisco in 1952 he drove to Mexico City, where he wrapped up work on *Visions of Cody* and wrote *Doctor Sax* while living with Burroughs.[35] It is unknown what Burroughs thought of *Cody* and Kerouac's use of the tape recorder, but not long thereafter Burroughs also took up the tape recorder and used it off and on throughout the 1950s and 1960s. Similar to Kerouac, Burroughs initially used tapes to help capture voices, and as he admitted in an interview with the *Paris Review* years later, "Many of my characters first come through strongly to me as voices. That's why I use a tape recorder" (http://theparisreview.org). Moreso than Kerouac, Burroughs became known for his experimental uses of the tape and the cut-up method – especially in *The Ticket That Exploded*, the second book of the Nova trilogy. Burroughs's renegade tape methods are usually attributed to his collaborations in the 1960s with the artist Brion Gysin and sound engineer Ian Sommerville, but one may also detect subtle inflections of Kerouac's tape methods in Burroughs's writing – inflections that include both attention to the sound of voices and the spliced-in elements of past recordings. The leftover sounds of past recordings were initially accidental, but these kinds of random splices became an important property of Burroughs's approach to experimental recording. Allen Ginsberg, reflecting on a passage from the final section of *Visions of Cody*, pointed out that "Jack's naked original mind's surreal cut-ups, [were] prophetic of later Burroughs conscious efforts the same" (*Cody* 419). The difference, as Ginsberg aptly notes, regards the level of consciousness in these efforts. Kerouac's approach began as a transcription project, but in the course of transcribing the tapes, with their mechanical glitches and remnants, Kerouac began to discover a potentially more playful use – one that transformed the listener's role from mere consumer to producer of sound. Whereas this discovery pushed Kerouac back toward his own voice and his deeply personal explorations, Burroughs took this tape function to its opposite extreme. In *The Ticket That Exploded*, Burroughs is more interested in the depersonalized voice and in performing fictionalized voices than in recording his own, and the tape recorder assumes a more insidious role.[36] Tapes, tape recorders, and tape cut-ups come to infuse the text both thematically and formally, and ultimately, *The Ticket That Exploded* becomes a kind of experimental how-to manual for using a tape recorder.

The Nova trilogy, which includes *The Soft Machine* (1961, 1968), *The Ticket That Exploded* (1962, 1967), and *Nova Express* (1964), is loosely organized around the struggle between an alien Nova Mob, who enact a violent, highly erotic brand of viral mind control, and the Nova Police who, along with the likes of Inspector Lee, are tasked with breaking up the Mob. For Burroughs, language was the ultimate form of mind control – or as he called it, a *virus* – and thus subverting the Nova Mob required the subversion of language. In *The Ticket That Exploded*, the tape recorder is the most prominent vehicle of brain washing, but paradoxically the tape recorder is also the means of subverting that very method of control by making one's own recordings and splicing them with other recordings. Of course, to give any kind of plot summary of the Nova books is a bit misleading. *The Ticket That Exploded* is a book without a traditional plot; it eschews narrative in favor of the cut-up. As such, the text is always on the move, and the characters are nearly impossible to follow as they come to the reader through the ear, which is to say through the sound of their voices.

The Ticket That Exploded may be read as a tale told by the tape recorder. From the outset, the voices are displaced and the characters are unknown: "It is a long trip. We are the only riders. So that is how we have come to know each other so well that the sound of his voice and his image flickering over the tape recorder are as familiar to me as the movement of my intestines the sound of my breathing the beating of my heart" (1).[37] But who is this "we"? The unnamed narrator has lost a sense of individual identity and conflates and confuses the sounds of his own body with that of another. Ihab Hassan has suggested that the book's "*aim is to make man bodiless and language silent*"—a kind of new twist on the Word made flesh (65). However, more often than not, the relation between the sound of the voice and the body is ambiguously dependent. "In fact his voice has been spliced in 24 times per second with the sound of my breathing and the beating of my heart so that my body is convinced that my breathing and heart will stop if his voice stops," the narrator continues (3). The scene is meant to familiarize the reader with a concept of mind control that is dependent upon sound. While the common trope about sound recording has been that it produces disembodied or invisible voices, in *The Ticket That Exploded* the sounds of the bodies and the tape recorder voices have become, if not interchangeable, much more closely related. Burroughs's tape recorder restructures the relationship between embodiment and sound, and interspliced voices produce a sound image at roughly the same rate that films do. One could call these voices *disembodied*, but to do so would diminish the forceful presence of bodily sounds within the text: "the beating of his heart, the gurgle of shifting secretions and food, the rattle of breath and scratches of throat gristle—crystal bubbles in the sinus chambers magnified from the recorders" (72). The novel does not reject the body; rather, it is full of the grotesque, the pornographic, and the scatological. Characters suffer morbid addictions to "Sex Skins" that involve "being slobbered down and shit out by an alien mollusk" (4).[38] In the topsy-turvy world of *Ticket*, bodies overcome by addiction and mechanically repetitive behaviors are the result of the mind control of the Nova Mob who are, in fact, bodiless.

The Nova Mob are a band of parasites who infect their human hosts with language and can only be detected by transferable personality traits or, in many cases, by their *sound*. One of the central stories in *Ticket* is the investigation of a particular parasite known as "Genial" in relation to an unsolved death by hanging. The difficulty of the case is that no one seems to know who Genial really is. The protagonist, Inspector Lee, whose sole purpose is to fight the Nova Mob, searches for tape recordings that might shed light on the case. It turns out that Genial has a recognizable laugh and is only detectable in the tape-recorded interactions with those he infects. In Lee's own tape-recorded field notes, he remarks:

> The sound track *illuminates* the image . . 'Genial's' image in this case . . almost tactile . . Well there it is . . biologists talk about creating life in a test tube . . all they need is a few tape recorders: 'Genial 23' at your service sir . . a virus of course . . The soundtrack is the only existence it has no one hears him he is not there except as a potential like the spheres and crystals that show up under an electron microscope. (19)

The tape does not simply keep a record or a copy of the virus; it holds the *potential* for new viral life forms in mutation. The tape recorder is the central metaphor for the prerecorded aspects of viral control; tapes contain all the information to infect or inoculate.

Those who have managed to escape the mind control of the Nova Mob are attributed with voices that have a mechanical, tape-like quality, namely, the DS (District Supervisor) that Inspector Lee encounters in his hopes of being inoculated against the Nova Mob's main means of control: "a computerized Garden of Delights" and the word virus (10). The DS is a member of a group of assassins called the White Hunters, and he is described as "talking in a voice without accent or inflection, a voice that no one could connect to the speaker or recognize on hearing it again. The man who used that voice had no native language. He had learned the use of an alien tool. The words floated in the air behind him as he walked" (9).[39] In other words, the DS speaks with the voice of the tape recorder itself, a voice that is disembodied and not spoken by any one particular person.

Burroughs also inserts descriptions of how actual tape recorders perform the effects into the narrative. In his investigation into the death of John Harrison and the possible involvement of Genial, Inspector Lee listens to tapes made by Harrison and Genial. Mr. Taylor, who initially investigated the death, plays the tapes and narrates how they work:

> "Now listen to this." The words were smudged together. They snarled and whined and barked. It was as if the words themselves were called in question and forced to give up their hidden meanings. "Inched tape . . the same recording you just heard pulled back and forth across the head . . You can get the same effect by switching a recording on and off at very short intervals. Listen carefully and you will hear words that were not in the original text: 'do it-do it-do it . . yes I will will will do it do it do it . . really really really do it do it do it . . neck neck neck . . oh yes oh yes oh yes . .'" (18)

The primal qualities of these sounds reduce words into a primordial state where new words are born from sound and erotic meanings revealed. Inching the tape – that is, pulling the tape back and forth over the tape head – leads to repetitions whose rhythmic qualities are themselves erotic, by Burroughs's measure. When reading *Ticket,* it can sometimes be difficult to imagine what this sounds like; the effect of prerecorded speech being used to create new speech is clearer when one listens to the actual recordings Burroughs made with Brion Gysin and Ian Sommerville. On a track called "Sound Piece" from the album *Break Through in Grey Room* (1986), one can hear these inching effects at work. The effect sounds similar to a DJ scratching a record, and when words emerge from the scratches, they sound as though they are being sucked through a vacuum. In the novel, Mr. Taylor explains, "the content of the tape doesn't seem to effect the result" (18). Throughout *Ticket*, one of the ways the Nova Mob exerts power is through erotic images and sounds, but Burroughs always includes clues for the inner workings of the mob's control strategies. Only in the course of listening to the recordings does Inspector Lee realize that Genial is a tape virus.

The cut-up method is generally considered Burroughs's most significant contribution to late twentieth-century writing. As its name implies, the process usually involves taking scissors to a page of text and rearranging the pieces in order to create new texts. Although, a cut-up can also be performed by cross-referencing folded pages of texts (as he frequently did while writing *Ticket*) and can be applied to tape recordings by cutting and rearranging prerecorded elements. Burroughs used scissors, folds, and splices of his own materials, but also introduced 'found' elements such as newspapers, novels, and radio shows into the mix. By adding a randomizing element to writing, Burroughs hoped to better reflect everyday experiences of sensory input and to undermine the predetermined aspects of language. The cut-up, rather than being an artificial activity, is "a juxtaposition of what's happening outside and what you're thinking of" (*The Job* 8). *The Third Mind* (1978), Burroughs's collaboration with Gysin, offers several definitions and demonstrations of the cut-up, and suggests that by reading texts written in this way, "you will hear the disembodied voice which speaks through any newspaper on lines of association and juxtaposition. The mechanism has no voice of its own and can only talk indirectly through the words of others" (178). Of course, even Burroughs recognized that the cut-up was not essentially new, citing precursors such as T. S. Eliot's *The Waste Land* and Tristan Tzara's Dadaist experiments – even "Dos Passos used the same idea in 'The Camera Eye' sequences in U.S.A. and I felt I had been working toward the same goal," Burroughs admitted (http://theparisreview.org). Similar to Glenn Gould, who hoped for a "participant listener," or even Barthes who said "listening speaks," Burroughs felt the cut-ups would "involve much more of the total capacity of the observer" (http://theparisreview.org). Listening to recorded sounds with a tape recorder was not just another form of consumption. Instead, the listener regained the possibility for agency and became a producer of new sounds. In other words, Burroughs's cut-ups require resonant reading.

There are a number of parallels between Burroughs's approach to the listener/reader's role and that of the classical pianist and recording pioneer, Glenn Gould. Gould, who at the height of his career gave up performing in favor of the recording studio, presented quite a challenge to the world of classical music, which privileged live performance. Evan Eisenberg has pointed out that Gould imagined a "situation in which the artist disappears and the listener, shaping the music to his environment and his 'project at hand', becomes the artist" (83). In Gould's 1966 essay "The Prospects of Recording," he predicts a "new kind of listener – a listener more participant in the musical experience" (121). This new "participant listener," Gould continues, "is no longer passively analytical; he is an associate whose tastes, preferences, and inclinations even now alter peripherally the experiences to which he gives his attention, and upon whose fuller participation the future art of music waits" (122). Gould even went as far as to suggest granting the listener "tape-edit options which he could exercise at his discretion" (122). At the time, this provocation seemed little more than fantasy, but in 2012, Sony Music released *Glenn Gould: The Acoustic Orchestrations*, which includes not only a spatial rendering of the score, but a CD with a "Gouldian 'sound mixing kit'" that includes the unmixed tracks so that anyone with a computer or mobile device with multitrack applications (e.g., Apple's Garage Band) can create their own mix. Gould predicted that the hierarchies between composer, performer, and listener would break down, as would the hierarchies between music and the environment. Without such hierarchies, "the audience would be the artist and their life would be art" (126). This dissolution of order reflected a larger shift during this period in aesthetic practices in music, but also in theater and writing. John Cage imagined his role as composer becoming that of listener; in the book *In Search of a Concrete Music* (1952; trans. 2012), Pierre Schaeffer was especially interested in the way "the listener evolves into the composer" (120). Poststructuralists like Roland Barthes proclaimed the death of the author and the birth of the reader. The pioneer of performance art, Allan Kaprow, and others expanded notions of breaking down the fourth wall in theater to include what they called "Happenings." The performance of poetry in cafes and clubs became more central to the poetry scene. Tom Wolfe described how the "acid tests" of Ken Kesey and the Merry Pranksters, for instance, were meant to be a "form of expression in which there would be no separation between himself and the audience" (Wolfe 8). One might even argue that the exchange of bootleg tapes of the Grateful Dead operate under similar auspices. In each of these scenarios, tape recorders were often present on the scene and the notion of *play* was central to the collaborative modes of artistic exploration.

Burroughs's collaboration with Gysin and Sommerville to make recordings that applied the techniques of the cut-up to magnetic tape began in the early 1960s while he was working on the Nova trilogy. The experimental recordings, a few of which were broadcast on the BBC, inspired the incorporation of the tape recorder in *The Ticket That Exploded*. The first tape cut-ups involved "dropping-in," recording fragments *over* previous recordings at random. Dropping-in replicates deliberately what Kerouac experienced inadvertently while making recordings with Cassady. As Burroughs, Gysin, and Sommerville became more aware of all the potential facilities of the tape, they incorporated them into their experiments: techniques such as slowing-down, speeding-up, running backward, inching the tape (also known as rubbing), playing several tracks at once, and cutting back and forth between two recorders. On "Silver Smoke of Dreams," made by Burroughs and Sommerville in the early 1960s, the recognizability of language diminishes significantly as new words and voices are *dropped in* the middle of others. Cutting between extremely short stretches of tape, perhaps no more than a couple of seconds, the voices of Burroughs and Sommerville (and sometimes Burroughs and Burroughs) intersect and interrupt one another as they read from the last page of *Ticket*. If the process does not exactly produce new words, it creates new word-like sounds. Especially prominent are the cut-ins of the nonverbal utterances ("uhm" "ah" "st") and short inhales of breath between words.[40] At times, the repetitions give the sounds a rhythmic musical quality. Certain recognizable words and phrases bleed through, hinting at their origin – "the still," "Billy," "smell of late morning," "how to do it," "of dreams" – but more frequently, the listener is faced with isolated vocables and half-words.[41] Any attempt to transcribe these sounds, of course, would involve an act of interpretation and would crystallize a word whose sound and interpretation is meant to be open. Gysin observed that the words produced by the drop-ins and splices "had never been said, by me or by anybody necessarily, onto tape" (Wilson 44). These were new words without any predetermined meaning, spoken by a new voice – a voice only the tape recorder could produce. For Burroughs, the possibilities of tape were both intoxicating and toxic, providing model for the sounds of *The Ticket That Exploded*.

Initial responses to *The Ticket That Exploded* when it was published in the United States in 1967 were mixed; Burroughs's cut-up style was no longer new, but the reading experience was no less harrowing. Eliot Fremont-Smith of the *New York Times* praised *Ticket* for its humor and described it as comprising "a painting, perhaps a jukebox, of lethal, writing images and wails." However, Samuel Bellman of the *Los Angeles Times* criticized that *Ticket* "really isn't a novel after all but a mere idea for relating deviant

behavior" and a "misuse of the machine for recording sounds."
Bellman's critique only adds to the sense that *Ticket* is a kind of
Anarchist Cookbook of tape technology and highlights the strange
relationship between the tape recorder and the text. Accusing *Ticket*
of *misusing* tape technology implies not simply objectionable writing,
but an objectionable methodology. Responses like those of Bellman,
however, are not surprising given the difficulty of Burroughs's weedy
prose. Indeed, *Ticket* is not a novel in the traditional sense, and
reading his cut-ups can be uncomfortable. One might even call it
revolting in the broad sense of the word – disgusting in subject matter,
but revolutionary in form.

Assessing Burroughs's radical formal methodologies in relation to his
subject matter continues to be one of the most divisive aspects of critical
responses. Critical interpretations of Burroughs are steeped in the myth-
ology of his association with the Beats, his drug use, his sexuality, and the
ambivalent morality of his texts, not to mention the overtly misogynistic
portrayals of women. Burroughs's first book *Junkie* (1953) chronicled his
experiences as a drug addict, and the explicit portrayal of sexuality, violence, and drugs in *Naked Lunch* (1959) led to his trial on charges of
obscenity. Burroughs's participation in the 1962 Edinburgh conference,
where he presented on censorship and the future of the novel, was controversial, and though he was championed by other writers like Mary
McCarthy and Norman Mailer, who praised the cut-up method and
compared his satirical wit to Jonathan Swift, many were still skeptical
and called his work "disgusting."[42] Robin Lydenberg and Jennie Skerl have
suggested that the poststructuralism of the late 1960s and 1970s made it
easier to read Burroughs's books as "texts rather than messages," which led
to his reconsideration among scholars (8).[43] N. Katherine Hayles points
out that, although Burroughs would not have read Derrida when working
on *Ticket* (*Of Grammatology* was published the same year), he came to
a similar conclusion about language (212). In a 1964 review in the *Nation*,
Marshall McLuhan said that Burroughs's work in *Naked Lunch* and in the
Nova trilogy was emblematic of the way the new media forms were shaping
consciousness: "It is the medium that is the message because the medium
creates an environment that is as indelible as it is lethal" (72).[44] At times, it
feels like McLuhan will apply his famous catch phrase to anything he can,
but in Burroughs's treatment of the tape recorder, the medium and the
message sometimes do appear interchangeable.

In the strange world Burroughs constructs, tape recorder viruses and
tape recorder voices are layered into tape recorder landscapes. Thus, the

tape recorder is a metaphor for mind control, but magnetic recording is also a way for Burroughs to imagine a kind of writing that is multilayered and constantly rewriting itself. In the following description of a phantasmagoric journey through "The Exhibition," the reader might not immediately recognize that they are inside a tape recorder:

> In a room with metal walls magnetic mobiles under flickering blue light and smell of ozone—jointed metal youths danced in a shower of blue sparks, erections twisted together shivering metal orgasms—Sheets of magnetized calligraphs drew colored iron filings that fell in clouds of color from patterns pulsing to metal music, off on, on off—(The spectators clicked through a maze of turnstiles)—Great sheets of magnetized print held color and disintegrated in cold mineral silence as word dust falls from demagnetized patterns [. . .] The magnetic pencil caught in calligraphs of Brion Gysin wrote back into the brain metal patterns of silence and space. (62–63)

The scene is steeped in psychedelic images of swirling color, and a reader less familiar with the mechanics of magnetic tape recording could easily miss the fact that Burroughs has taken the reader down to the microscopic level of the tape where "metal music" pulses the long sheet into magnetized patterns. Whereas these recorded patterns are impossible to see with the naked eye, Burroughs zooms in on the technology to the point where sound becomes an image – amplified to the point of silence. Even the turnstiles evoke the rotating spindles around which the tape turns. Located within a routine titled *"writing machine,"* the tape recorder shape-shifts and the spooling tapes become "conveyor belts" that, instead of spilling "talk and metal music fountains," take Shakespeare and Rimbaud and "shifts one half one text and half the other through a page frame" that in turn spits out new literary works. The scene is emblematic of the strange, associative relationship between tape and text throughout *The Ticket That Exploded*, where it is not always clear that Burroughs distinguishes between recording and writing, or between medium and message. Although Burroughs was deeply invested in sound and recording experiments, their role in the text continually fluctuates between metaphor and formal model.

The image of the conveyor belt-tape is also useful for understanding the ever shifting and contingent relationship that Burroughs imagines his reader will have to the text as a result of the cut-ups and fold-ins – a relationship that I would argue is more like that of a listener than a reader. In interviews, Burroughs asserts that everything he writes is in the service of the "juxtaposition of word and image" and their "very complex association lines," which he calls "coordinates" (http://theparisreview.org).[45] Not only does Burroughs encourage readers to cut-in and start reading at any point in his texts, but through the cut-up method of assembling text, the writing performs the juxtaposition of unmatched text.[46] Thus, the writing does not always comply to expected rules of grammar, and the meaning of sentences can prove elusive. Instead, meaning depends upon the associations that percolate in the mind of the reader. This is resonant reading at its core. Rather than operating on the basis of a cohesive narrative – which, when it appears, lasts no more than a few pages – cohesion in *The Ticket That Exploded* arises from "coordinates" and refrain-like words and phrases that recur throughout the book and the trilogy as a whole.[47] For example, phrases that appear in the passage above, such as "cold mineral silence," repeat verbatim, but there is also a repetition of similar images (such as metallic dust) in various contexts, including "magnetic silver flakes" (66), "iron from pale word dust" (79), and "silver morning smoke" (202), each of which evokes a resonant sense of association.

Listening depends upon our capacity to perceive resonance. In the case of Burroughs's experiments with inching the tape, the reader is invited to partake in the role of "participant listener" in order to hear the words *between* words through resonant reading. These "coordinates" of association allow the text to cohere as a kind of constellation of moments, without being tied to a particular narrative time. Whereas these kinds of associations require listening in a more metaphoric sense, there are moments in *The Ticket That Exploded* that explicitly play upon musical memory to demonstrate the degree to which recordings have programmed contemporary readers' minds. In "*do you love me?*" the young monk Bradly is tortured into painfully contorted ecstasies through tape-recorded sounds of love making and popular songs:

> All the tunes and sound effects of '*Love*' spit from the recorder permuting sex whine of a sick picture planet: Do you love me?—But i exploded in cosmic laughter—Old acquaintance be forgot?—Oh darling, just a photograph—Mary I love you I do do you know i love you through—I would run till i feel the thrill of long ago—Now my inspiration but it won't last and we'll be just a photograph [. . .] Tell Laura i love my blue heaven—Get up woman off your big fat earth out into cosmic space with all your diamond rings—Do you do you do you love me? (44)[48]

Burroughs might have imagined this section as emulating the sound created by turning the radio dial at random, but for today's reader, the "do you love me" section is immediately recognizable as an elaborate mashup – a form which Burroughs arguably pioneered. A mashup is the combination of two or more songs to create a new song, and it is a form that has become a staple of early twenty-first-century cultural production (the practice is also sometimes applied to text and video). In sections like these, it is easy to see why so many musicians, bands, and DJs have been drawn to Burroughs's work. Through lyrical reference, Burroughs is deliberately drawing on the Newsreel and Camera Eye strategies of John Dos Passos and playing on the way that recordings (through repetition) have been able to ingrain particular culturally inscribed sounds into the minds of the masses. On the one hand, the reader's familiarity with well-known songs like "Stardust" and "Do You Love Me" enables Burroughs to create a pleasurable, even erotic, effect that draws upon the emotional associations the individual reader has with the music. But on the other hand, there is an inherent critique of the way that popular songs have affected a kind of mind control by ingraining themselves in the memories of unwitting listeners, which illustrates the problem with a passive kind of listening. Whereas a writer like Dos Passos seemed to want to evoke songs in their entirety (even specific recordings) through strategic reference, Burroughs's interspicing of the song lyrics with one another to create new lyrical lines offers a way of obliterating the "association blocks" and creating new relationships to the words. This is Burroughs's innovation. Rather than treating popular song recordings as something static, he treats sound and lyrics like the materials for making art. In a 1972 *Rolling Stone* interview with Robert Palmer, Burroughs explained how his relationship with Gysin gave him a new attitude toward the materiality of making text: "The cut-up method treats words as the painter treats his paint, raw material with rules and reasons of its own" (67). When Burroughs turns this strategy to tapes of recorded music, it not only creates new sentences with new meanings, but the juxtaposition creates new melodic lines. For the reader who is familiar with these songs, reading the lyrics causes the melodies to sound in the mind. And as the fragments connect to one another, new and original melodies emerge.

Through the processes of reworking songs, texts, and other materials, Burroughs hopes to break open and rewrite the memory. "We think of the past as being there unchangeable," he suggested. "Actually the past is ours to shape and change as we will" (*The Job* 20). To illustrate this point, Burroughs uses the example of two men having a conversation. If the conversation is not recorded, it just exists in memory. But play back an altered tape recording over the conversation and "the two actors will *remember* the altered recording" (*The Job* 20). This scenario, of course, could describe the tape recorder sessions between Jack Kerouac and Neal

Cassady, who struggle with the relationship between recording, memory, and writing. In *The Ticket That Exploded*, this scenario is represented by "engrams" and "engram clearing," which is a process by which memory can be written and rewritten via tape and repetition. Engrams are part of a strategy devised by the Logos group to control people with word combos. In a therapy called *clearing*, "you 'run' traumatic material which they call 'engrams' until it loses emotional connotation through repetition and is then refiled as neutral memory" (21). However, the system is open to abuses and "these 'engram' tapes are living organisms viruses in fact" (21). In other words, engram clearing is a kind of inoculation. The section that follows enacts the engram clearing through its form. Characterized by a lack of punctuation and text strung together in an endless line of em-dashes, this section consists of a montage of disturbing erotic images, samples of text from books, and unidentified voices.

In the manipulation of word and image, Burroughs was drawing on principles of advertising he had been exposed to as a copywriter, and in resisting the mind control aspects of language, he ends up adopting the strategies of the enemy.[49] Doing so, however, places Burroughs in a double bind. The problem with writing a book that tries to resist language (through the random reordering of text via the cut-up method) is that print inevitably freezes language. The risk to the reader is that rather than being freed from the so-called mind control, one simply becomes reprogrammed. In other words, by writing a book, Burroughs is also exerting a kind of mind control over the reader via text, which undermines his aims of subverting language. However, Burroughs has tried to account for this possibility. Throughout *The Ticket That Exploded*, Burroughs includes implicit instructions for using the tape recorder by describing how the various processes of Nova mind control is performed; in the epilogue of the book, "The Invisible Generation," he includes overt instructions (written with Brion Gysin) for experimenting with tape recorders, and even suggests to the reader which brand to purchase: "a Philips compact cassette recorder" (208). Reading alone is not enough – Burroughs instructs the reader to actively engage the gadgetry and *perform* the cut-up process.[50] To read *The Ticket That Exploded* as a novel would therefore seem to be a mistake; it is not a novel, but a revolutionary how-to manual.[51]

"It's all done with tape recorders," Burroughs and Gysin assert in the epilogue (205).[52] Adopting the tone and language of tape recorder manuals and advertisements, the final section titled "*the invisible generation*" provides detailed instructions for innovative ways to use the tape recorder.

Some of the instructions seem innocuous, if a bit silly, such as saying a sentence backward to unlearn it: "a tape recorder can play back fast slow or backwards you can learn to do these things record a sentence and speed it up now try imitating your accelerated voice play a sentence backwards and learn to unsay what you just said" (206). In this way, one could be freed from the "old association locks" of language (206). The tone of the instructions fluctuates wildly, from humorous and jovial, to absurd, to morbidly serious. One moment the narrator encourages the reader to go to the zoo to listen to the gorillas, the next moment he asks, "why not give tape recorder parties?" (209). In a more serious turn, the tape recorder becomes a tool for political resistance at a freedom march or rally: "suppose you record the ugliest snarling southern law men several hundred tape recorders spitting it back and forth and chewing it around like a cow with the aftosa you now have a sound that could make any neighborhood unattractive" (210). Burroughs was not known as a civil rights activist – if anything, the Beats had a complicated attitude toward race with naïve ideas about integration – but the reference here to the civil rights movement implies that to fight hate speech one must take that hate speech and reinvent it until the sound itself becomes a weapon.[53] It is an instruction that might be said to resonate with the recordings of Amiri Baraka on *It's Nation Time*, even if Baraka did not use the tape recorder specifically. The only way to move past the fighting and arguing, for Burroughs, is to let the tape recorder do it for you. According to Burroughs, everybody must "splice himself in with everybody else" (212). Borrowing the language of the pioneering performance artist Allan Kaprow, Burroughs and Gysin claim that "tape recorders can create a happening anywhere" (214). Ultimately, "*the invisible generation*" manifesto asks "you" to take control of your own message by turning tape recorder listening into an active mode of sound production.

In a parallel development, the elaborate system of programmed, looped tape recorders that Burroughs and Gysin describe was made a reality by the ultimate purveyors of the "Happening," Ken Kesey and the Merry Pranksters, as described in *The Electric Kool-Aid Acid Test*. In a scene where Neal Cassady was once again both literally and figuratively at the wheel, the Kesey compound was a kind of vast experimental recording studio where even the trees were wired for sound. Like Burroughs, Kesey felt that tape recorders represented a way not simply to record and reproduce sounds, but to solve larger philosophical problems of sensory experience. As Tom Wolfe describes it in *The Electric Kool-Aid Acid Test* (1968):

[Kesey] starts talking about the lag systems he is trying to work out with tape recorders. Out in the backhouse he has variable lag systems in which a microphone broadcasts over a speaker, and in front of the speaker is a second microphone. This microphone picks up what you just broadcast, but an instant later ... A person has all sorts of lags built into him, Kesey is saying. One, the most basic, is the sensory lag, the lag between the time your senses receive something and you are able to react. One thirtieth of a second is the time it takes, if you're the most alert person alive ... [Neal Cassady] is going as fast as a human can go, but even he can't overcome it. (144–45)

The result of Kesey's variable lag system is that one is constantly speaking over echoes of echoes. Whether the system leads to harmonious sounds or merely cacophonous noise is left unaddressed. Having left his writing career behind, the Happenings, the Grateful Dead concerts, the acid tests, and the tape recordings became Kesey's main mode of artistic production. It was a mode in which one's life becomes one's art – a mode that Neal Cassady arguably pioneered and which inspired Jack Kerouac to write about him in the first place.

* * *

During the last two decades of the twentieth century, Burroughs achieved a level of pop notoriety not usually afforded writers, recording with rock musicians and even appearing on *Saturday Night Live*.[54] As is well documented, his writings have inspired numerous songs and band names (from Steely Dan and Soft Machine to DJ Spooky, That Subliminal Kid), and in more recent years there have been several attempts to set parts of the Nova trilogy to music, including John Zorn's 2011 album *Nova Express* and James Ilgenfritz's 2011 opera *The Ticket That Exploded*. Indeed, there is a good reason that William Burroughs appears on the cover of the Beatles' 1967 album *Sgt. Pepper's Lonely Hearts Club Band* – and it is not simply because the publication of *Naked Lunch* had made him a cult figure. Burroughs, through his tape recorder experiments in the early 1960s with Ian Sommerville and Brion Gysin, had become one of the influences on how the Beatles were beginning to use the recording studio. In 1966, shortly after Burroughs returned to London, Paul McCartney invited Burroughs to listen to an early cut of *Rubber Soul* at the studio they had set up for Ian Sommerville (Morgan 454). *Rubber Soul* was not nearly as experimental as *Revolver* (1966) or *Sgt. Pepper's* (1967) would be, but it did include some early experiments with the tape, such as playing a recorded piano back at double speed for the harpsichord effect on "In My Life."[55] As Burroughs recalled, he had several conversations with McCartney and Sommerville around this time about the possibilities of the tape recorder, such as overlaying and running backward,[56] and McCartney considered Burroughs something of a mentor.[57] McCartney had even planned to launch a spoken-word label with Sommerville, Burroughs, and Barry Miles that would incorporate poetry, interviews, and experimental music (T. Morton 8890). It is easy to forget the connection between these experimental pop albums and the avant-garde literary and tape recorder experiments of a fringe figure like Burroughs.

Burroughs himself was not a huge fan of Rock and Roll music, but his subversive approach to sound would anticipate and give forward momentum to hard rock and punk rock to come. Figures from Mick Jagger to Kurt Cobain revered Burroughs and in their screams, the squeals of their guitars, and their obscured vocals, one can hear the resonance of the kinds of sound Burroughs brings forth in his written and recorded work and encourages through nontraditional uses of the recorded medium: the sounds in between the words, the feedback, the peals of sped-up-speech, the rubbing of the tape. When Burroughs applied his cut-up method to the realm of tape, he not only shifted how we think about the malleability of recorded sound, but he created a link between modernist collage and the aesthetic gestures that have come to define much of late twentieth- and early twenty-first-century aesthetics, including the remix and the mashup.

CHAPTER 4

The Stereophonic Poetics of
Langston Hughes and Amiri Baraka[1]

> If you play James Brown (say, "Money Won't Change You ... but time will take you out") in a bank, the total environment is changed. Not only the sardonic comment of the lyrics, but the total emotional placement of the rhythm, instrumentation and sound. An energy is released in the bank, a summoning of images that take the bank, and everybody in it, on a trip. That is, they visit another place. A place where Black People live.
>
> Amiri Baraka, *Black Music*

When James Brown released *Live at the Apollo* in 1963, no one but Brown could have predicted the phenomenon it would become. King Records, Brown's label, initially declined to make the record because Brown did not plan to feature any new songs, but Brown could feel that the timing was right and that his band was primed so he made the record at his own expense. The album, which was recorded in stereo, captures not only the energy of Brown's singing and signature falsetto scream but also the supercharged waves of the audience's shouts and wails as they resound in the large Harlem theater. But what does it mean to be "live" and "at the Apollo"? When listening to the album in one's living room, the sounds of one's own environment are interpenetrated by and reverberate with those of the Apollo theater, such that when Brown calls out "I want to hear you scream!" he could be speaking to you. In critical circles and among record collectors, *Live at the Apollo* is frequently cited as one of the greatest "live" albums of all time. Yet, at time, the excitement of the album seems to have less to do with the music than the vicarious crowd experience, which Phillip Auslander has argued is the only real difference between a live album and a studio recording.[2] One might argue that the audience performs a kind of useful listening frame, and yet, on this album, something else is going on. As Amiri Baraka has said of James Brown's records, his music "makes an image," and, as the passage above suggests, if you are listening to James Brown in some ordinary place like a bank, "an energy is released in the bank, a summoning of images that take the bank, and every body in it, on a trip. That is, they visit another place. A place where Black People live" (*Black Music* 186). But where is this place, and where are we when we listen to such an album? When listening to *Live at the Apollo*, the answer is not simply that we are simultaneously in our own home and at the Apollo theater; there is an implied third, more complicated audio space – one that is also strangely visual: a stereophonic dimension. Listening is always a complicated act, and the ways one listens to records are as varied as there are listeners, but while music has always had trans-portative qualities, the stereo LP, with its long-play form and two channels of sound, created a new frame for understanding sonic space. In this chapter, I turn to works by two authors whose poetry directly engages with the stereo LP – Langston Hughes and Amiri Baraka – as a way to explore how stereo enabled the possibility of new Black sonic spaces.

We do not often think of the stereo LP as a tool for radical thought, and yet Langston Hughes's book *Ask Your Mama: 12 Moods for Jazz* (1961) and Amiri Baraka's album *It's Nation Time* (1972) remind us to consider the ways that sonic space became an important imaginative forum for both political and social thought. In histories of recorded sound, the popular-ization of stereo recordings has generally been thought of as a marketing ploy on the part of record companies (Milner 142). But such histories tend to focus on stereo's role in relation to the music industry rather than its social history. Stereo would reshape the way listeners thought about sonic space, and when the first commercial stereo album was released in 1957, it was not only the same year as the Civil Rights Act, but it was also the year usually acknowledged as the beginning of the "space age." One could argue that "space" as a theoretical concept dominated the 1960s, and as Amiri Baraka himself had said, the issue surrounding racial integration and later Black Nationalism was always a "space question" (qtd. in Szwed 311). Resonant readings of the works of Hughes and Baraka reveal writers exploring the radical potential of stereophonic sound.

Baraka and Hughes were not the first, nor the only poets to make albums – and importantly, both poets were known for life-long commit-ments to poetry that engages with jazz, blues, and other forms of Black music – but what distinguishes *Ask Your Mama* and *It's Nation Time* is the ongoing dialogue with the specificities of stereo technology and the album as a cultural form. In this chapter, I am purposefully extending the idea of what "stereophonic" can mean and use the term broadly to refer to sound in its technological-spatial dimension. What makes this *stereophonic dimension* different from ordinary audition, however, is the way it opens a space within a space: one that is neither outside nor in between, but central and simultaneous. Whether sitting in your living room with an LP on the stereo or listening on your headphones, suddenly you are participating in two (or more) spaces.[3] It is, on some level, a fundamental modeling of the modern multimedia environment. With just two channels of sound, stereo promises to project a total sound image before you.

Generationally speaking, we tend to consider Hughes and Baraka separately – Hughes as part of the Harlem Renaissance, and Baraka as part of the Black Arts Movement. This is the unfortunate effect of periodizing authors for the purposes of anthologies and surveys. However, in the poetry they wrote during the 1960s and early 1970s, we can track overlapping concerns marked by the civil rights era, the political commitments of their art, Black music, and technological advances in recorded sound. Stereo ushered in a wave of experimentation by musicians, audiophiles, and sound engineers; but the stakes of sonic space are heightened when considered in light of historical circumstances. In the United States, the 1960s were marked by the struggle to end segregation and systematized discrimination against African Americans, but globally the 1960s were also an incredibly tumultuous time for African and Afro-diasporic people. There was civil war in the Congo, protests against apartheid in South Africa, and a renewed sense among Black intellectuals in America that the struggles of African Americans were linked to those of African people everywhere.[4] While *Ask Your Mama* alludes to an emerging global Black consciousness, *It's Nation Time* attempts to use sound to establish a new Black Nation with a poetry that screamed and raged in dynamic engagement with free jazz, R&B, and African drumming. Although Hughes and Baraka were working in different media, stereophonic poetics allowed both poets to pry open new sonic spaces for poetic protest at two quite different moments in the civil rights era. Hughes was primarily concerned with the geography of *place* during integration – that is, what happens to the "quarter of the Negroes" – but Baraka was more interested in opening a *space* into which a new Black Nation could be born. The stereophonic is musical but also philosophical. Thus, the album *It's Nation Time* taps into a stereo imagination of infinite new spaces, including previously unimagined Black sonic spaces.

Critical discussions of both Hughes and Baraka have pointed out the importance of the spatial dimensions of their poetry. Larry Scanlon's "News from Heaven: Vernacular Time in Langston Hughes's 'Ask Your Mama,'" briefly alludes to the interesting tension between the spatial and temporal dimensions of the text, citing the repeating figure of the shadow or shade in the poem, which, "paradoxically, because it is spatial, . . . is also an image of simultaneity" (55). Fred Moten takes us a step closer to the issue regarding Baraka's work, noting that "syncopation, performance, and the anarchic organization of phonic substance delineate an ontological field wherein Black radicalism is set to work" (*In the Break* 85). In addressing Baraka's radical poetic turn in the mid-1960s, Moten argues that "Baraka plays: from question to assertion, from line to line (spatial reorientations) from sight to sound," adding that "we might look at that temporal-spatial discontinuity as a generative break, one wherein action becomes possible" (95, 99). Although critics like Scanlon and Moten have alluded to the sonic spatial dimension of these works, they have paid less attention to the role of stereophonic sound in negotiating the issues of racial segregation, integration, and later Black Nationalism.

My own intervention draws upon Alexander Weheliye's *Phonographies: Grooves in Sonic Afro-Modernity* (2005), in which Weheliye usefully points to the ways Black culture and its uses of sonic technologies have shaped modernity more broadly.[5] Weheliye has noted that despite cultural historians' interest in space as it relates to the postmodern moment, few have thought about the sonic dimensions of space. In his readings of Ralph Ellison's "Living with Music" (1955) and Darnell Martin's film *I Like It Like That* (1994), Weheliye maintains that music influences and shapes the spaces in which we dwell, arguing that "*consuming* sonic technologies and *being consumed* by them suggest specifically modern ways of be(com)ing in the world" (107). However, while Weheliye makes an important point about how sonic technologies shape the places we already inhabit, he fails to consider either the projective aspects of sonic space or the connection between spatialized uses of sound and the development of stereo technology.

Although Weheliye overlooks the relationship between stereophonic recordings and the importance of sonic space, I am not the first to use the term *stereophonic* to describe the Pan-Africanist consciousness. In *The Black Atlantic: Modernity and Double Consciousness* (1993), Paul Gilroy describes the double consciousness experienced by Afro-diasporic people as "stereophonic, bilingual, or bifocal" (3). Though Gilroy uses the term only in passing, his invocation of the term stereophonic reveals how we have come to understand the stereophonic in terms of the temporal and spatial dimensions created by *two* channels of sound. Gilroy's metaphoric use of stereo and its dual-channeled sound in the context of Black studies reverberates with the many tropes of intertextuality and doubleness that flow from W.E.B. Du Bois's "double consciousness" to Henry Louis Gates Jr.'s Bahktinian "double-voiced utterance" to what Julian Henriques sees as the double in "dub." And yet, as recent discussions in Black sound studies have shown, we might be wise to reconsider the binaries that too often "other" blackness as outside Western modernity.[6] It can be helpful to remember that stereo, rather than referring to binaurality or two channels of sound, comes from the Greek *stereo-* meaning solid or three-dimensional.

Tsitsi Ella Jaji has borrowed the metaphor of stereo to describe Africa's own reciprocal relationship with creative and political movements throughout the diaspora. Jaji's book, *Africa in Stereo: Modernism, Music, and Pan-African Solidarity* (2014), offers a "perspective on diaspora that includes and inscribes Africa as a constitutive locus rather than viewing it as a 'source' for diasporic populations and practices but not an active participant" (6). While Gilroy invokes the dual channels of a modern stereophonic metaphor precisely for its double-ness, Jaji reaches back to the Greek etymology of stereo defined as "solid" in an attempt to break down the binary. As she puts it, she is "dubbing stereo in for solidarity" (11). Jaji's turn of phrase is provocative, but the leap from stereo to solidarity is less frequently concerned with a direct consideration of the technology itself.[7] And yet, both Gilroy's and Jaji's suggestive uses of stereo as a metaphor invite a resituation of the stereophonic within its historical and cultural contexts, and it is from this position that I hope to touch upon the very real ways stereo technologies became a way for established poets like Hughes and Baraka to explore Black sonic space. For although Sun Ra declared in 1973 that "*Space Is the Place*," most listeners have struggled to follow what he meant.

Now in Stereo: Mid-Century Developments in Sound Recording Technology

Within the histories of recorded music, stereo rarely registers as more than a benchmark in the audiophile's pursuit of high fidelity. Using two (or more) microphones, stereo recordings inscribe both sides of the record's groove with two channels of sound that, when replayed, produce the illusion of hearing sound in a real space. Stereo thus plays upon what cognitive psychologists refer to as the interaural time difference and the interaural level difference – or, the difference in time as sound hits one ear and then the other, and the difference in volume as it encounters the ear that is closer to the sound source (Goldstein 378). The high fidelity movement began with the introduction of vinyl records in the late 1940s.[8] With longer playing time and vinyl's improved sound, high-fidelity albums promised to recreate the continuous listening experience of the concert hall or the jazz club in one's living room, "as though he were hearing it live" (Milner 139). Prior to long-playing vinyl records, "albums" of recordings did exist, but were sold as books with sleeves holding several 78 rpm discs that had typically been released individually. The combined developments of long-playing vinyl and stereo recording along with advances in magnetic tape recording technology (such as Ampex that enabled multitracking) not only allowed for a more "live" sound, but made it practical to record a "live" album because the technology itself was more portable. However, it is worth noting that the desire for stereo hi-fi by audio engineers was not simply about replicating the original performance, but rather about presenting the sound of that performance within a culturally inscribed setting, such as the concert hall; stereo recordings reproduce not just the sound of the instruments but the sound of the space in which they are produced. Audio engineers refer to this as a "sound image," but some, including composer and theorist Paul Théberge, have taken to describing the audio space of a stereo recording as a "sound stage."[9] In this way, stereo became a theater of sound: both a performance space and a performance *of* space.

Although stereo LPs did not appear until 1957–58, research into stereo-phonic sound began in the 1930s when film companies started looking for a sound to complement cinematic realism.[10] One of the ironies is that the first commercial film to incorporate stereo sound was Walt Disney's surrealist *Fantasia* in 1940, an animated film in which dancing hippos and other animals are accompanied by classical orchestral pieces; in other words, sound was being used to enhance the dimensionality of a visual medium, and in the case of animation, a determinedly flat medium.[11] Audiophile publications were quick to marvel at the promise of stereo and its visual sound. As Joseph Enock put it in a 1956 issue of *Gramophone*, there was a sense of "anticipatory gilt" in the coming synesthetic technology "which together would make up the complete moving sound picture that was being presented for the enjoyment of the listener. Or should I say 'viewer'" (101). Even at this early moment in the technology's development, stereo was embedded with a paradox: on the one hand, stereo promised greater realism and the reproduction of sounds in real spaces; on the other hand, it enabled a kind of sublime fantasy and the creation of spaces that could never exist in 'real' life – such spaces are not unreal, but a kind of simulacra.[12]

By the early 1960s, the album had reached a point where its cultural currency rivaled the book, and hi-fi stereos and record libraries were prominent features in the average living room. For an audiophile like Langston Hughes, who had an extensive record collection and even wrote a children's book about rhythm that included technical explanations of sound waves, an appeal to the LP was not simply an attempt to be hip to the changing times, but demonstrated an attentiveness to technological form and the cultural role of LPs and stereo sound.[13]

Langston Hughes and the LP Book

Langston Hughes began writing *Ask Your Mama: 12 Moods for Jazz* on July 4, 1960, just two days after a riot at the Newport Jazz Festival brought the event to a premature end. Hughes, who was on the board of the festival and was engaged to give a demonstration lecture on the history of the blues with John Lee Hooker, Muddy Waters, Sammy Price, and others, saw the riot as a significant event.[14] Though the rioters were primarily white college-aged men, Hughes recognized that it was Black jazz that had ignited them.[15] Just a few months earlier, Hughes had also witnessed youth protests beginning to flare in the South while giving a reading in Atlanta, where he saw the Black students of Atlanta University engaged in tension with the police, and this along with the Newport riots ignited a new awareness in Hughes (Rampersad 309). Hughes had a premonition that the struggles of African Americans would soon erupt and, emboldened by the young Black protestors and the fiery power that Black music held over young white people, put down on record a more caustic poetic protest of his own. Hughes furiously began scribbling the first lines of *Ask Your Mama* in pencil on scraps of pocket notebook paper and hotel stationary, returning again and again to the line: *In the quarter of the Negroes* . . .[16]

As Hughes's longest and arguably most ambitious poem, the wide-ranging scope of *Ask Your Mama* lends itself to a variety of different readings. Nearly all studies point to Hughes's protest against racism in the face of the civil rights movement (Hughes termed it a "polite protest"). Larry Scanlon has a studied the poem as a meditation on the "dozens" – an African American form of ritual insult, the most recognizable example being "yo' mama" jokes. Arnold Rampersad has drawn parallels between *Ask Your Mama* and modernist epics such as T. S. Eliot's *The Waste Land* and Ezra Pound's *The Cantos*. Others have studied both Hughes's critique of the white-dominated music industry and the relationship between music and the text. Meta DuEwa Jones has revisited the performative voice of Hughes, and Josh Kun writes about the exchange of African American and Afro-Cuban music. More recently, scholars have turned to the international consciousness of the poem, and John Lowney argues that "the jazz form of *Ask Your Mama* enacts the challenge of developing a progressive black transnationalist public" (564). That the poem has elicited such rich and varied readings is a testament to its multifaceted qualities. But here, I want to focus on how Hughes's "disc-tortions" of the poetic form exploited the new technologies of the stereo LP, as well as how the stereophonic dimension opened new avenues for Hughes to rethink the geopolitical spaces inhabited by Afro-diasporic peoples.

By the time Hughes began writing *Ask Your Mama*, he had already established himself as one of the most famous poets in America, known primarily for his short lyric works, his characteristic invocation of Black vernacular speech, and especially his blues poems. Having read his poetry with Harlem jazz musicians since the mid-1920s, decades before Beat generation writers began reading poetry to jazz, Hughes experienced something of a revival in the late 1950s with the downtown scene. But despite the fact that Hughes wrote prolifically until his death in 1967, including a weekly column for the *Chicago Defender* from 1942–63, today he is often taught and anthologized as simply a Harlem Renaissance figure; his politics, compared to the Black radical poets of the sixties, seem tame. Hughes's sanitized reputation may have something to do with his own attempts to rehabilitate his public image following the 1953 McCarthy hearings. During the 1950s he did more work as an editor and wrote books for children, among other projects. Privately, Hughes was critical of Black writers like Ralph Ellison and James Baldwin, who he felt were not concerned enough with the plight of Black Americans (Rampersad 297). He was skeptical of the integrationist Beats and even questioned whether the young Amiri Baraka (then Le Roi Jones) was really Black (Rampersad 311). The bitter irony that tinges his mid-century writings can be mistaken for retreat, but his book-length poetry from that era, such as *Montage of a Dream Deferred* (1951), reveals Hughes's increasing impatience with the slowness of change ("What happens to a dream deferred?") and the decline of Black urban centers like Harlem. In *Montage*, one can witness how Hughes was adapting the rhythms of his poetry to the sounds of bebop, as "Little cullud boys with fears, / frantic, kick their draftee years / into flatted fifths and flatter beers" (*Collected Poems* 404). His interest in Black music as a source of inspiration, rather than being trapped in a 1930s folk vision of the blues, was attuned to both the changing sounds of the music and to the technology of the time.

The disc had long been on Hughes's mind. An avid record collector, Hughes had dragged a portable phonograph along with jazz and blues records across Europe and Russia in the 1930s.[17] As Hughes put it, "there is something about Louis Armstrong's horn that creates spontaneous friendships" (*I Wonder as I Wander* 133). In the preface to *Montage of Dream Deferred*, Hughes remarked that "Harlem, like be-bop, is marked by conflicting changes," and thus *Montage*, with its many variations and versions (of the blues and of its own poems), reflects what Hughes called the "disc-tortions of the music of a community in transition" (*Collected Poems* 387). These *disc-tortions* register the increasingly central role records had come to play in American culture and recording's economic and cultural significance for Black Americans. In the 1950s and 1960s, Hughes would make several recordings of his poetry, including the album, *Weary Blues* (MGM 1958), which he recorded with Leonard Feather and Charles Mingus.[18] However, Hughes's collaboration with Mingus and Feather did not quite live up to his ideas about an album of poetry. Longer and much grander in scope than his earlier blues and short works, *Ask Your Mama* consists of twelve poems or "tracks," coyly explanatory "liner notes" for the "unhep," and a prefatory note stating that the "Hesitation Blues" is the *leitmotif* of the poem. But what is perhaps more notable is the unique form the poems assume on the page. The book itself is squareish in shape, much like an album, and the poems run in two columns: on the left, poetry written in all capital letters (Hughes sometimes called this column the "voice"), and on the right, evocative musical descriptions meant to accompany the poetry (Figure 4.1). As one can see in Hughes's papers at Yale's Beinecke Library, *Ask Your Mama* went through more than thirteen drafts before the poet settled upon the form we now know. In its earlier stages, the poem grew amorphously, riffing lightly on the oft-repeated line "IN THE QUARTER OF THE NEGROES," but in Hughes's later drafts the concept of the LP – with its twelve tracks, cohesive artistic vision, and cultural status – gave form, structure, and dimension to *Ask Your Mama*.[19] The book takes the disc-tortions he began in *Montage* to new levels. He does not merely distort the disc by recording multiple versions, like so many bebop musicians did, but by playing upon the new developments in long-play, the stereophonic elements of the poem open up a new relationship to space as the first rumbles of integration after *Brown v. Board of Education* were shifting the kinds of spaces Black Americans could inhabit. The result was a radical, revolutionary form with a recursive relationship between text and music, poetry and album.

Figure 4.1 Langston Hughes, *Ask Your Mama: 12 Moods for Jazz*

Hughes's use of the LP as a formal inspiration for writing is usually overlooked or treated as incidental, but the intermediality of the book functionally shapes the way we read and hear *Ask Your Mama*. Critical readings have attempted to reclaim the vernacularity of the book in the face of modernist difficulty by focusing on Hughes's use of the dozens. But what if we rethink the LP *as a vernacular form*? Hughes's approach to the LP manifested itself in a number of ways. As Judith Jones at Knopf described, "He saw the book as different, and he wanted it to look different," and so its squareish shape gestures toward an album sleeve (qtd. Rampersad 329).[20] In the press materials that accompany his archival drafts, Hughes suggested that these were more than visual allusions:

> In his new book of poetry, Ask Your Mama, Langston Hughes employs liner notes as commentary at the back of the volume. The book, subtitled 12 Moods for Jazz, Hughes feels is like a recording with six tracks to a side. Since current LP records all have liner notes, why not a poem? The notes by Hughes comment not only upon the moods and meanings of the poetry, but go beyond them into the realm of free association – which the poet claims jazz itself does – so when you have finished the liner notes, you return to the poems to find out what the notes mean.[21]

Of course, it would be impossible to make a one-to-one comparison between Hughes's book and an actual LP, but in encouraging a recursive, resonant relationship between reading and listening, Hughes constructs a multimedia experience on the page that challenges these distinctions and makes use of the visual aspects of text to illuminate the visual-spatial elements of sound.

The most recognizable attempt to unsettle our reading practice is the poem's layout in dual channels. In the multisensorial opening poem, "CULTURAL EXCHANGE," Hughes establishes the dialogic relationship between poetry and music with lines that stutter like a needle dropped in the groove:

IN THE	*The*
IN THE QUARTER	*rhythmically*
IN THE QUARTER OF THE NEGROES	*rough*
WHERE THE DOORS ARE DOORS OF PAPER	*scraping*
DUST OF DINGY ATOMS	*of a guira*
BLOWS A SCRATCHY SOUND.	*continues*
AMORPHOUS JACK-O'-LANTERNS CAPER	*monotonously*
AND THE WIND WON'T WAIT FOR MIDNIGHT	*until a lonely*
FOR FUN TO BLOW DOORS DOWN.	*flute call,*
	high and
BY THE RIVER AND THE RAILROAD	*far away,*
WITH FLUID FAR-OFF GOING	*merges*
BOUNDARIES BIND UNBINDING	*into piano*
A WHIRL OF WHISTLES BLOWING	*variations*
NO TRAINS OR STEAMBOATS GOING –	*on German*
YET LEONTYNE'S UNPACKING.	*lieder*
	gradually
IN THE QUARTER OF THE NEGROES	*changing*
WHERE THE DOORKNOB LETS IN LIEDER	*into*
MORE THAN GERMAN EVER BORE,	*old-time*
HER YESTERDAY PAST GRANDPA –	*traditional*
NOT OF HER OWN DOING –	*12-bar*
IN A POT OF COLLARD GREENS	*blues*
IS GENTLY STEWING.	*up strong*
	between verses
THERE, FORBID US TO REMEMBER,	*until*
COMES AN AFRICAN IN MID-DECEMBER	*African*
SENT BY THE STATE DEPARTMENT	*drums*
AMONG THE SHACKS TO MEET THE BLACKS:	*throb*
LEONTYNE SAMMY HARRY POITIER	*against*
LOVELY LENA MARIAN LOUIS PEARLIE MAE	*blues*
(3–4)	

Before one even begins to think about content, the reader is faced with the question: *how do I read this?* Ought one read each column separately and try to imagine them together? Should one read the musical description at right first, and then the poetic verse, or the other way around? When we read "lonely flute call" do we hear it, or must we play it? Perhaps we are meant to read all the way across, each column intersecting the sense of the other, like a cut-up. While reading from left to right across the line is standard reading practice, doing so in this case would seem to interrupt the poetic flow and lead to a cacophonous nonsense; Hughes's use of two different font styles (all-caps and italics) seems to resist this kind of reading. Although there is no prescribed reading practice and no consensus as to the best approach to the text, the tendency among readers is to read each channel separately (treating the right channel descriptions as the musical accompaniment to the poem, thus secondary), and most critical treatments of the poem tend to analyze the left channel and may or may not mention the right. Reading in this manner, however, would suggest that the music and the poetry are two completely separate entities, when, in fact, both columns contain music that is in constant dialogue with one another.

Difficult and jarring though it may be, some degree of reading across the lines is necessary to hear the full extent of the rhythms at play in *Ask Your Mama*. Meta DuEwa Jones has argued in favor of an "oppositional reading practice" that moves vertically as well as horizontally, "even though, admittedly, it goes against the grain of how listeners would hear Hughes's recital of *Ask Your Mama*" on the recording that he made for Buddah Records in 1961 in which he only read the overtly poetic left column (*Muse is Music* 68). Extending Jones's claim, I would even say that reading across is a practice invited by the strong rhythms of his opening lines. In "CULTURAL EXCHANGE," Hughes sets the tempo of the poem in the rhythms of the musical descriptions, reinforced by the rhythmic poetic line, "IN THE QUARTER OF THE NEGROES." Mimicking the *"rhythmically rough scraping of a guira"* (a cylindrical metal percussion instrument played with a brush, typically with a short-short-long rhythm), the oft-repeated line takes on a three-dimensional acoustic as its rhythms are echoed both horizontally and vertically across the plane of the page. Although the free verse poem has no set meter, in this line we can hear both an anapestic quality (˘ ˘ ¯) as well as the more standard trochaic tetrameter (¯ ˘), a poetic echo of a "three-over-two" polyrhythm that is the hallmark of jazz's sense of swing and most African-based music. The reader is placed in the position of overhearing through paper-thin doors a "scratchy sound" that from the outset evokes both the guira and the scratch of the record as the needle is set in the groove. As the wind blows in breathy alliteration in the left column, so blows the flute *"high and faraway"* in the right column. These resonant sonic reflections work their way throughout *Ask Your Mama* and call into question the notion of the musical accompaniment as simply supplementary or secondary.[22]

As we read *Ask Your Mama*, the parallel right and left channels have the effect of the dual-sided groove of the stereo record. Although a stereo recording produces two separate streams of sound, our ear is inclined to unite them. Slight differences in each channel (volume, orientation of the instruments, and an imperceptible delay) lend the illusion of space. Depending on the placement of microphones in the recording space, and depending on how the engineer mixed the final cut, when we listen to a stereo recording, we hear certain instruments as coming from one side more than from the other. For example, we might hear more drum or bass on the right side, the flute on the left, and the piano as centered. But even if we isolate each channel, we will usually still hear all instruments in both channels, only at different levels. In attracting the ear to musical elements across both channels, Hughes draws a kind of imperfect diagram of the sound image – one in which the poetic lyrics are always in the left channel and music primarily on the right, but each always interpenetrating the other.

The musical descriptions are score-like, but their impulse is frequently more poetic than musical, and a blues gets described as "like a neon swamp-fire cooled by dry ice" (77). Thus reading the poem requires that we enlist our eyes to struggle at the task our ears perform so naturally: perceiving the two channels as an aggregated, single sound. These audio-visual acrobatics are fascinating in their own right, but for Hughes, the aesthetic cannot be untangled from the political. By interpolating Western trochaic patterns with the Caribbean guira and African 3:2 polyrhythms, this innovative form allows Hughes to hold these geographically disparate sounds in tension with one another even as they blend and interpenetrate. In this way Hughes sonically performs the difficult patterns of cultural exchange that mirror the more official, institutional forms that he references, such as when "COMES AN AFRICAN IN MID-DECEMBER / SENT BY THE STATE DEPARTMENT / AMONG THE SHACKS TO MEET THE BLACKS." Cultural exchange is always multidirectional for Hughes – often paradoxically so; the poem evokes the trips organized by the US State Department during the Cold War that sent jazz musicians such as Louis Armstrong, Dizzy Gillespie, and Dave Brubeck around the globe to promote American culture and freedom, but Hughes also references trips by African leaders to the United States, such as Guinean President Ahmed Sékou Touré's visit in 1959, which was interrupted by racial violence in the South.[23] Juxtaposing these multidirectional forms of cultural exchange, Hughes also brings forward an irony that he offers more explicitly in the "liner notes" to the poem where he calls America "an IBM land that pays more attention to Moscow than to Mississippi" (86). For what good is cultural exchange among nations when America understands "even so little about itself" (86).

In light of this lack of understanding, *Ask Your Mama* is, at its core, about the negotiation of Black spaces within America, and particularly Black sonic space. With its insistent repetition of "IN THE QUARTER OF THE NEGROES," the poem is partly about the quarter or *place* where Black people live, but it is also about the place they occupy in America and in the world as part of the broader African Diaspora.[24] It is the story of Black neighborhoods from Harlem to Haiti, and the opening lines hesitate on the preposition "IN" as a way of opening the door, so to speak, to the question of *where* Negroes stand in America. Evoking the smells of a pot of collard greens stewing, and the sounds of trains and steamboats, Hughes takes the reader across the tracks into a segregated universe where "THE ENTRANCE TO THE MOVIE'S / UP AN ALLEY UP THE SIDE" (5). The repeated imagery of doors and the frequent use of prepositions (especially "in") at the beginning of lines help to position and situate the reader within the three-dimensional space of the poem, and specifically, within the quarter of the Negroes – an acoustically rich and resonant space.

Visually, one could read the two columns on the page as a reflection of this preoccupation with segregated space as the columns literally command a dis-unified and separate reading; sonically, they enact a different kind of spatial orientation, one that requires the ear to take in their rhythms at once. But as we read, a delay is always perceptible, and this visualization of the delays and disjuncture already at work gestures toward a stereophonic effect. Hughes's poem highlights the aspects of binaural hearing and stereophonic sound that are, in fact, visual. The dual columns of the poetry are perhaps the most recognizable stereophonic effect, as they physically divide the space on the page; however, the poem also incorporates stereo techniques in more nuanced ways through manipulation of the "Hesitation Blues" and the use of echoes. An echo might be thought of as a temporal delay that registers as a marker of space. On the level of cognition, the interaural time difference is usually too insignificant to register as two separate sounds, but after a threshold of five milliseconds our ears begin to hear this time difference as an *echo*, or repetition of sound.[25] As the poem's leitmotif, the "Hesitation Blues" thematizes this delay and echoes Hughes's "dream deferred."

Echoes and doubling in *Ask Your Mama* are often indicative of a collapse of historical time, musical time, or general delay, and open the tension between time and space. When Hughes repeats a phrase or word to even-out the line (metrically), this poetic echo visually amplifies the amount of space that his writing inhabits on the page, in addition to reinforcing the word and placing pressure on the meaning:

WHOSE HAYMOW WAS A *MANGER MANGER*	[*"Battle Hymn of the*
WHERE THE CHRIST CHILD ONCE HAD LAIN	*Republic"*] ...
SO THE WHITENESS AND THE *WATER*	*repeated*
MELT TO *WATER* ONCE AGAIN	*ever*
AND THE ROAR OF NIAGARA	*softer*
DROWNS THE RUMBLE OF THAT TRAIN	*to*
DISTANT ALMOST NOW AS *DISTANT*	*fade*
AS FORGOTTEN PAIN IN THE *QUARTER*	*out*
QUARTER OF THE NEGROES	*slowly*
("ODE TO DINAH" 27 emphasis mine)	*here*
	tacit

Thematically, this is another instance in which Hughes is drawing together large swaths of history, quilting together a Biblical journey with those made along the Underground Railroad, all the while referencing the present-day living spaces of the Negroes. The repetitive doubling reinforces the ways that cyclical historical moments fade into the noise created by their echoes. Across time and across great distances, the pains of slavery and the Underground Railroad get forgotten. On the one hand, the echo amplifies a sound by repeating it, but the noise it creates also threatens to drown out the original message or sound – repetition degrades the fidelity of reproduction. Here, Hughes reinforces the image of sound's degradation across distance with a fade out effect in the music. Interestingly, many of these echoes would appear to be the direct result of Hughes's own use of a tape recorder in the process of drafting his poem, including the addition of a second "MANGER." This addition was among a number of edits that Hughes listed in a note on an early draft from January 8, 1961, titled "Changes made after verbal taping." It would seem that something about hearing his own voice displaced and echoed back at him via the tape recorder enabled Hughes to incorporate that element of recording phenomena.

Musically and thematically, this interaural time difference is embodied by the "Hesitation Blues," a song that resonates with the theme of deferral present in so many of Hughes's poems. As you may recall, the song also appeared in in John Dos Passos's *U.S.A.,* and it was sung by Jelly Roll

Morton at the Library of Congress. In "Ode to Dinah," Hughes's paean to Dinah Washington, the "Hesitation Blues" express themselves across both channels as Hughes explores the way that Black artists have been exploited by the recording industry and jukebox culture.[26]

AS EACH QUARTER CLINKS	*"Hesitation*
INTO A MILLION POOLS OF QUARTERS	*Blues"*
TO BE CARTED OFF BY BRINK'S	*softly*
THE SHADES OF DINAH'S SINGING	*asking*
MAKE A SPANGLE OUT OF QUARTERS RINGING	*over*
TO KEEP FAR-OFF CANARIES	*and*
IN SILVER CAGES SINGING.	*over*
***TELL ME**, PRETTY PAPA,*	*its old*
WHAT TIME IS IT NOW?	*question.*
PRETTY PAPA, PRETTY PAPA,	*"Tell*
WHAT TIME IS IT NOW?	**me**
DON'T CARE WHAT TIME IT IS –	*how*
GONNA LOVE YOU ANYHOW	*long?"*
WHILE NIAGARA FALLS IS FROZEN.	*until*
	music
	dies . . .
	(28; emphasis mine)

The voice singing "TELL ME, PRETTY PAPA, / WHAT TIME IS IT NOW?" is echoed by another question in the right channel: "*Tell me how long?*" These reflections of the Hesitation Blues are also the musical manifestations of the dozens in which questions are answered with questions, resulting in a reverberation effect. As the questions redouble back upon themselves and the "Hesitation Blues" is re-versioned across the columns, Hughes draws out the irony of the continued delay of justice for Black Americans, and gives the irony space to resonate.

Ask Your Mama treats not only the technical aspects of recording but also the socioeconomic aspects of the recording industry. While a number of Black entertainers and athletes managed to achieve success and moved into the white suburbs, they were still largely exploited by white-owned industries, and their individual wealth did not trickle down to Black communities as a whole. As the "liner notes" to "Ode to Dinah" state, "Most of the money spent goes downtown. Only a little comes back in the form of relief checks" (88). Dinah Washington is a particularly fraught figure in the poem and offers insight into the paradox of the successful African American artist: she was the epitome of "crossover" and one of the most popular singers of the 1950s and 1960s, but in retrospect, her records

Figure 4.2 Dinah Washington, *Dinah Jams*

have sometimes been criticized for having a whitewashed sound that compromised her roots.[27] A singer in the blues tradition who grew up singing in the church, her distinctive voice and phrasing style was indicative of the recorded era's dependence upon recognizable voices and distinct audio identities; in album cover images from the era, such as *Dinah Jams* (1955), Dinah and her microphone are seldom far apart (see Figure 4.2).

In 1956, she even released an album called, *In the Land of Hi-Fi,* as though hi-fi were not merely an aspect of the technology, but a place one might go. Dinah Washington's marketed image reveals the conflation of the recording artist with the technology itself. Hughes alludes to the sense in which "Dinah" is manufactured; she does not make her songs, the jukebox does:

> DARK SHADOWS BECOME DARKER BY A SHADE
> SUCKED IN BY FAT JUKEBOXES
> WHERE DINAH'S SONGS ARE MADE
> FROM SLABS OF SILVER SHADOWS
> AS EACH QUARTER CLINKS
> INTO A MILLION POOLS OF QUARTERS
> TO BE CARTED OFF BY BRINKS (28)

Though her records were top sellers, that money was "CARTED OFF" in armored trucks with the implication that it never made it to the quarter of the Negroes, where the arrival of prosperity is always deferred. In "Horn of Plenty," this faulty accounting manifests on the page where incoming dollars "$$$$" become only cents "¢¢¢¢" (another "quarter" of the Negroes) in a poetic accounting that recalls Ezra Pound's *The Cantos* and his endless obsession with debt. There are great costs to success and integration, and Dinah Washington's voice was the sonic manifestation of both costs and gains.

Despite the inherent contradictions contained within a figure like Dinah Washington, the poem reclaims the African American roots of her sound through an elaborate mashup. Hughes calls upon readers to hear the resonance across the time and space of musical references by calling up records in the jukebox of the mind, allowing sounds to accumulate and infiltrate one another.[28] In the space of the poem, Dinah is all at once southern, tinged by a Caribbean past, and born of both the gospel music of Mahalia Jackson and the gutbucket blues of Blind Lemon Jefferson. This history is exemplified by the image of a fruitcake from Georgia crumbling into Caribbean rum "TO A DISC BY DINAH," as Hughes asks us to hear between two distant Negro neighborhoods. However, this kind of listening *across* is not without difficulty or hesitation, and the disc by Dinah hiccups as the record skips and repeats; Blind Lemon is not a real father but a step-father, and he literally steps over the enjambed lines ("STEP-FATHERED BY BLIND LEMON / STEP-FATHERED BY / BLIND LEMON" [26]). The melding of both blues and gospel roots is reinforced across the channel with a blues played *à la* Ray Charles, the artist who is usually charged with secularizing gospel music.

In moments like these, Hughes plays disc jockey, matching beat for beat as he switches between records, long before beat matching was the purview of the DJ.[29] This mode of collage is common to modernist epic poetry, but the specific references to recordings give the practice a closer affinity to that of DJs today. Hughes is *timestretching* and *pitchshifting* to bring these records closer together; he deploys the recorded form's ability to transcend temporal boundaries in a poetic move that Larry Scanlon calls "diachronic."[30] In "Ride, Red, Ride," for example, Hughes works across the channels to create the ultimate protest-song mashup, bringing together the "Hesitation Blues" with "When the Saints Go Marching In" and an obscure reference to the French Revolutionary song, "Ah, Ça Ira!" (13). A casual reader of French might see *ÇA IRA!* and translate the phrase as "it will go." However, colloquially, *ÇA IRA!* means "it'll be fine" or, by some accounts, "we will win!" The phrase became the refrain of an important song during the French Revolution as early as 1790 and was revived by Edith Piaf in the 1953 film *Si Versailles m'était conté*. Even more surprising is that Benjamin Franklin is said to have originated the phrase; when asked about the Revolution in America, he would reply, "Ah, ça ira!"[31] Taken together, these songs express the complex emotions around civil rights issues: the exasperation of the "how long do I have to wait?" with the promise of the glory at the end of days ("when the saints go marching in") and the self-assured conviction that it will all turn out alright. Writing about jazz recordings more generally, Peter Elsdon has suggested that this kind of "intertextuality works against semantic stability and the concept of the closed work" (Elsdon 159). In Hughes's writing, the density of audible reference pushes on the capacity of the recorded medium and calls into question the ability of the record to contain such a vast black space. The resonant reader's critical ear must make sense of these multilayered schemes of reference; listening is therefore a strategy for hearing the blend of references without sacrificing their distinct sounds.

It is not without irony that the poem titled "Blues in Stereo" recounts instances in which the new media technologies fail. Dominated by images of broken down media and the failure to get a signal, "Blues in Stereo" announces that the "TV KEEPS ON SNOWING," and repetition in the poem creates self-reflexive echoes that challenge the LP's musical status (37). The record itself does not *play* the horn – an image that implies both phonograph and trumpet – but echoes it; the music is in effect "BORROWED" and the LP has no memory of itself: music is played "ON LPs THAT WONDER / HOW THEY EVER GOT THAT WAY" (36). Hughes may be a master of the media in its various forms, but his mastery does not dilute his contentious relationship with the media. Part of what Hughes is doing is not simply mimicking the LP or trying to induce stereo effects but rather questioning and reimagining how media function. It is something of an antidote to Marshall McLuhan's technodeterminist readings of media technologies.

If *Ask Your Mama* has received renewed attention in the twenty-first century, it may have something to do with the fact that, as John Lowney has noted, "it resembles a DJ's mix of converging sounds rather than a more conventional jazz poem" (566). Since the early 2000s, there have been a number of attempts to stage the poem using multimedia, including Laura Karpman's multimedia composition and collaboration with the Roots and Jessye Norman (premiered in 2009 at Carnegie Hall, and released as a Grammy-winning recording in 2015), Ron McCurdy's Langston Hughes

Project (since 2009), and Dr. John S. Wright's reading with Jon Faddis and the Carnegie Hall Jazz Band in 2000. Of course, these performances and recordings reflect the paradox of *Ask Your Mama*: it is a book that models itself on a record and, in doing so, becomes a score for performance. Laura Karpman has argued vehemently for the need to reconsider the importance of *Ask Your Mama,* and, in a phone interview in June 2012, called Hughes a "multimedia visionary" whose ideas could not be realized in his time.[32] For Karpman – a composer for film and television who has worked with the likes of Steven Spielberg – part of the attraction of *Ask Your Mama* lies in the slippages between the sonic and visual elements and the exhaustive references to recordings, which she incorporates into her composition. In considering *Ask Your Mama* anew, we find that while Hughes takes inspiration from the LP as a way to give form to his poem, he just as actively theorizes and critiques that form by illuminating the already spatial-visual nature of sound. This is made vivid on the page, where Hughes visualizes the stereophonic dimension of recorded sound and confounds our typical understanding of the aural and the visual as distinct. In working across that space on the page and challenging readers to listen for resonance (as well as for moments of disjuncture), Hughes's work clarifies an attitude toward listening that was just beginning to take shape while foreshadowing the possibility of a recording that did not just reproduce but actually produced new kinds of spaces. Through his experimental poetics, Hughes illustrated a new possibility for the LP – both as a tool for opening new spaces and as a protest space – and laid the foundation for a recorded poetic that would influence poets of the Black Arts Movement.

Creating a Black Forum: The Poetry Album and the Black Arts Movement

By the mid-1960s, the cultural status of albums had come to rival books as more artists and audiences began to view the long-play format as a critical medium for artistic and even political expression. One could cite any number of albums that ushered in this transformation, from John Coltrane's *A Love Supreme* (1965) to the Beatles' self-titled "white album" (1968) – a title which Joan Didion would later borrow for her own collection of essays about the 1960s.[33] As an LP book that understood the cultural currency of its form, Langston Hughes's *Ask Your Mama* was ahead of its time, both in scope and in its appeal to the long-play stereo album as a site of poetic protest. However, as the decade rushed ahead, and in the wake of the assassinations of Malcolm X and Dr. Martin Luther King, Jr., it became clear that the time for "polite" protest had passed. Hughes's muted, ironic critique soon gave way to the louder, more aggressive sounds and demands of Black Nationalism and the Black Arts Movement.[34] Even still, Hughes's LP book reflects a transitional moment in which the notion of what the "publication" of poetry meant was beginning to shift. Public readings were becoming de rigueur, and spoken-word recordings were highly popular.[35] Gil Scott-Heron's first album, *Small Talk at 125th and Lenox* (1970), exemplified "a new era of poets making the crossover from books to albums," as Pat Thomas has noted, and the album cover itself depicts Scott-Heron with a book of poetry in his hands (19).[36] But it was the album with Scott-Heron's voice – not the book – that became the primary means of disseminating his Black radical message.

The Black Arts Movement emerged around 1965 as the cultural wing of Black Power and Black Nationalism in response to the growing unrest among Black Americans and to the assassination of Malcolm X. As the poet and dramatist Larry Neal described it in 1968, both Black Arts and Black Power were nationalistic, but "one is concerned with the relationship between art and politics; the other with the art of politics" (qtd. in Collins and Crawford 7). However, at the center of both movements was the "necessity for black people to define the world in their own terms," a point made by Black artists in terms of aesthetics (7). Having rejected the liberals' push for nonviolence and integration during the late 1950s and early 1960s, activists like Larry Neal and Amiri Baraka advocated that African Americans make art addressing Black audiences, rather than protesting against white ones, expressing visions for the future. It was in essence a separatist movement. Blaming the mass media for programming Black Americans with negative images and racial self-hatred, Black Arts proponents supported efforts to reprogram the Black psyche.[37] Lisa Gail Collins and Margo Crawford have written of the importance of visual culture to the Black Arts Movement in making these new images, but in some ways the visual could prove more difficult to reprogram. Sonic spaces were less explored, and spoken-word albums became a crucial means of getting the message heard in an era when the LP was increasingly viewed as art. Amiri Barka and others began establishing small independent presses and record labels to disseminate their works to Black audiences.

Although Hughes passed away in 1967 and was conflicted about the anger of the new generation of Black artists, his life-long advocacy for the connections between poetry, jazz, and other forms of Black music resonates clearly on many of the albums made by poets of the Black Arts Movement.[38] The early 1970s saw an explosion of such poetry albums. In

1970, The Last Poets, usually credited as the "godfathers of rap," released their eponymous debut, as did poet Gil Scott-Heron on the independent label Douglas Records; both records feature poetry accompanied by conga drums and a flowing style of delivery that would heavily influence rap (Thomas 15). Poets like Scott-Heron frequently mentioned the influence of Hughes, and on *Boss Soul: 12 Poems by Sarah Webster Fabio set to Drum Talk, Rhythms and Images* (Folkways 1972), Sarah Webster Fabio incorporates folk songs, African rhythms, and R&B – calling out Hughes and *Ask Your Mama* by name on "Soul Through a Lickin Stick." The poetry album became a prominent form for female poets associated with Black Arts, including Jayne Cortez, Maya Angelou, and Nikki Giovani.[39] On Jayne Cortez's *Celebrations and Solitude* (1974), a collaboration with bassist Richard Davis, she echoes the "Hesitation Blues" in her ode to John Coltrane, "How Long Has Trane Been Gone." Echoing the refrain, she asks "How long, how long has that Trane been gone. John palpitating love notes in a lost found nation within a nation, his music resounding discovery." The poem laments that Black communities may be forgetting their history and music – it is indicative of the anxieties of integration's threat to erase or ignore cultural differences and mask continuing forms of racism. On such albums, one hears not only a clear need to redefine the *place* of Black Americans in America, but also to carve out new *spaces*.

One such space was "Black Forum" – a short-lived sublabel of Motown Records. Given Motown's reputation for inoffensive crossover music and Berry Gordy Jr.'s reluctance to release albums by radical Black artists, the creation of the Black Forum sublabel was surprising. Between 1970 and 1973 Black Forum released a limited selection of spoken-word recordings, including Amiri Baraka's *It's Nation Time,* and others by Martin Luther King, Jr., Langston Hughes and Margaret Danner, Elaine Brown, Stokely Carmichael, and others. Black Forum was formed by a small group of producers at Motown who were empowered by the efforts of mainstream Black artists on Motown and other labels to take more vocal political stances in their music. Songs like James Brown's 1968 anthem "Say it Loud, (I'm Black and I'm Proud)" became a huge force in the movement and opened the door for other mainstream Black recording artists to write political music. Such music included the Temptations' "Message from a Black Man" and Sly Stone's "Don't Call me Nigger, Whitey," both released in 1969, and Marvin Gaye's "What's Going On" in 1971.[40]

The albums released on the Black Forum label were part of a small but growing trend; in the era before video, spoken-word and commemorative albums played an important role in preserving historical events and speeches. Those associated with Black Arts, Baraka included, advocated for independent modes of dissemination, and Baraka himself created his own record label and publishing company, Jihad, to this end. Black Forum, however, created an important space within the mainstream for artists and activists with nonmainstream messages.

Compared to *Ask Your Mama*, *It's Nation Time* takes the stereophonic poetic in a somewhat different direction. Hughes was intimately concerned with issues of *place* – that is, the sounds and scenes of the Black neighborhood – but for Baraka the audible *space* was a realm that could be harnessed in the service of a new Black nation. Whereas *place* usually denotes a specific geographic or historical location, *space* is unbounded, expansive, and can have a temporal as well as physical dimension. Therefore, the acoustic spaces Baraka inhabits are projective, hyperbolic, and imagined. They are attempts to push beyond the constrictions of place and history in order to produce a new, contingent sonic space. Such a move also reflects a turn in the studio stereo recording that would take place around this time as engineers discovered that sonic spaces could not only be reproduced but manipulated and produced. *It's Nation Time* strives toward a theory of sonic space that might redefine the parameters of a national space and create a new conception of blackness.

Amiri Baraka and the Audio Nation

When Amiri Baraka passed away in January 2014, the words most often used to describe his legacy were "polarizing" and "controversial" – as a writer who came of age among the Beats, who broke away to participate in the Black radicalism of the 1960s, and who later became a Marxist, his artistic output has been diverse and his message at times contradictory. His outspoken, often violent, critiques of white bourgeois culture and the treatment of Black Americans led many to accuse him of race baiting, but his simultaneous insistence on the beauty and spirituality of Black culture would galvanize a generation of Black poets and artists. As a poet, playwright, essayist, activist, teacher, and founder of the Black Arts Movement – Baraka was prolific. His performances of poetry with jazz, which continued the legacy of Hughes, would help set the stage for the emergence of hip-hop, and Ishmael Reed has argued that Baraka "did for the English syntax what [Thelonious] Monk did with the chord. He was an original" (http://wsj.com). And yet, while Baraka was known for his engagement with Black music in his poetry, many have overlooked *It's Nation Time* – the 1972 LP that he recorded for Motown's Black Forum

Figure 4.3 *It's Nation Time*

label.[41] Chanting, singing, and screaming his poetry over the rhythms of African drums, free jazz, and R&B, Baraka asked his listeners: "Can you imagine something other than what you see? Something Big, Big & Black. Purple yellow red & green (but Big, Big & Black)."[42] It was a call to action for Black people to imagine new futures for themselves – an album that put into action his ideas about Black music and Black Nationalism by creating new Black sonic space within the dimensions of the stereo LP.

When Baraka recorded *It's Nation Time,* he had just returned from the 1970 Congress of African People (CAP) in Atlanta (Figure 4.3). Black Nationalism, self-determination, and Pan-Africanism had been important themes at the Congress, which aspired to create a governing body that could put the ideas of Black Power into action. But one of the biggest questions that the Congress and Black Nationalists had yet to resolve was: where should such a nation reside? Did a people so geographically dispersed constitute a nation? Some still advocated for a return to Africa, but others questioned whether a nation needed to have a geographic location in order to exist. While the term "nation" has historically meant many things – from a loosely constituted group of people united by language, religion, or common heritage to a geographically bound political state – the questions raised at CAP were indicative of a struggle with the concept of nationhood in the context of the late twentieth-century nation-states.[43] For Baraka, however, the concept of "nation" retained its plasticity and is perhaps more in line with Benedict Anderson's redefinition of nations as "imagined communities."[44]

Energized by the ideas and questions raised at CAP, Baraka considered *It's Nation Time* to be a kind of founding document of Black Nationalism, stating assertively on the liner notes: "This recording is an institution." But how can a recording be an institution? Can a nation have a sound? The Congress of African People in some ways marked the high point of Black Nationalism, but it was also the beginning of Black Power's demise.[45] The mandate for a unified nation with its own governing body was nearly impossible to actualize on a geopolitical level, and nationalism proved to be a fraught subject that divided Black radical thought. By 1974, even Baraka would separate himself from the nationalists. However, on *It's Nation Time*, one can hear Baraka struggling with how to bring a Black nation into being while rethinking the idea of what a nation might look and sound like; the album registers the imaginative, hyperbolic, and ultimately never-realized creation of a Pan-African nation.

Of course, *It's Nation Time* was not Baraka's first foray into the political realm, nor was it his first recording. Following his break with the racially integrated Beat crowd in the mid-1960s, he had become increasingly political. With poems like "Black Art," he helped to ignite the Black Arts Movement.[46] Baraka changed his name from LeRoi Jones to Imamu Amiri Baraka and wrote poetry with a more radical edge, including "Against Bourgeois Art," and "Black Dada Nihilismus" – poems which he frequently performed and also recorded with musicians such as Sun Ra, Sonny Murray, the New York Art Quartet, Albert Ayler, and others on albums such as: *Sonny's Time Now* (Jihad Productions, 1965); *New York Art Quartet* (ESP Disk, 1965); and *A Black Mass* with Sun Ra (Jihad Productions, 1968). What distinguishes *It's Nation Time* from these earlier efforts, however, is Baraka's poetic dialogue with the specificities of stereo sound, the LP, and his theoretical model of sound in its spatial dimensions.

Admittedly, the stereo effects of *It's Nation Time* are not revolutionary. If I had wanted to write simply about experimental stereophonic techniques, there are better albums to feature – for instance, Pink Floyd's *Dark Side of the Moon* (1973). But the stereophonics of *It's Nation Time* are particularly interesting because the soundscape it creates reinforces the thematic aspects of space in Baraka's poetry in a combination of electroacoustic effects and speech acts. At a rudimentary level, the album attempts to construct a sonic environment that expresses a relationship between the different genres of music and their geographic-temporal relations to one another: African drums, as an ancestral music, feel "farther" away, while the R&B tracks, with electric amplified instruments like electric guitar, bass, and keyboards, feel "closer" and more direct. On the two opening tracks, "Chant" and "Answers," the unison female voices and the African hand-drums and shakers sound distant, especially when contrasted to Baraka's voice, which is not just significantly louder but lacks the ambient acoustic quality, feeling instead flat and close to the ear as a result of close mic'ing. "All praises due to the black man. All praises due to the creator," he intones. The track hearkens to the sounds of ritual at the moment that establishes the stereophonic landscape. The African instrumentation overlaps with African American jazz, the drumming slowly and seamlessly gives way to Lonnie Liston Smith on piano, who plays a series of ascending and descending arpeggiated tone clusters to a dreamlike effect, finally leading into the track "All in the Street." The lyrics, as printed in the Jihad pamphlet *Spirit Reach* (1972), encourage the listener to transpose sound into the visual dimension:

> Can you Imagine something other
> than what you
> see Something
> Big Big & Black
> Purple yellow
> Red & green (but Big, Big & Black)
> Something look like a city
> like a Sun Island gold-noon
> Flame emptied out of heaven
> grown swollen in the center
> of the earth
> Can you imagine who would live
> there (10)[47]

Asking his listeners to "imagine" this new world that seems to exist simultaneously at the center of the earth and out in the "Big & Black" (i.e., outer space), Baraka induces the audio-eye of the listener, creating a moment of synesthesia through lyrics and sonic effects. In the liner notes, the will to listen in order to see is part of the album's philosophy: "These are projections of (image/sound) which represent the new life-sense of African men and women here in the west, it is the African man's vision/version of music." As these opening tracks illustrate, the album itself wants to complicate the line between vision and sound.

There is a growing body of literature about what R. Murray Schafer has called the "soundscape" – defined as "any acoustic field of study" ranging from musical works to acoustic environments, including urban environmental noise (*Soundscape* 7). The elasticity of the term has allowed it to be adopted by a range of scholars to suit various ends, but as Jonathan Sterne notes, we ought to consider the concept of the soundscape in its historical context: "soundscape is very much a creature of mid-century sound media culture, first radio, then hi-fi (a term Schafer directly borrows), then stereo" (*Living Stereo* 67). In *Spaces Speak: Are you Listening?* (2009), Barry Blesser and Linda-Ruth Salter compare the ability to create virtual auditory space to the ability of Renaissance painters to represent perspective in their paintings. With technologies for recording and manipulating sound, "Musical space is unconstrained by the requirements for normal living, and musical artists are inclined to conceive of surreal spatial concepts" (164). However, discussions of real or virtual soundscapes tend to rely on visual language and metaphors. Sound engineers and acousticians talk about the "sound image," but as Peter Damaske points out in his book, *Acoustics and Hearing* (2008), "acoustical quality is basically defined by *subjective sound impressions,*" and even technical data gathered by machines only gives partial information (vi). In other words, listeners always play an important role in constructing a sound image – often through descriptive language. Thus, my readings of Baraka are interested in the ways Baraka himself, through his poetry, describes and reinforces the idea of these new sonic spaces.

By the mid-1960s, there were a number of record labels and producers interested in using the recording studio as an instrument, but not all were convinced of the benefits of stereo sound. For example, Phil Spector ("wall of sound") and Brian Wilson (the Beach Boys' *Pet Sounds*) used multitracking to create new sonic environments, but preferred mono recordings. The Beatles' "Revolution 9" on their self-titled white album (1968) became one of the most notable experimental stereo recordings, pioneering panning, looping, sampling, and other studio techniques as a way of representing revolution in sonic space, and yet the Beatles' released both stereo and mono versions of their early records (with many preferring mono).[48] Within the world of soul and R&B, both Stax and Motown were known for their recognizable *sounds* and used stereo to enhance these effects. Whereas Stax's sound relied largely on the fact that it recorded in an old movie theater in Memphis (i.e., a real space), the "Motown Sound" (as it is often called) was achieved through instrumentation and studio recording effects. This sonic signature was created by a recognizable blend of pop and soul, characterized by the tambourine, electric bass, and call-and-response vocals; it is a prime example of how *sound*, rather than simply music or a musician, came to dominate commercially successful recordings. Motown's sound, however, was more than simply its instrumentation, but its arrangement of the vocals, the use of reverb, and its particular use of the stereo space. One of the best examples is the Supremes' 1964 album *Where Did Our Love Go?* As Greg Milner describes, on the title track "For the entire song, quarter-note handclaps keep the rhythm. They begin the song in the right channel, quickly migrate to the left, and remain there until the last few seconds, when they merrily skip across the stereo field and back, as though daring the listener to figure out the secret of their sound" (155). A similar strategy can be heard on the track "Come See About Me" – also produced by Brian Holland and Lamont Dozier – which Baraka reimagines on *It's Nation Time*. In the Supremes' version the drums enter in the left channel but gradually fill the entire stereo field. Diana Ross's lead vocal emerges front and center, while the backup vocals truly sound like they are *in the back*, giving the illusion of a larger space because they have the echoing quality of acoustic sound. Although other companies would try to reproduce the Motown sound, it was nearly impossible to do because it was not merely the sound of the Detroit studio or some real place, rather, it was an audio space constructed by record producers and engineers who knew how to wield the voices and the instrumentation of Motown's stable of talent within the stereo frame.

With *It's Nation Time,* Baraka seems to have been aware of the ironies of recording a Black nationalist album for Motown and used the opportunity to reinforce his ideas about the spiritual nature of all Black music, even R&B. For instance, on "Come See About Me," he overlays the Supremes' original song lyrics about getting over lost love with poetry calling to "the deity." Some critics of Motown claimed that the record label whitewashed Black music in order to make it palatable to white listeners. Baraka, however, felt that there was a spirituality to be unearthed from Motown's version of R&B – "even The Miracles are spiritual," he said (*Black Music* 188). Although it is not entirely possible to transcribe the interplay between the two sets of lyrics, whose rhythmic relation to one another is elastic, I attempt to do so here to show how the spiritual and secular intersect one another. On the left I have transcribed Baraka's voice, and on the right, the backing vocals with a few references to instrumentation:

OAllah, all deity, jinn, spirit creation on the earth, where we live, cut off from righteousness by devil in corporated (*repeat*) come see about we us black people your first creations	(*African drums and electric bass*)
All deity Hey God Hey God Hey God Spirit Interior animation of existence we here cut off in a devil land we need something to be strong god	(*Music shifts to Motown sound*) I've been Praying (for you) 'Cause I'm lonely (so blue) Smiles have all turned to tears But tears won't wash away my fears That you're never ever gonna return To ease the fire that within me burns
all spirit flesh us with strength to Allah give us will to get up and split [. . .]	It keeps me crying baby for you Keeps me sighin' baby for you So won't you hurry? Come on boy, see about me (Come see about me) [. . .]
	("Come See About Me," *Side A* 11:13–12:30)

In terms of the stereo arrangement, the Supremes-esque backing vocals play in the right channel, while Baraka's vocals play in both – an arrangement which spatially orients his lyrics as central and yet interpenetrated.[49] On the page, I can easily separate the streams of music, but such separation is more difficult in the moment of listening because the lyrical lines overlap and overtake one another, smudging to the point of interference. The lyrics call and respond to one another – "Hey God" is answered by "I've been praying (for you)." In this instance, the stereophonic works on two levels: that of the album's engineering and the aesthetic decision to mashup (as it were) two separate lyrical trajectories. Doing so allows the track to perform the task of bringing the secularized (and saccharine) R&B closer to its spiritual roots – later trading "come see about me" for "come see about we" and making the individual or personal plural. By bringing together the spiritual and popular aspects of Black music, Baraka's attentiveness to the stereophonic dimensions of the album extend beyond the album's engineering and inflect the poetry as well.

For Baraka, the music was already a technology of sonic space in the stereophonic dimension. Baraka's trifecta of Black sonic space philosophers included James Brown, Ornette Coleman, and Sun Ra, and in "The Changing Same" from *Black Music*, Baraka utilizes a spatial vocabulary to describe a new theory of social expression at work in both R&B and Free Jazz. This marked shift from the typical musical discourse gives sound a multidimensional, even visual orientation – similar to the way James Brown can transport even passive listeners standing in line at the bank to "a place where Black People live" (186). By this same measure, Ornette Coleman is "the elemental land change, the migratory earth man" (197); "Ornette was a cool breath of open space. Space, to move. So freedom already exists. The change is spiritual" (198). The descriptions chart a new definition of space, one that better lends itself to a philosophical and spiritual account of geography and nationhood. As a central text and "institution" of the Black Nation, *It's Nation Time* attempts to locate *where* such a new nation would exist by redefining space.

Perhaps the most instrumental figure in Baraka's development of a theory of Black sonic space was Sun Ra. While some activists were more literal-minded about the need for a Black space, in the music of Baraka and of Sun Ra we can hear a philosophical rethinking of what space means.[50] Sun Ra's 1973 album *Space is the Place* helped to catalyze this more celestial and philosophical thinking (now referred to as Afrofuturism) because, as Baraka noted early on, "Sun-Ra is spiritually oriented. He understands 'the future' as an ever widening comprehension of what space is, even to the 'physical' travel between the planets as we do anyway in the long human chain of progress" (199). After Baraka's collaboration with Sun Ra in 1968 on the play and recording *The Black Mass*, Sun Ra's influence would continue to inflect his work, helping him to rethink the sonic space of the album as infinitely more flexible than physical space and "sticks and stones" institutions (*It's Nation Time* liner notes).[51]

In the sonic space of the album, Baraka could more freely explore the connections among Afro-diasporic peoples in the stereophonic sense proposed by Gilroy and Jaji, transcending not just geographic boundaries but temporal boundaries as well. Space is "way out waaaay out way way out" he tells us, stretching the elastic "ay" with each repetition ("All in the Street" 11). But in order to reach this place, he appeals to the ear:

> Hear each other miles apart (without no telephones)
> "Love I hear you from way cross the
> sea ... in East Africa ... Arabia ...
> Reconstructing the grace of our
> long past – I hear you love
> whisper at the soft air as it bathes
> you – I hear and see you"   (11)[52]

Baraka invokes the listening ear to access an African past but without the technology of the telegraph or telephone. As Ingrid Monson reminds us, "In many West African musics, for example, the boundaries between language and music are much blurrier, since speech may literally be spoken through instruments, most usually drums" (211). The performance of the lyrics themselves emulates spatial effects such as echoes. The chorus of men and women repeat Baraka's words in a fugal pattern: "lovelovelove I I I hearhearhear youyouyou," and so on. Each word decrescendos in its repetition, and in doing so the words issue ripples as they reverberate against each other. The effect resonates like a voice speaking in a vast and vaulted space. The repetitions are orchestrated as part of the performance, but it is a self-contained stereo effect. Literally resounding the words reinforces the act of listening: love, I hear you.

The efforts to double and perform the resonant technology only become more clear when Baraka himself becomes the medium as "All in the Street" continues, claiming that that ancestors in Africa will speak through him if only we listen:

> I am in touch
> w/ them. They speak and
> beckon to me
> Listen they speak thru
> my mouth
> "Come on –
> "Come on –
> "Come on –   (12)[53]

In a moment of frenzied improvisation, Baraka becomes the "medium" – the body through which the message speaks – speaking both in his voice and in the voice of the ancestors across space and time. Sound's spatial qualities are largely a result of the fact that sound requires a medium through which to travel – sound must resonate in other things. Shouting "come on" in quick succession, the words take on a percussive quality; the exclamation is also a call to the band to catch up with him as together they drive the tempo ever faster. By increasing the noise level of the album through wailing and scatting, Baraka also increases the track's resonance within the space it is played. But these resonant spaces can only exist for a time. At the end of the poem as the band fades out, he says, "Here the contact is broken," for as the music ends and the poetry ends, the auditory space closes and so does the communion of African peoples across time and space.[54] The space no longer exists when sound is replaced by silence. Sonic spaces thus only exist in time, even on a recording.

Through time, speed of delivery, and noise, Baraka tries to explode the audio space into the projective, prospective realm. Baraka's conception of the projective stereophonic space echoes Charles Olson's 1950 essay "Projective Verse." Olson's manifesto aimed to bring the breath of the poet (and the poet's listening) back into poetry, calling for poetry that was "(projectile (percussive (prospective." As Lorenzo Thomas points out, when redefined by African Americans, the return to speech and the breath has political implications (308). But when poetry becomes a record, certain aspects of "Projective Verse" become literalized, and the contact with Baraka's voice and breath is not just projected but amplified. Olson exclaims, "Get on with it, keep moving, keep in, speed, the nerves, their speed, . . . keep it moving as fast as you can, citizen" – Baraka performs the speed and makes his poem the "high-energy construct" necessary to move into a stereophonic dimension (Olson "Projective Verse").

On "Peace in Place," his voice rips and fries on the "*CR*" of "CRACKLE" and explodes on the plosive p in "hotpunctures," rupturing with uneven repetitions and words that suggest fissures, breaks, and burns (*Spirit Reach* 5). Pushing upon the onomatopoetic capacity of words to articulate the sounds they describe, the poetry approaches the musical and sensual, leaving less and less space for silence:

I AM USING ALL OF THE SPACE ALL OF THE SPACE FILL THE
SPACE ALL THE
SPACE MY VOICE IS NOT HEARD MY FLESH IS NOT SEEN IT IS
ALL THE SAME (6)[55]

The enjambment of the lines and clustering of capitalized words emphasize the use of "all of the space" on the page, while on the recording these lines seem to run into each other, breaking only so briefly for Baraka to take a breath (similar to Allen Ginsberg's *Howl*). One gets the sense that the space of the present listening moment might actually be stretched and expanded, like a balloon filling with air. In this flexible expansion of the audio space, Baraka and the instrumentalists push and pull against one another. Through the accumulation of undifferentiated sounds, nonsense words, screams, and shouts, language itself seems to break down in the flaming primordial heat of a new space erupting

Walter Benjamin, writing in the 1930s before the era of the stereo LP, famously said that technological reproducibility "emancipates the work of art from its parasitic subservience to ritual" (24). Benjamin stressed the absence of "the here and now" of recorded works (21) and suggested that technologies that abstract sounds and images from a particular place and time purportedly free them from *aura* (24). The assertion was controversial, but the general acceptance of Benjamin's claim that film, recordings, and other kinds of technological reproduction removed the "aura" of the original performance would lay the foundation for media studies. Ever since, his ideas have dominated debates around recording and liveness. But do Benjamin's claims about aura still hold true when stereo sound reproduction technology can arguably reproduce the spatial qualities of sound? *It's Nation Time*, which explicitly aspires toward the performance of ritual, challenges a number of generally accepted notions about the qualities of recorded sound, and in particular, Benjamin's assertions about aura. The title track of the album was originally published in a 1970 pamphlet of the same name distributed by Third World Press, and the phrase "It's Nation Time" became an important chant at gatherings of the Black Nationalist movement. On the album, the track produces a radical rupturing of the aural/visual and spatial/temporal divide through its noisy screams and the insertion of an "eye" into "time," but the phrase had a broader life span. Strongly influenced by Baraka's poetry, Rev. Jesse Jackson adopted the phrase during his speeches at rallies. When he asked his audiences, "What time is it?" they would respond: "It's Nation Time!"[56] The call-and-response form is central to a number of Black art forms and religious practices, and the phrase as well as the poem engages in the rhetoric of ritual in order to foster a sense of collectivity and unity. The poem itself calls out to listeners to come together in service of the Black nation:

> Time to get
> together
> time to be one strong fast black enrgy space (21)[57]

The stylized vocal performance is reminiscent of a Pentecostal preacher, and Baraka moves seamlessly between the sacred voice, the vernacular voice of a James Brown style falsetto, and the voice of ritualized violence. In his readings and performances, Baraka was sometimes known to bring a gun on stage and point it at the audience. On the album, he uses his voice to mimic the fire of bombs and machine guns ("Boom BOOOM Boom Dadadadadadadadadadadadada" 22), recalling F. T. Marinetti's Futurist Manifesto.[58] The performance of a ritual of violence opens into an assertion that "Christ was black / Krishna was black [. . .] Shango budda black" (23). By blackening the world religions and the sonic space, the recording opens a possibility that this new nation can be accessed through listening as Baraka stereophonically melds sight with sound.

The *eye*'s intersection of *time* in the course of this chant could be thought of in terms of Baraka's work at what Fred Moten refers to as the "interstitial break," but there is something more projective here: he is no longer working between but *beyond* – simultaneously inside and outside. Shouting "it's nation time" in repetition, Baraka aspirates the "i" in "time" repeatedly so that we hear all the homophonic associations: time, eye, I. The synesthetic meaning is also made explicit in the printed version of the poem from the 1970 pamphlet *It's Nation Time*:

> It's nation time eye ime
> it's nation ti eye ime
> chant with bells and drum
> it's nation time (24)[59]

As he bursts open time, Baraka's voice is rough and hoarse with use, and it breaks and squeaks like the saxophones of James Wheeler (alto) and Philip Eley (tenor) as they play at the limit of their own upper registers. Fred Moten, when discussing Baraka's earlier works, argues that his poetry is *in the break*: "This location, at once internal and interstitial, determines the character of Baraka's political and aesthetic intervention. Syncopation, performance, and the anarchic organization of phonic substance delineate an ontological field wherein Black radicalism is set to work" (85). It is a break that refuses to close and that resists a single, settled meaning. Here, time is not just time, but the eye through which to look outward toward a new space and inward toward the "I." These words rupture an opening that is both internal (that is, literally within the ears) and external (inscribed on the album). Although the album is called *It's Nation **Time***, time and space are intricately linked, creating not just an imagined space, but a real, audible one that can only be accessed in the moment of listening. As Paul Gilroy notes in his essay, "Soundscapes of the Black Atlantic," "remote listening had acquired both social and political significance in the black Atlantic world" and helped to create a "community of listeners" (*Audio Cultures* 385). While it is perhaps tempting to assume that all recordings lack aura and to think of all experimental stereo recordings as simulacra, by reasserting presence, *It's Nation Time* does something different. The space it creates is imaginative and hyperbolic to be sure, but the community of listeners who enter that space (who are, in fact, created by that space) *are* real.

Because of the phrase's popular use by the Black Nationalists, its presence and reiteration here on the record directly participate both in the performative ritual of nation building and in the institutionalizing of the LP itself. To say "It's Nation Time" is thus a speech act in the declarative order: the phrase does not simply describe reality but ushers a new one into being. Saying the phrase creates the nation. This idea is central to understanding the way in which Baraka and the Black Nationalists were negotiating the desire for a unified Pan-Africanism. From a political standpoint, the album's status as an art object appears to reinforce Benjamin's ideas about the political potential of art in the age of its technological reproducibility, but not because the aura of ritual (the here and now) has been removed. Baraka's sense of nation ti-eye-ime and the assertion of a Black sonic space in its stereophonic dimensions challenges Benjamin's argument that technologically reproduced art necessarily lacks a "unique existence in a particular place" (21). Here the audio space itself is its own unique existence and when sound takes on spatial dimensions, as it does in stereo, it can perform the space of a new nation, however impermanent and fleeting it may be.

***

While Baraka's interest in Nationalism turned out to be but one phase in his career, his interest in Black sonic spaces was not. Traces of what I've been calling a stereophonic poetic continue to inflect his later works, especially his evolving book-length opus *Wise Whys Y's* (1995) and the CD album *Real Song* (1994). *Wise*, as a poem that chronicles African American history, adopts a shifting narrative voice that moves across geographic and temporal boundaries. In the print edition, each poem is "accompanied" by a piece of music. But rather than include musical notation, as W.E.B. Du Bois did in *The Souls of Black Folk* (1903), or descriptions of sounds, as Langston Hughes did in *Ask Your Mama: 12 Moods for Jazz*, Baraka's musical cues most often direct readers to a particular recorded version of a song, for example W-15, which calls for "(*Creole Love Call*) / *Duke Ellington* / (*Sidney Bechet Version*)" (*Wise* 40). Like so many of Baraka's poems, *Wise* was written to be sounded – to be heard. In a 1980 interview with William J. Harris, author of *The Poetry and Poetics of Amiri Baraka: Jazz Aesthetics*, Baraka explained:

AB: . . . "To me it [the text] is a score.
WJH: What does this mean? In 200 years when you aren't around, are you
going to expect people to be listening to tapes of your work?
AB: Yeah, I hope. (147)

As for the future of text, Baraka felt that "the page will be used by people
who want to read it aloud" (147). Today, there are hundreds of recordings
of Baraka's various performances circulating among bootleg tape collectors, but also on YouTube and websites like PennSound.

When we think of the legacy and of the afterlife of an album like *It's
Nation Time,* or of Hughes's *Ask Your Mama,* it would be hard not to hear
the reverberations in hip-hop (and later, Afrofuturism), whose sonic landscapes began to take shape around this time. Baraka's influence, however, is
not only felt in the performance style of rappers, but in the stereophonic
poetics and spatial politics of hip-hop. As Davarian L. Baldwin points out,
because the mainstream acceptance of hip-hop coincided with the rise of
Reagan-era nationalism in the 1980s, a kind of Afrocentric "nation-
conscious" counter-rhetoric reemerged in hip-hop. We can hear it in the
recordings of Afrika Bambaataa, Public Enemy, and the Native Tongues
collective (which included De La Soul, Jungle Brothers, and Queen Latifah,
among others). Baraka himself would lament the loss of social consciousness
in the commercialized rap that followed, and yet, his projective sonic
landscapes continue to find resonance today in the Afrofuturism of artists
like Janelle Monáe, Kendrick Lamar, and others. Stereophonic poetics
reoriented the listener's relationship to space. What Langston Hughes hinted
at and Amiri Baraka made explosively clear was that stereophonic reproduction had the capacity not just to reproduce the sound of spaces but to create
entirely new ones. Opening other dimensions was not simply the domain of
science fiction but was made real via stereo sound. Today, we think very little
about the produced environments from which our popular music emanates;
the idea that they would replicate some *real* acoustic space is hardly
a consideration, and recordings are mixed for headphones and car stereos.
Listening in one's living room situated perfectly between two speakers seems
almost quaint now. And yet, the stereophonic dimension continues to be an
important space for cultural exploration.

CHAPTER 5

From Cut-up to Mashup
Literary Remix in the Digital Age,
feat. Kevin Young and Chuck Palahniuk

> A good read is the equivalent of a good mix. Think of 'em as a kind of
> "amicus curiae brief" for the sonically perplexed – render judgment
> not on the singular track but on the mix as a whole. It's philosophy for
> the audio-splice generation – on a mix tape made by Burroughs VS
> Grand Master Flash etc. – anything goes.
>
> DJ Spooky, that Subliminal Kid (aka Paul D. Miller)

In a special issue of *Wired* magazine titled "Remix the Planet," from
July 2005, the novelist William Gibson – best known for cyberpunk
works such as *Neuromancer* (1984) – attempted to offer an explanation of
the role of remix in the digital age. For Gibson, "the record, not the remix,
is the anomaly today. The remix is the very nature of the digital" ("God's
Little Toys"). However, Gibson begins his essay not with a discussion of
DJs or record producers but with his own first encounter with William
S. Burroughs as young teen:

> Burroughs was then as radical a literary man as the world had to offer, and in
> my opinion, he still holds the title. Nothing, in all my experience of
> literature since, has ever been quite as remarkable for me, and nothing has
> ever had as strong an effect on my sense of the sheer possibilities of writing.
>
> Later, attempting to understand this impact, I discovered that Burroughs
> had incorporated snippets of other writers' texts into his work, an action
> I knew my teachers would have called plagiarism. Some of these borrowings
> had been lifted from American science fiction of the '40s and '50s, adding
> a secondary shock of recognition for me.
>
> Sampling. Burroughs was interrogating the universe with scissors and
> a paste pot, and the least imitative of authors was no plagiarist at all. ("Gods
> Little Toys")

As a writer in the era of the word processor, where cut, copy, and paste are
built into the software itself, Gibson felt that "everything I wrote, I believed
instinctively, was to some extent collage" – but it was Burroughs who had
allowed Gibson to embrace that aesthetic practice. The affinity between

Burroughs's cut-up method and *sampling* has long been acknowledged inside and outside music circles. The musician and writer Paul D. Miller (aka DJ Spooky that Subliminal Kid) takes his DJ name from Burroughs's Nova trilogy. Indeed, of all the writers of the twentieth century to influence art outside the realm of literature, few have been as influential (or as infamous) as William S. Burroughs. In the cultural imagination of the late twentieth and early twenty-first centuries, Burroughs's approaches to text, composition, and meaning making have appeared in the unlikeliest of places. From band names (Steely Dan and Soft Machine) and lyrics (Iggy Pop), to avant-garde musical compositions (Frank Zappa and David Bowie), to collaborations with grunge rockers (Kurt Cobain, REM), the words of Burroughs reverberate literally and figuratively across the post-modern soundscape. But to think of Burroughs as a kind of godfather of remix invites us to ask: what genre are we talking about when we talk about remix? Burroughs, of course, was drawing on Dadaist techniques of chance operations when he first began making his cut-ups, but ought we consider remix, collage, and cut-up as interchangeable? What makes remix different? Given the proliferation of remix across genres, is remix a practice, a theoretical concern, or both?

A number of scholars and artists, from Eduardo Navas, Mark America, and Lawrence Lessig to the novelist Jonathan Lethem and DJ Spooky (Paul D. Miller), have suggested that we are living in a "remix culture," asserting that remix is the defining aesthetic of the digital age.[1] Today we use the term promiscuously to describe a variety of cultural practices (from recordings, to high fashion and cuisine, to art and literature), but the word itself first emerged in the recording studio in the 1960s, not long after multitracked recordings became widespread. Recording vocals and instrumentals on separate "tracks" or tapes, recording engineers would "mix" or blend these recordings together to create a single record. The most common definition of remix points specifically to sound recordings that reinterpret or rework existing recordings in order to make a new one.[2] In common usage, remix in its musical context might refer to a more danceable version of a pop song with an accentuated drum or bass track, or an entirely new setting of a piece. When two or more recordings are combined, these remixes are sometimes referred to as *mashups*.[3] However, the question that often accompanies remix is whether a remix is ever actually *new* work – whether it constitutes something original?

Part of the reason for this skepticism of originality stems from the practice of sampling, which became associated with remix starting in the late 1970s and 1980s when it emerged from Jamaican dance hall "dub" music, disco, and early hip-hop in the United States. By manipulating previously recorded materials, DJs and recording engineers realized that they could create not just slightly different versions of a song, but entirely new ones based upon samples of multiple recordings. Since then, the practice has spread beyond sound recording to other media. In *Keywords in Remix Studies* (2018), theorists such as Steffan Sonvilla-Weiss and Eduardo Navas define remix as a multimedia practice characterized by its transformative properties. Sonvilla-Weiss, in defining the practice of sampling, has argued that "through alteration, re-combination, manipulation, [and] copying," DJs "create a whole new piece" (qtd. in *Keywords in Remix Studies* 260).[4] Part of the reason for this insistence on the transformative properties of remix has to do with copyright laws surrounding "fair use," which allows for the use of previous works if deemed transformative. Both David Gunkel and Lawrence Lessig have compared sampling to the act of citation (*Keywords in Remix Studies* 262). In this sense, remix is related to intertextuality and other writing practices such as quotation, but given the lack of norms surrounding sonic attribution, remix artists have often faced lawsuits and other legal repercussions.[5] Part of the difficulty with remix and issues of appropriation is that in the digital space the ethics of reuse, originality, and citation are still being contested even as they remediate text-based citation practices. Walter Benjamin famously argued that the concepts of copy and original collapsed in the age of technological reproducibility. But only in the last twenty years or so has art in the digital era seriously contested the transparency of the recorded medium.

In this chapter, I will set to the side the debates surrounding remix and copyright law – which are lively and numerous – and instead focus my attention on remix as a cross-disciplinary aesthetic mode with roots in sound recording technologies and practices. To treat remix as merely a development in the history of sound recording technology, however, is too limiting. Remix is a *practice* that relies on several interrelated technological developments whose timelines overlap and sometimes intersect. In many cases, technologies were developed in response to the desire to remix rather than the other way around. And, as a number of theorists have increasingly noted, remix might be better thought of not as a cultural product (like a song or video or novel) but as a *culture*. While I am somewhat skeptical of such sweeping claims about the scope of remix, it is important to acknowledge the ways remix does not conform to normal constraints of media or genre. It might be more accurate to say that remix is a *form* in Caroline Levine's sense – a portable constraint that blends the aesthetic and the social.

One of the key tropes that one finds in the discourse surrounding remix is the insistence on the relationship between remix practices and modernist collage. Jessica Pressman's *Digital Modernism: Making it New in New Media* (2013) makes this connection particularly cogently, noting how artists such as Young-hae Chang borrow from modernist poets like Ezra Pound and others. Remix theorists and practitioners alike (including Navas, Amerika, and DJ Spooky) refer back to modernist poets like Ezra Pound, Jean Cocteau, T. S. Eliot, and Gertrude Stein not only to explain the aesthetic and formal aspects of remix, but also to legitimize remix as a cultural form. This desire to connect remix to modernism may be a reflex born of anxiety – the worry that remix as a popular form might not be legitimate as an area of academic study or high art; however, that concern makes these aesthetic parallels no less convincing. What are the newsreels of John Dos Passos if not remixes? When Kendrick Lamar samples clips of Geraldo Rivera of Fox News on his Pultizer Prize–winning album *DAMN.* (2017), or juxtaposes those clips with music by Rick James, is his act of remixing those samples so different from what Dos Passos tore from the pages of the *Chicago Tribune* or from the recordings of Bessie Smith? Dos Passos quotes from records, Lamar samples the recordings themselves. One can draw these connections easily enough and show how they are alike, how they resonate, but perhaps we ought to go one step further. Modernist literature isn't just *like* remix (or vice versa): it makes remix possible because modernist textual practices have been bound up in and shaped by recording practice all along.

"Jammin' on the One": The Origins of Remix

In his popular musical memoir *Mo' Meta Blues: The World According to Questlove* (2013), Ahmir Thompson (aka Questlove), best known as a drummer and bandleader for the Roots and as a DJ, argues that the single most influential moment in the history of hip-hop had nothing to do with a particular album or musician or night in the club; rather, it was an episode of *The Cosby Show* from 1986 featuring Stevie Wonder using a sampler (66).[6] In the episode, Wonder has invited the Huxtables to his recording studio to make amends for a traffic accident, and in the course of their studio visit, he weaves samples of their individual voices into a new song. For Questlove and others of the 1980s hip-hop generation, seeing the sampler in use was a revelation. About a year later, Questlove would acquire a Casio SK-1, a toy keyboard that featured rudimentary sampling technology. At the time, most samplers were incredibly expensive, but musicians like Wonder had been using samplers as early as *The Secret Life of Plants* album in 1979, which employs a Computer Music Melodian (Wickman). On *The Cosby Show*, he features the Synclavier keyboard, which included a 16-bit polyphonic sampler, which meant that Wonder could "pitch-shift" the samples using the keyboard, musicalizing their spoken words.

Whether an episode of *The Cosby Show* is indeed the most important moment in hip-hop history is, of course, debatable, but the point that Questlove makes here is more about a catalytic moment in hip-hop that changes it going forward – that is, the centrality of sampling. For Questlove, there is something *textual* and even readerly about the practice of mixing samples, and in a surprising turn in his explanation, he cites Roland Barthes to explain how sampling works:

> Much later in life, I had a friend who tried to explain Roland Barthes to me; not all of it, of course, but that one little principle about how a text is not a unified thing, but a fragmentary or divisible thing, and that the reader is the one who divides it up, arbitrarily. Reading is the act that creates the pieces. I wasn't totally sure I understood it – I'm still not sure – but it sounded like what was happening with the SK-1. You, as the listener, pick a piece of sound, a snippet of speech, or a drumbeat, and you separate that from everything around it. That's now a brick that you have in your hand, and you use it to build a new wall. It also lets you take things that were transparent, that were previously thought of as words and sounds that you look through to see other words, and make them opaque. You can take the invisible and make them visible. (67–68)

In paraphrasing some of the key theoretical claims that Barthes makes throughout his works in books like *S/Z* and *The Pleasure of the Text*, Questlove not only argues for an approach to sampling that is inherently tied to the textual but also implies that there is something about reading that is akin to sampling.[7] It is a journey from text to recording and back again. "Classic hip-hop is a sentence," he argues (112). Describing two of his favorite albums from 1993, A Tribe Called Quest's *Midnight Marauders* and Wu-Tang Clan's *Enter the Wu-Tang (36 Chambers)*, he writes, "We debated every song, analyzed every lyric. We picked through those things like they were academic texts" (113). Known as a music geek with an encyclopedic knowledge of songs and records, Questlove wears the academic tone lightly; however, here and elsewhere in his memoir, the allusions to the academic and the literary are less affectation than an attempt to reflect on the larger cultural implications of hip-hop and remix practices.

Intertextuality and connections between literary texts and hip-hop are a key feature of Questlove's own music, as is evident on albums like the Roots' *Things Fall Apart* (1999), whose title references Chinua Achebe's 1959 novel (which is in turn sampled from William Butler Yeats's 1919 poem "The Second Coming"). The album has a track titled "Table of Contents," and it also has tracks indicating the album's structure, "Act Won (Things Fall Apart)"; "Act Too (The Love of My Life)"; and "3rd Acts: ? vs. Scratch 2 . . . Electric Boogaloo." The album marked a transition for Questlove from drummer to producer, as he recorded (to two-inch tape), sampled, and looped his own drumbeats in order to play with the plasticity of their sound.[8] However, literary and textual approaches to sampling are not unique to Questlove and the Roots. In Aram Sinnreich's book on mashup, his interviews with DJs about their practices reveal just how prevalent the sampling-as-writing, sample-as-text metaphors are. The mashup artist TradeMark G (Mark Gunderson), founder of the Evolution Control Committee, for instance, suggested that, "I look at this whole progression of samples in music as a linguistic thing. If a song is a sentence, made up of words and letters, if you're DJing, the samples are probably words. If I'm composing, the samples are probably letters" (qtd. in Sinnreich 151). Of course, even Sidney Bechet thought of his music as telling a story, and Kevin Young in *The Grey Album* stresses the "storying" aspects of Black music across generations. But for DJs, the impulse is not always narrative in a traditional sense, but rather seems to be about textuality more broadly. As sound recording technology – understood as inscriptive technology – entered the digital age, the lines between writing and producing continued to blur.

The concept of remix, which first appeared around 1969 in reference to multitrack studio practices, coincided with the rise of the DJ as a performer in Jamaican dancehalls, discos, and later, underground hip-hop parties. In contemporary parlance, the term "DJ" usually refers to a celebrity music producer, remixer, and nightclub impresario. In Las Vegas (where I currently live and teach), the DJ reigns supreme over the world of nightclubs, and the faces of famous DJs like Calvin Harris, DJ Khaled, and Kaskade rise above the streets on enormous billboards. These DJs do not merely spin records in clubs but release their own tracks and albums of electronic dance music, much of which is produced using digital sound editing and sequencing software such as ProTools and Ableton Live, with a vinyl LP rarely in sight. While today's DJs have roots in disco and hip-hop culture, the moniker of DJ, which was originally short for disc jockey, is one that started in radio and only later migrated to the dancehall.[9]

Although early radio DJs sometimes hosted dances at nightclubs, the transition of the term from radio to a dance or nightclub DJ was first noted in the *Chicago Defender* in 1966. Meanwhile, the first use of DJ as a prefix was for DJ Kool Herc in 1973. As Jeff Chang notes in his history of hip-hop, *Can't Stop, Won't Stop*, DJ Kool Herc, who was born in Kingston, Jamaica, was critical in bringing the sound of Jamaican dancehall sound systems to the Bronx. Herc, along with Afrika Bambaataa and others, pioneered the use of breakbeats. Both hip-hop and disco, however, were predated by Jamaican dub.

In *Dub: Soundscapes & Shattered Songs in Jamaican Reggae*, Michael Veal links the emergence of remix culture to the kinds of technological innovations pioneered in the late 1960s by Jamaican dub artists such as Lee "Scratch" Perry, Osbourne "King Tubby" Ruddock, and Error "Errol T." Thomson, and others. According to Veal, the significance of dub as a style "lies in the deconstructive manner in which these engineers remixed reggae songs, applying sound processing technology in unusual ways to create a unique pop music language of fragmented song forms and reverberating soundscapes" (2). The term dub has a complex etymology, but its origin is usually associated with the "dub plates" or acetate discs originally used for mastering prior to producing them on vinyl (dub here referring to dubbing or doubling). Dub plates often included a B-side that was the "rhythm version" without the vocal track – often called the "riddim" – which dancehall MCs used to "toast" or rap over. The emergence of dub plates was critical to the stylistic practices of remix to follow and constituted a convergence of multitrack recording and booming sound systems.[10] Remix in its dub plate iteration, therefore, had dual origins in the studio and in DJ practices. For Veal, there is a direct lineage between contemporary pop and dance music and Jamaican dub that runs through hip-hop and disco. Significantly, dub artists (and later disco DJs) were among the first musicians to treat recordings as something malleable and performative – and it is this practice that characterizes remix culture today.[11]

The performance-oriented aspect of hip-hop gave rise to turntablism, which Aram Sinnreich has defined as "a variety of configurable music – often considered an offshoot of hip-hop – in which a DJ spinning vinyl emphasizes his skill through extended improvisation, using a rapid sequence of difficult techniques such as backspinning, cutting, scratching, and beat juggling" (Sinnreich 154). These feats of turntablism were often complemented by the improvisatory linguistic acrobatics of MCs or rappers. On the one hand, the role of the MC was to encourage the energy of the dancers in the club, and many of their verbal toasts began to take on poetic feats that drew directly on the practices of spoken-word poets of the era like Amiri Baraka, Gil Scott-Heron, and The Last Poets, as discussed in Chapter 3. However, starting in the 1980s and into the 1990s, remix began to be perceived as a *style* – not just as something that happened in the disco or hip-hop club (Navas 20). DJs and budding MCs released "mix tapes" of their collaborations through underground channels, not unlike the underground publishing of 1960s era Black Arts Movement poets. With more socially conscious lyrics, mixtapes tended to circulate within the communities from which the music arose and might be seen as an extension of the kinds of Black sonic spaces that Baraka envisioned with albums like *It's Nation Time*.[12]

As the distinguishing feature of remix, sampling has become deeply politicized. Sound recordings only began to receive protection under Federal Copyright Law in 1972 (nearly a hundred years after the technology's invention). Since then, copyright laws have become increasingly stringent, and listeners have changed how they think about the nature and status of recordings. Even as recording technology aimed at higher "fidelity" and greater realism in capturing "original" sounds, it also became easier to manipulate sounds in the recording studio to create "performances" that never occurred in any traditional sense. Without this tie to the aura of so-called *live* performance, the link between the performer and ownership eroded too. The idea that a record was not merely a finished product, but something that could be continually edited, remixed and sampled represented not just an evolution in studio recording techniques but a revolution in how listeners thought about the malleability and manipulation of sound more generally. This is evident in the way that artists talk about sampling.

By some measures, the golden age of sampling was 1986–1992, before highly publicized lawsuits led to a crackdown on the practice.[13] In her oral history of sampling, Kimbrew McLeod weaves together interviews with several originators of sampling in order to recreate a sense of the creative freedom of the era. As Chuck D of Public Enemy put it: "Sampling is playing with sound, or playing sound – like it's like an instrument, or a game" (84). However, as hip-hop and remix started to enter the mainstream recording industry, the nature of sampling soon led record companies to sue artists for using samples of recordings without permission.

EL-P (MC AND PRODUCER): During the golden age, you had these records that were these extreme collage records, you know, producers like Prince Paul, who helped create the early De La Soul records.

DE LA SOUL (HIP-HOP GROUP): We used to sit there with a bunch of records and try to find something to go into a song. That process alone, that's what is so great about it, because we didn't censor ourselves.

HARRY ALLEN: What you are hearing on those records is true experimentation, unrestrained by suits.

MATT BLACK: Public Enemy were iconoclastic, definitely. You'd never heard collage music like that.

EL-P: One song would have five, six, seven, eight layered samples from really famous records, but completely reworked so that it didn't sound like the original sources.

MR. LEN (DJ AND IT TAKES A NATION OF MILLIONS PRODUCER): You listen to the song "Night of the Living Base Heads," if you really listen to that song, it changes so many times.

GEORGE CLINTON: They actually did arrangements. They took small parts and had a whole 24-track arrangement that created one song. (McLeod 97–98)

The intricate collaging and reworking of previous recordings recontextualized the music in such a way that practitioners of the art recognized the transformational aspects of these records. But all that older listeners and record company lawyers heard was theft – theft from musicians, but more often from the record companies that owned the copyrights. The practice of versioning had been one of the central creative aspects of jazz and blues practices, and quoting the solos of famous jazz recordings in one's own improvisations was seen as standard practice, and even a sign of great art. So why was the practice of DJ sampling any different?

McLeod's oral histories reveal the extent to which artists view sample-based music as *archival* practice. Chuck D, for example, says that the song "Fight the Power" "contains a great deal of black music history from a 25-year period" (89). As Drew Daniel of Matmore has argued, "What's exciting about sampling and collage is that it makes sound referential – it's not abstract. Sound contains a specific reference to a specific time and place. That's what's cool about sampling: that it transports the listener, if they're willing, to move in a pathway back to a specific action. It's like an archive of memories of real experiences" (89). This approach to listening is often thought of as "audio archeology" because of the layers one can dig through. Of course, the use of samples of actual recordings that remain, at least in part, recognizable is part of what lends remix its status as archive; but to the extent that samples are transformed, one also can take pleasure in witnessing the new. It may be the combination of the creative, archival, and referential aspects of remixes that causes so many to think about remix as a textual practice.

Writing about the future of media in a 2016 essay, "Remix, Rewind, Reinvent: Predicting the Future of Media," Kevin Kelly, the founding executive editor of *WIRED* (and former editor of the *Whole Earth Review*), has argued that, "We live in a golden age of new mediums," and while old mediums still persist, "digital technology unbundles those forms into their elements so they can be recombined in new ways" (Kelly). As these media become "unbundled" new genres emerge, are combined, and reconfigured.[14] Of the most potent new genres emerging from the remix economy, according to Kelly, are literary remixes: "Behind every bestselling book are legions of fans who write their own sequels or fanfic. They may mix elements from more than one book or author." Kelly, who has been a kind of evangelist for the new media forms such as mashup and remix, talks about the necessity of developing a "new grammar" for new media, as well as the need for new technologies of citation and footnote that will render video and sound recordings as citable as text. Digital technologies, he asserts, "permit any literate person to cut and paste ideas, annotate them with her own thoughts, link them to related ideas, search through vast libraries of work, browse subjects quickly, resequence texts, re-find material, remix ideas, quote experts and sample bits of beloved artists. These tools, more than just reading, are the foundations of literacy." Or, at least, they could be the foundations of a new literacy if the right conventions are developed. Ultimately, what Kelly is arguing for is the digital to establish new codes and conventions for citation. Copyright law for digital texts and recordings is unlikely to disappear, but the development of a digital equivalent of the quotation mark and of the footnote would allow writers and artists to continue sampling and citing in a legal and ethical manner. But regardless of what system emerges in the new media, it seems almost certain that it will have roots in textual practice.

Kevin Young Remixes Jean-Michel Basquiat

While there is no doubt that remix as a form has been most prevalent in popular music, as DJs themselves have attested, the line between writing and remixing is a thin and malleable one. That more "traditional" writers have taken up remix as a textual practice is thus a natural extension of the form's multimodal qualities.[15] One such example is Kevin Young's *To Repel Ghosts* (2001) and *To Repel Ghosts: The Remix* (2005). Young, who is not just a poet and essayist, but poetry editor for *The New Yorker* magazine and Director of the Schomburg Center for Research in Black Culture, is known for his capacious approach to Black subjects and history.

As a collection of poetry that treats the life and works of the visual artist Jean-Michel Basquiat, *To Repel Ghosts: The Remix* takes the form of the album as its guide. Structured with A-sides and B-sides, the book seems to have "tracks" rather poems, a nod to Langston Hughes's *Ask Your Mama*. In the "liner notes," Young self-describes *To Repel Ghosts* as "not a biography, but an extended riff – Basquiat and his work serves as a bass line, a rhythm section, a melody from which the poems improvise" (295). He samples text from Basquiat's paintings and graffiti works (made under the alias of SAMO©) and splices these samples in between his own poetic riffs on ideas, musicians, and public figures depicted in Basquiat's art. Young's text is less a rewrite than it is, in his words, a trimmed down "more danceable remix version" meant not to supersede the original but coexist alongside it.[16]

In addition to slimming down the volume, Young rearranges the tracks. The subtle changes to the ordering of the poems might not seem monumental at first, until one considers how the order in which you read things changes the resonances you are able to hear – a fact to which Young, as poet, editor, and music-essayist, is particularly attuned. Even in an earlier poetry collection like *Jelly Roll: A Blues* (2003), one gets a sense of Young's resonant arranging. Talking in a *Paris Review* interview about the connections between a poet editing a collection of verses and a DJ mixing a selection of tracks, Young remarked that,

> In a long poem or a sequence of poems, you're trying to formalize your obsessions and give them a shape and a name. The key is to realize if the connections you are making are ones with resonance. That is something a DJ does. A DJ draws a connection between two seemingly disparate things and says, "Look, they are alike. You can dance to them." (Hoover)

One of the pleasures of a great remix lies in spotting the connections you might not have noticed before: the strange serendipitous overlapping, the just-right juxtaposition. Of course, those who remix rely to some extent on the reader or the listener's ability to recognize the references and hear their reverberations in just the right places. While the 2001 Zoland edition groups poems together generically, as though packaged for the different audiences of radio, club DJs, and true fans (Bootlegs, Hits, Takes, B-Sides, Solos), the 2005 Knopf *Remix* edition is more of a producer's mix, amplifying the sounds of some of the other featured artists and themes in the book ({Side B} Portrait of the Artist as a Young Derelict, Jack Johnson, Famous Negro Athletes, Quality Meats for the Public; {Side A} King Zulu, The Mechanics that Always Have a Gear Left Over, Out Getting Ribs, Pentimento, Pegasus). In other words, *To Repel Ghosts* was always conceived in terms of discs and tracks, which makes the decision to offer a remixed version a choice related to the poem's genre as well as the subject matter. Even in the original 2001 edition for Zoland Books, the table of contents is divided into two "discs" and five "sides."

While we know Basquiat as a visual artist, he was also known by his contemporaries for his audiophile tendencies, having amassed a record collection of over 3,000 albums, most of which were jazz, but which included an eclectic mix of artists, ranging from Curtis Mayfield, Donna Summer, Bach, Beethoven, David Byrne, Charlie Parker, Miles Davis, Aretha Franklin, and David Bowie (Eshun). Jazz musicians in particular, such as Miles Davis, Charlie Parker, and Louis Armstrong, were featured subjects in Basquiat's paintings. But his musical tastes were not limited to jazz, and he found himself bridging the worlds of New York's hip-hop and punk scenes. He was close friends with Fab 5 Freddy but also appeared in a music video for Blondie and designed an album cover for the punk/ska band the Offs. He even had his own noise-music group called Gray, claiming the influence of John Cage (Buchart 38–39). For a time, he famously dated the pop singer Madonna and deejayed the occasional set at the Mudd Club in TriBeCa – an underground club known for featuring New Wave and hip-hop music as well as art exhibitions and literary guests (including William S. Burroughs and Allen Ginsberg). Basquiat-as-DJ at the Mudd Club appears in Young's "Beyond Words," a poem that portrays Basquiat tagging subway cars while lyrics from Rock Master Scott & the Dynamic Three's "The Roof Is on Fire" (1984) intersplice the lines:

> or press yourselves
> betw. train
> & the wall
>
> spray can rattling
> like a tooth – *The roof*
> *the roof*
>
> *the roof is on*
> *fire* – soon
> the 6 will whistle (Young *Remix* 25)

Through internal rhymes, the poem draws together the renegade artistry of graffiti with the energy of the underground club scene, blending the sounds of the trains with the sounds of early hip-hop. Young's decision to organize his book of poems riffing on Basquiat as an album, and later a remix, makes sense in the context of Basquiat's interests.

However, even with its rhythmic organization, the poems of *To Repel Ghosts: The Remix* still largely reference Basquiat's visual art. If you do not know the works of Basquiat and do not know his biography, reading a poem like the ekphrastic "VNDRZ {1982}" can feel alienating.[17]

> Antennae, antlers,
> Rabbit ears
> For better reception
>
> Basquiat's hair
> a bundle of dread-
> locks, coiled, clenched (36)

Young's taut poetic lines begin by giving the reader a fragmented visual description of the painting, but it is a description that is always shifting between the portrait's subject and Basquiat himself. On an initial reading, one might know that "VNDRZ" is a painting made by Basquiat but might not know that the letters stand in for the photographer James Van der Zee, who was a famous photographer of the Harlem Renaissance who also photographed Basquiat.[18] The reader might not know that that phrase "MOST YOUNG KINGS GET THEIR HEADS CUT OFF" in the sixth stanza is sampled from a different portrait – one of Charlie Parker titled "Charles the First" – and appears elsewhere in Basquiat's paintings. Then again, that phrase might ring familiar to a contemporary reader if only because it became the inspiration for a lyric by the rapper Jay-Z on his 2011 track "Most Kingz."[19] To read Young's poetry, therefore, invites the reader to do a bit of googling. While modernist writers like John Dos Passos (and to a lesser extent, T. S. Eliot) were dependent upon the memory of their readers to enliven allusions to popular culture, literature, and world events, they accepted that some references would pass by unnoticed. By contrast, writers in the digital era implicitly understand that their readers can (and will) just as easily google obscure references. With digital editions of texts for Kindle and other e-readers, the ability to search unfamiliar words is often a built-in function of the software. Some references will no doubt still pass a reader by, but readers in the digital era, attuned to reading for resonance (the repeated words or images that reverberate across tracks and album "sides") are far more likely to notice these patterns and seek their meaning.

That Basquiat has become inspiration to poets and rapper-producers and continues to be sampled by artists across genres pays homage to the ways his art was already sample-based. As Dieter Buchart writes in the catalog for *Basquiat: The Unknown Notebooks*:

> Basquiat's art can thus be located in the field of concrete poetry, Burroughs's cut-up technique, the rise of hip-hop, and the rap of his friends Fab 5 Freddy, DJ High Priest (Nicholas Taylor), and Michael Holman. The hip-hop techniques of sampling and scratching relate to his artistic practice: he tests letters and words both for their sounds and their constellations of meaning, trying out word mutations and permutations, and he crosses out words in his notebooks and oilstick drawings, and places actual scratches in his paintings. (38)

Moving between the visual, linguistic, and auditory concepts of the sample and the remix, Kevin Young both embraces and troubles the ways sampling and citation can effect meaning. In the "Liner Notes," Young reveals that just as Basquiat was "an artist who appropriated & copyrighted as many images & sayings as he created," he too includes "'found' text & imagery" in his poems and proceeds to offer something like end notes (295). But like the "liner notes" in Langston Hughes's *Ask Your Mama* (or even like the footnotes in T. S. Eliot's *The Waste Land*), these references are frequently elusive, cheeky, even ironic. For example, "8 Poison Oasis: To be read *al dente*, slowly" tells us little about the references embedded in this poem, instead offering cryptic instructions on reading that mix metaphors of cooking and musical performance. As a book of poems that sample from Basquiat and jazz poetry and hip-hop, *To Repel Ghosts: The Remix* is also dabbling in the ways that even the remixing of samples in hip-hop distorts and misleads the listener. But by working in the citational conventions of literature, Young also reveals that this is something poets do too.

By looking to Basquiat (as well as music) as his model for remix, Young reveals the ways that even in the earliest days of sampling, it was a cross-disciplinary mode. The point is not to draw parallels between Basquiat and the music of his era, but rather to show the ways Basquiat was already doing with images and text what the DJs *would* do. If Kevin Young's collection of poetry more explicitly engages hip-hop culture and the musical form of the album, Chuck Palahniuk's novel takes up remix aesthetics of *sampling* and *looping* and applies them to the structure of the novel in order to shift the reader's engagement with text.

Chuck Palahniuk's Loops and Dance Tracks

Readers familiar with Chuck Palahniuk probably know him for his popular novel *Fight Club* (1996) and its successful 1999 film adaptation. The novel was lauded for its dark satirical edge, its tortuous plotline, and its highly cinematic style; but while we think of that style as being pioneered in *Fight*

Club, Palahniuk first used it when writing *Invisible Monsters* (1999) – an early novel that satirizes the drug- and plastic surgery-fueled fashion industry. Similar to *Fight Club*, *Invisible Monsters* (and *Invisible Monsters Remix* (2012)) is what Palahniuk has called "transgressional fiction," characterized by violence, plot twists, and inversions, as it withholds certain information from the reader and lands shocking reveals. Written not long before *Fight Club*, the novel's narrative voice foreshadows the recognizable use of an unreliable second-person/first-person narration that Palahniuk favors: "Where you're supposed to be is some big West Hills wedding reception," the unnamed narrator tells us (*Invisible Monsters Remix* 284). The effect of such narration is meant to imply the slipperiness of identity in an era in which one is constantly remaking themself.[20] For a novel that skewers the world of high fashion, celebrity, plastic surgery, gender performance, and image-making, it is a narrative technique particularly well suited to the plot.

The story follows the unnamed narrator, who is later revealed as Shannon MacFarland (aka Daisy St. Patience, aka Bubba Joan, aka Miss Kay MacIsaac). Shannon, we learn, was a budding fashion model who is now recovering from a gunshot wound to the face that left her mangled, without a jaw, and unable to speak. During her recovery, she meets the transgender "queen supreme" Brandy Alexander, who promises to give her a new narrative. Much of the story covers the road trip the narrator takes with Brandy, interspersed with flashbacks to the narrator's childhood, the alleged death of her brother from AIDS, her failed attempts to capture the attention of her parents, and her eventual rise in the modeling world. Written in a highly ironic voice, the events of the novel walk the line between gonzo absurdity and a Raymond Chandler whodunit. While the novel met some positive reviews and a degree of popularity after its initial publication in 1999, its form was never satisfying to Palahniuk.

In the "Reintroduction" to *Invisible Monsters Remix* (2012), Chuck Palahniuk explains that the original structure that he imaged for his satirical novel about modeling and the image industry was meant to resemble the effect of reading a story in a fashion magazine or catalog in which the pages are set "chockablock with artsy photos and quotes" and the articles start on one page and swiftly ask the reader to "jump" to the pages at the back of the magazine. It was meant to be "a little unknowable" (vi). In a magazine, "trying to read a story was like trying to navigate through a Las Vegas casino. It was designed to entice and seduce you. It was designed to trap you. I got lost. I loved it. I told myself, *Why can't a novel do this?*" (vii). The answer to this question had less to do with actual mechanics of writing and more to do with marketing. When the novel was originally published in 1999, Palahniuk's editors worried that readers would not be willing to flip back and forth between chapters, and so he shelved the more experimental features of the text and restructured the book into a more linear form. But in Palahniuk's 2012 *Remix* version, the novel is "restored" to the author's original vision. As the narrator warns in the first chapter, "Don't expect this to be the kind of story that goes and then, and then, and then" (1). Some reviews of the remix have referred to the new edition as a "director's cut,"[21] which leads one to ask, why call the book a *remix* at all, given the cinematic instructions to "jump" from scene to scene? Is it merely a superficial gimmick? An attempt to rebrand a novel that did not initially impress readers the way *Fight Club* had? While it might be tempting to dismiss the remix title as simply a hip way to entice readers to buy the new edition, there are ways in which *Invisible Monsters* was *already* recognizable as a remix, a fact that the new edition was able to highlight through its experimental form.

The most identifiable aspect of Palahniuk's remix aesthetic is, of course, his use of chapter loops. Structuring the chapters in such a way that the reader must flip back and forth in order to navigate the novel, one is inevitably faced with the task of keeping track of which chapters one has actually read. If you simply follow Palahniuk's instructions to the letter – starting with chapter 41, then to jumping to chapter 1, moving from 40 to 2, and so on – you invariably miss chapters. These skips and breaks are by design, and they invite the reader to meddle with and rupture the flow of the narrative. The novel consists of four intersecting loops – (1) the large narrative of Shannon's story; (2 and 3) bonus chapters, including "mirror chapters," which are printed backward; and (4) Palahniuk's autobiographical commentary, which include details that inspired the book. The longest loop by far is Shannon's story, which consists of thirty-two chapters and has a kind of spiral logic as the chapters move from the outsides to the center. The second and third loops contain three and four chapters each, while the fourth loop has just three chapters. With the exception of the first loop, which concludes with a "the end" at chapter 21 (roughly the center of the book), each of the smaller loops are self-enclosed and when you reach the "end" of one, it sends you back to its the beginning.

The logic of these loops is meant to subvert the reader's desire for the additive, progressive qualities of narrative – to interrupt the desire for "and then, and then, and then" (1). Palahniuk has adopted instead the logic of the pop song remix, with its repetitive looped beats and samples, its choruses, its breaks and drops. In a musical remix, some beats loop repetitively in the background; some samples come back at predictable moments. The verses repeat the "melody," but the lyrics move the arc of the song forward. In pop remixes, the jumps between discontinuous sounds, samples, and lyrical motifs of a multitracked recording do not jar the listener because of the underlying, unifying beat. But for better or worse, the reader of Palahniuk's novel cannot keep all tracks moving simultaneously; she can read only one chapter at a time. Although Palahniuk offers the reader his own "mix" with his instructions to jump from chapter to chapter, because of the sequential nature of the pages in a book and also because of the chapters which get left out of the central narrative loop, the novel seems to invite the reader to disobey, to read the chapters in an order of one's choosing (even sequentially), in effect offering their own "remix" of the book through the process of reading. These versions exist concurrently within the book.

There is, of course, some precedent for this kind of disjunctured narrative, including the popular "choose-your-own-adventure" stories written for young adults and the hypertext fictions of the late 1990s and early 2000s.[22] The most notable literary precursor is Julio Cortazar's 1966 *Hopscotch* (published in Spanish as *Rayuela* in 1963), a nonlinear novel about a bohemian group of intellectuals living in Paris and Argentina in the 1950s, which includes instructions to the reader who wishes to "hopscotch" through the vignette-like chapters, as well as optional chapters that fill in backstory and gaps. Like Palahniuk, Cortazar traffics in and takes inspiration from musical forms, in particular jazz and bebop, but also tango, and their attendant tensions and dissonances. But while Cortazar's novel invites nonlinear hopscotching, it does not contain the premeditated loops that we find in *Invisible Monsters Remix*.

In Palahniuk's novel, loops not only serve as an organizing principle, they also serve as metaphors for the mediation of everyday life in the postmodern era. Describing tourists who took part in the filming of an infomercial, Shannon notices how the tourists cannot help looking at themselves in the monitor while being filmed. The seduction of screens is "eerie, but what's happening is the folks are staring at themselves in the monitor staring at themselves in the monitor staring at themselves in the monitor, on and on, completely trapped in a reality loop that never ends" (46). For Palahniuk, there is something sinister about these mediated reality loops, which lure people with their own reflections, that anticipates selfie culture in which the "I" and "phone" are conjoined. Writing his reintroduction with the context of the glossy flat screens and smartphones of 2012, Pahlaniuk reflects how "the moment that monitor goes black, you're looking at yourself, not smiling, not anything. Here's your worst-ever passport photo enlarged to life size. Swimming behind the eBook words of Jane Austen, that slack, dead-eyed zombie face, that's yours. That's you" (v–vi). Besides the oblique reference here to Seth Grahame-Smith's popular 2009 mashup novel *Pride and Prejudice and Zombies*, what Palahniuk is describing is a kind of literal face-book. And yet, as *Invisible Monsters* seems to suggest, those links between the face, the body, the self are contentious, conditional, and precarious.

As a novel that is explicitly about the image industry and how it shapes modern selfhood, *Invisible Monsters* targets the beauty business at a critical moment in the emergence of digital culture, just before phone cameras and social media make everyone a kind of budding fashion model or reality star. In addition to employing the loops that emerge as a result of the novel's organization, Palahniuk uses the photographic and cinematic language of "flash" and "jump cut" to splice together scenes that do not take place in linear time; however, he does so in highly rhythmic, lyrical ways that invite the reader to listen across the novel for resonance, repetition, and clues that may help one to anticipate the many twists and reveals of the story. Although he uses visual language, the logic of Palahniuk's splices resembles the way DJs and recording engineers assemble samples of music. Blurring the lines between interior and exterior, the language of the fashion photoshoot is deployed to express the narrator's interior thoughts, and Shannon's emotions are filtered through jargon. In many scenes, the consciousness of the narrator is interrupted by the flash-bulb of the camera and the half-remembered platitudes fed to her by fashion photographers:

Give me attention.
Flash.
Give me beauty. (201)

The instructions are initially superficial, but in a later chapter, the photographer's instructions point to something at least vaguely interior:

Give me homesickness.
Flash.
Give me nostalgic childhood yearnings.
Flash.
What's the word for the opposite of glamour (237)

In response, instead of real emotions, the narrator gives the reader poses – a fragmented representation of an interior life. Initially, the imperative flashes and references to fashion magazines seem to denote merely a visual signifier, but their rhythmic recurrence may also bring to mind Madonna's 1990 hit "Vogue," which commands its listeners to "strike a pose."

Palahniuk's references to Madonna's billboard hit are made only indirectly, but one might read the novel and its flashes as a kind of remix of "Vogue." In a chapter in which Shannon sees Brandy Alexander for the first time at a speech therapist office where Brandy is retraining her voice to sound more like that of a woman, Shannon remarks, "The queen supreme is the most beautiful anything I've ever seen, so I just vogue there to watch from the doorway" – that is, she stands there posing (279). It is a passing allusion, but in his introduction to the *Remix,* Pahlaniuk acknowledges that he watched music videos on MTV in the early 1990s while writing the initial drafts of the novel (vii). "Vogue," which was written by Madonna and produced by renowned DJ and remixer Shep Pettibone, pays homage both to the dance style vogueing that was popular in underground gay clubs like New York's Sound Factory, and to the famous faces that appeared in *Vogue* magazine.[23] Vogueing is a dance characterized by runway walking and striking poses. It originated in the performative aesthetics of 1960s drag queens in Harlem, but by the 1980s and 1990s, vogueing and other forms of runway had become central to the underground nightclub scene. In MTV News coverage of the Runway phenomenon at Sound Factory in 1993, one dancer described how "Runway is just something that happens . . . at 6 o'clock in the morning when everyone else is asleep. It's just like something from a dream." It required DJs who could respond to the dancers. Madonna was drawn to the freedom and expressive qualities of the dancers and recruited a number of them for her own music videos and concerts. "Vogue" itself was rhythmically and lyrically born on the dancefloor.

Madonna's lyrics contain thematic and even rhythmic resonance with *Invisible Monsters*:

> Strike a pose
> Strike a pose
> (Vogue, vogue, vogue)
> (Vogue, vogue, vogue)[24]

Like Palahniuk, Madonna mobilizes the language of fashion photography to the rhythmic landscape of the underground clubs (which she and one-time lover Jean-Michel Basquiat frequented). The lyrics stress that, when "everywhere you turn is heartache," the dancefloor is a place you can go to "escape." In later verses, the lyrics speak more broadly to identity perform-ance and the centrality of imagination:

> It makes no difference if you're black or white
> If you're a boy or a girl
> If the music's pumping it will give you new life
> You're a superstar, yes, that's what you are, you know it

The song, which promotes the self-acceptance one can find on the under-ground dance floor, declares, "Beauty's where you find it." Madonna's words echo in what Brandy Alexander tells Shannon about the need to craft a "new narrative" for herself, encouraging Shannon to take on new names and new identities. The challenges of crafting a new self are especially challenging for Shannon because she is literally without a voice following her accident. But as a posterchild of a gender-bending identity in flux, Brandy Alexander is happy to be her mentor.

Attempting to help Shannon during her sessions in the speech therapy office, Brandy makes an argument that she repeats elsewhere in the novel: "'You're a product'" (180). Echoing Baudrillard's concept of the simulacra, Brandy compares life to a recording: "'The same way a compact disk isn't responsible for what's recorded on it, that's how we are. You're about as free to act as a programmed computer'" (181). In other words, Shannon is a medium, but one with the power to be remade – or remixed. Remixes – both official and underground – are recordings for which no *original* performance exists, in the conventional sense. "'There isn't any real *you* in *you*,' she says. 'Even your physical body, all your cells will be replaced within eight years,'" Brandy explains (181). But the solution to this world-view is "the opposite of following your bliss" – it is postmodern:

> Give me attention.
> Flash.
> Give me beauty.
> Flash.
> Give me peace and happiness, a loving relationship, and a perfect home.
> Flash.
> Brandy says, "The best way is not to fight it, just go." (183)

The logic of Brandy Alexander's approach to identity echoes Judith Butler's concept of performativity in *Gender Trouble* (which also, inciden-tally, was published in 1990), where she famously refers to gender as a "style" of being (2551).[25] Because the bodies in the novel are constantly in a state of flux as characters undergo plastic surgery and hormone therapy, they are the perfect stage for a novel of mistaken and disguised identity. Palahniuk uses the drag-elements of modeling to skewer the fashion industry; but his satire edges toward morality tale as it critiques the more grotesque aspects of the business, offering a parable not just of self-acceptance, but of self-obliteration in the pursuit of an "authentic" way of being in the world. The novel's mocking, even moralistic tone seems to foreclose the possibility that the performance (and its remix) is also real. By contrast, Madonna's "Vogue" and the underground dance clubs the song celebrates take what Palahniuk critiques as grotesque and instead glorify the performative expressiveness of the body in its adornment. In Madonna's remix, the grotesque is made danceable.

And yet, the novel's rhythmic, danceable cadences and themes have made it incredibly popular among musicians who have turned to the novel for inspiration. The band Panic! at the Disco based the lyrics for their hit song "Time to Dance" (2005) on *Invisible Monsters*, and the song's chorus even samples language from the novel's pages: "Give me envy, give me malice, give me your attention." The Walkmen's 2006 "Brandy Alexander" loosely references images from Palahniuk's novel, and the relationship between Brandy and Shannon: "Set a fire and watch it burnin' / Come here sit next to me / I'll tell you about a dream." Motion City Soundtrack's song "Invisible Monsters" (2005) is likewise based on the novel. The internet celebrity Jeffree Star also drew inspiration from the novel for his 2009 album *Beauty Killer*, which makes references to Brandy Alexander and other themes from the novel across its tracks.

Part of what makes Palahniuk and *Invisible Monsters Remix* such an interesting example of literary remix is the way that it, along with Palahniuk's other novels, has achieved cult status among Palahniuk's very active online fan culture. The official fan site for Chuck Palahniuk, http://chuckpalahniuk.net, which refers to itself as "The Cult," not only promotes his work, but highlights fanfiction as well, including a graphic novel version of *Invisible Monsters* with artwork by KGZ aka Gabor Kiss – an artist whose name sounds like that of a DJ. As the disclaimer on the site makes clear, "Although this is Chuck Palahniuk's official website, we are in essence, more an official 'fansite,'" which is to say, Palahniuk has endorsed the site but does not control its content. It includes his tour dates and Palahniuk's book recommendations, among other things. Perhaps this level of fan engagement should be expected – Palahniuk's approach to writing has always seemed to invite a certain level of collaboration from the reader. But more recently, he has tried to make this collaboration more explicit, publishing two adult coloring books, promising in the press-release that, "Each reader will bring his or her final details to the story" and create a "piece of collaborative art worth keeping for the ages!" To the extent that remix practices have inflected contemporary literature, one of the most active and potent sources for such remixes are not novels or books of poetry that title themselves remixes but rather the endlessly proliferating websites for fan fiction and other derivative works.

Iterative Writing and Fanfiction Remixed

The kinds of iterative works based on the writings of Palahniuk are but a small sample of the millions of works of *fanfiction* found on sites such as Wattpad.com, Archive of Our Own (AO3), and FanFiction.net. Wattpad alone claims to have 65 million users and 400 million stories uploaded globally.[26] In these online communities, contributors write, post, and comment upon new works of fiction based upon their favorite books and movies, and sometimes on the lives of celebrities. In *Vulture's* extensive 2015 survey of fanfiction and its cultural impact, Laura Miller argued that "in the global village that the internet has facilitated, all of pop culture has become a kind of folklore whose mix-and-match components can be passed from storyteller to storyteller, ad infinitum" ("Fanfiction Guide"). However, as she points out, not all published authors are enthusiastic about fanfiction. While some, including J. K. Rowling and Stephanie Meyer (of *Twilight*), have seemed to embrace their readers' fanfic, writers such as "George R.R. Martin, Anne Rice, and Diana Gabaldon . . . protest fic's appropriation of their creations and ask fans to refrain from writing it." While FanFiction.net will take town stories at the authors' request, the world of fanfiction is difficult to police. Amazon and other outlets have attempted to capitalize on the popularity of fanfic but have largely been unable to make it profitable or attractive to authors.[27]

Fanfiction as a genre is not interchangeable with remix, and yet elements of remix have long been part of the phenomena. Describing the links between fanfiction and remix, Natalie Zutter writes,

> Modern fandom's tendency to retweet and reblog content has its roots in the fanfiction community's tradition of remixing and reduxing stories. Starting in 2003, fanfic authors, not unlike music producers, remixed one another's work. There were a few ground rules: You couldn't change the basic plotline, the setting, or the pairing (whether by swapping in new characters or making a het pairing slash, or vice versa). But from there, anything goes! Those who got matched with their favorite writers got to turn the story over in their hands, to add or subtract characters, to layer new themes or motifs over the preexisting plot. The results were often

enchanting, as new POVs were revealed or remixers introduced techniques
that match the original story while bringing in a new dimension. (Zutter)

Using platforms like LiveJournal, the fanfic communities of the early
2000s, such as the membership-based community remix_redux, would
match users via algorithms for the "We Invented the Remix" challenge.[28]
What ties these works of fanfiction and their communities to more
traditional forms of musical remixes – even more so than their use of
digital technology to sample from and rework existing works – is precisely
this underground, competitive quality. Not unlike the underground scene
of mixtapes and unauthorized dance club remixes, fanfic communities are
able to function outside the constraints of copyright infringement by virtue
of existing outside the traditional market economy. Value is instead
assigned through a kind of digital street cred.

But what is the difference between iterative and derivative in such
works? This question continues to be asked of fanfiction communities as
well as remix and mashup artists. Even the most successful fanfic writers
like Anna Todd (author of *After*, based on the fandom and celebrity of
Harry Styles) will admit that "there's a big difference" between the kind of
fiction she writes and, say, Jane Austen's (Miller "Fanfiction"). E. L. James
(*Fifty Shades of Grey*) and Seth Grahame-Smith (*Pride and Prejudice and
Zombies*) have achieved popularity but certainly not critical success. While
most proponents of remix culture, from Kevin Kelly to Lawrence Lessig,
argue in favor of remix's transformative qualities, there is also something
seductive and pleasurable about repetition and resonance that would
suggest that originality is not always the most important element of an
iterative work's success.

Theorizing the RO/RW Era

The emerging critical discourse surrounding remix culture insists that
what makes this emerging culture unique is its *participatory* quality. If it
doesn't exactly require additional work on the part of the reader or listener,
it at least invites it. Steffan Sonvilla-Weiss, editor of *Mashup Culture*, has
suggested that remix and mashup offer the "democratization and active
engagement of the user, who is now empowered by means of user-friendly
technology to actively take part in the making and shaping of public
opinion" (12). No doubt drawing from Roland Barthes's essay on listening,
Sonvilla-Weiss asserts, "This means making the listeners not only listen but
also speak" (12). Legal scholar Lawrence Lessig theorizes this participatory

element of remix culture as the difference between an RO and an RW culture – a "read-only" versus a "read/write" culture (Lessig 28–30). For Lessig, one of the chief legal architects behind the Creative Commons license, this distinction between RO and RW is one of the defining features of how intellectual property functions in the digital age.[29] As a kind of work-around for restrictive copyright laws, creative commons licenses allow creators to set the parameters for the reuse of their work and its attribution (essentially, allowing creators to waive some of their rights to encourage others to remix). If copyright laws promote a "read-only" approach to creative works, creative commons licenses actively encourage "read/write."

Although there are ways that both Kevin Young and Chuck Palahniuk's books resist the digital by playing upon the media specificities of print, both invite reader participation in ways that echo RW culture. They demand a more active reading – a reading that is a kind of remixing in its own right. For *Invisible Monsters Remix*, this means flipping back and forth between the pages to navigate the narrative. For *To Repel Ghosts Remix*, the reader is implicitly invited to google the veiled references layered into the poetry. As the epigraph from DJ Spooky at the beginning of this chapter suggested, "A good read is the equivalent of a good mix" (*Sound Unbound* 16).

One of the unique features of the critical discourse to emerge from remix is that the theory often attempts to perform the remix; that is to say, the line between remix, literature, and theory is often blurred. DJ Spooky's essay, "In Through the Out Door," which forms part of the introduction to his collection of essays, *Sound Unbound: Sampling Digital Music and Culture* (2008), is itself an essay written as a kind of collage of ideas arranged along associative, rhythmic lines. Jonathan Lethem's 'The Ecstasy of Influence," which is a self-proclaimed "plagiarism" of the words of other writers, both theorizes and performs its subject matter. Similarly, Kimbrew McLeod uses the logic of the remix to arrange her "Oral History of Sampling" so that even DJs who did not speak to one another seem to be in conversation through her careful restructuring of quotes taken from recorded interviews. On twitter, @remixtheory (the project of Joel Katelnikoff) uses remix and cut-up techniques in order to offer new ways of reading and processing critical theory, ranging from Lyn Heijinian to Roland Barthes. But perhaps the most extensive project to offer remix *as* theory is Mark Amerika's *Remix the Book* (2011), which calls itself "a hybridized publication and performance art project" and includes chapters that remix the ideas and words of Allen Ginsberg, Alfred North

Whitehead, and Nam June Paik. With an accompanying website and an invitation to other scholar/artists to remix his book, Amerika's project attempts to break open the scholarly-critical practice in order to make it something more expansive, creative, and (ideally) generative. The success of these critical remixes *as* theory or even as art is debatable. And yet, if these impulses within the critical discourse are any indication of where remix might lead, it would appear that theory is already stitched into the code of remix as practice – the two cannot be extricated.

Recording and Remix Onstage

If the electrical grid were suddenly wiped out, what would happen to the cultural productions of the digital era? Would they simply disappear? This is the question at the heart of Anne Washburn's popular 2012 play *Mr. Burns: A Post-Electric Play*. Set in a postapocalyptic near-future, the play opens with a small band of survivors sitting around a fire as they try to remember a specific episode of *The Simpsons*. Over the course of three acts and seventy-five years, the play becomes a meditation on the persistence of storytelling – and in particular oral storytelling and theater – in a postelectric era. As several reviewers have noted, the play offers a remix of popular culture; the survivors of the unnamed disaster not only remediate *The Simpsons*, but in the second act, they also perform elaborate mashups of television commercials and music videos of everything from Beyoncé to Britney Spears.[1] Because the play insists on the centrality of live theater and critiques recorded media more generally, one might hesitate before applying the label remix; but the larger questions that the play raises about the relationships between new and old media, and between sound recording, writing, and performance resonate across many of the works discussed in this book.

Since its debut, *Mr. Burns* has become one of the most widely performed and critically acclaimed new works of theater to emerge in the post-2000 era.[2] It has had dozens of successful regional productions across the United States, as well as in Canada, the United Kingdom, and Australia, including a 2015 production that I attended in Las Vegas.[3] Given the play's premise, I was surprised to find myself thinking about the production for weeks after seeing it. In Act I, the characters are trying to recall the "Cape Feare" Episode from season 5 of *The Simpsons*. In itself, the subject is not particularly interesting, but the language is delightful. As written, the play's dialogue is naturalistic and filled with all the "ums" and "ahs" that plague speech when one is working against the limits of memory. The character with the most complete memory of the episode is Matt, who was portrayed by the actor Matthew Maher in the original 2013 Off-Broadway production at Playwrights Horizon.

MATT: So he has parole and they find out and (*Ah ha it comes to him.*) the Simpsons find out because they go to the movies and it's again a spoof of a scene in *Cape Fear* like they all go to the movies and De Niro is sitting in front of them with a cigar

MARIA: Mh hm

MATT: Smoking a cigar and like laughing, Sideshow Bob is sitting in front of them like going: hah hah

[. . .]

MATT: But in front of Sideshow Bob, Homer is sitting with like an even bigger cigar laughing and laughing even louder and going "Hoh!" and Sideshow Bob is like "oh now really that's just inappropriate" and that's and Bart and uh Bart says uh: "it's you you're threatening to kill me!"

And Sideshow Bob says . . . . . . What does he say do you remember what he says what the dialogue is?

MARIA: . . . no.

MATT: "It's you!" Bart says "you're the one who keeps sending me threatening letters," um . . . and Sideshow Bob says . . .

Matt laughs

oh god wait a minute – uh – uh there's some I remember it's like . . . there's some, *thing*, where Sideshow Bob keeps meaning to say something dreadful but he says it's some linguistic thing where he says it wrong "*I'm –*" – oh, god it's really hard to. (Washburn 20)[4]

As written, the scene incorporates the pauses, hesitations, and breaks in speech one expects of a person plumbing their memory for the minutiae of an old television episode, but in performance, one will also notice the particularity of Matthew Maher's vocal performance (see a video of Maher's performance of this scene on the New York Times Arts Beat Blog [Piepenburg]).[5] He performs the voices of the characters in a sort of loose way, but you might also notice the swift and rhythmic qualities of his speech as he speaks with the breathlessness of an overexcited kid. The sounds of his speech are also marked by the body of the actor Matt Maher – his S's are slightly exaggerated with the hint of a slur, the result of slight speech impediment from cleft palate surgery.[6] The cadences and affect of his speech are important because much of the character Matt's speech is actually based on that of the actor Matthew Maher, who participated in an early workshop during the play's construction.

The scene also stages the limitations of memory in the context of late twentieth-century media. Through repetitive reruns, memes, on-demand YouTube clips, and other forms of digital content, mediatized narratives are ingrained in our memories but also accessible as instant replay. This scene is not just about remembering one episode of *The Simpsons*; it points to the way that the TV show itself – through its satirical form – constantly "samples" from twentieth-century popular culture, both high and low. Since *The Simpsons* has always trafficked in elaborate cultural layers and parody, it becomes a kind of warehouse of cultural artifacts. Through his act of remembering, Matt is reconstructing and preserving not only the 1993 "Cape Feare" episode of the *The Simpsons*, but also the 1991 Robert DeNiro/ Martin Scorsese remake of the 1962 film *Cape Fear* starring Robert Mitchum, which is in turn based on John D MacDonald's 1957 novel *The Executioners*. Later, the characters of *Mr. Burns* also mine references to Mitchum's role in *Night of the Hunter* (1955) and lengthy digressions into Gilbert & Sullivan's *HMS Pinafore* (1878), including the singing of "Three Little Maids from School." But ultimately, individual memory fails, and the entire group is needed to piece together this nearly forgotten episode.

To reconstruct "Cape Feare," however, the characters can only reproduce these multimedia works *orally* through labored acts of recollection and performative speech. It is an act of *remediation* (in Jay David Bolter and Richard Grusin's sense of the term) but in reverse, as a newer, recorded media is pitched through the old. In the post-electric world of *Mr. Burns,* the episodes themselves no longer exist – without electricity, there is no way to *play* them. The characters must remember, reenact, and even *remix* the "Cape Feare" episode. Their performance is transformative, but the pleasure for the audience is not necessarily in recognizing the details of the episode – it is rather in the resonant associations brought forward by the characters' serendipitous memories. Like the DJ who draws connections between seemingly disparate sounds and ideas, Washburn draws from a wide range of pop culture references of the late 1990s and early 2000s. This can be seen in a more direct way in Act II.

Act II takes place seven years later, when the characters from the campfire have started a makeshift theater troupe that performs episodes of *The Simpsons* with accompanying commercials and mashups of popular music. They rehearse these skits throughout the act, which ends in a rather dramatic gunfight with a competing theatrical troupe. Although most productions seem to use the version of the mashup arranged by the composer Michael Friedman, the script itself leaves open the structure and content of the mashup, stating only that, "*What follows is a medley of popular hits from the last 10 years*" arranged for "*group singing*" – the "*overall effect should be highly choreographed, polished, entertaining, and without irony. The really characteristic instrumentations of these songs should be rendered as well, but vocally"* (66). In the versions I was able to view (first in Las Vegas, and then an archival video of the New Playwrights Horizons 2013 production in New York), the mashup is performed in the style of an a cappella group and, as specified in Friedman's arrangement, included songs such as Britney Spears's "Toxic," Baha Men's "Who Let the Dogs Out," Lady Gaga's "Bad Romance," Rihanna's "Umbrella," Ricky Martin's "Living la Vida Loca," Beyoncé's "Single Ladies," and Eminem's "Lose Yourself." At least twenty different pop songs are referenced.[7] As with all mashups, success is dependent upon the listener's ability to recognize the intertextual references and quotations; to a certain extent, it plays on the listener's sense of nostalgia. However, in the context of the play, these remixes and mashups are a mode of survival in the proto-economy that emerges among the survivors seven years after the disaster, as well as a way of preserving the fragments of a digital culture seemingly no longer accessible in a post-electric world.

The third act takes place seventy-five years in the future. The band of survivors from the first two acts are gone; instead, we are presented with an operatic setting of *The Simpsons* with a Greek-style chorus and characters wearing highly stylized masks. Although the "Cape Feare" episode of *The Simpsons* (and Bernard Hermann's ominous theme music from the 1962 film) still provides the most discernable plot points, there are some notable changes. The villain is now played by Mr. Burns (rather than by Sideshow Bob), and in the opening chorus, details of the nuclear disaster that lead to the postapocalyptic conditions are woven into the story such that when the Simpsons family flees Springfield for a houseboat on Cape Feare, the impetus seems to be nuclear disaster, embodied by Mr. Burns (a fact which is made more terrifying when he reprises a sinister version of Britney Spears's "Toxic").

As an opera, the third act frames *The Simpsons* as an apocalyptic origin myth, and in doing so, elements of the commercials and musical mashups from Act II are seamlessly woven into the larger performance. What was once popular culture is now high art. The opera also stages the failing electric grid through media-glitches, and television announcer Troy McClure's voice pulses rhythmically:

> Kent? Kent? You're breaking up, Kent. Ka-ka-ka-ka Kent?
> Ka-ka-ka-ka-ka-ka-ka-ka (77)

Moments such as these, which aestheticize the breakages and repetitive rupturing of language echo the scratching and breakbeats of hip-hop, but in this example, the sounding of media failure also symbolizes the breaking up of a community following a cataclysmic disaster.

On the one hand, the staging of the third act as a highly stylized opera that harkens back to classical theatrical traditions such as Greek tragedy, Japanese Noh theater, and European opera is meant to reassure the audience that the oral traditions of storytelling – and in particular of live theater – will survive the apocalypse. Theater reviewers are quick to point out the ways that this is a play *about* theater and its persistence even in the digital era.[8] However, because of the way that the play remediates and remixes our most salient digital and sonic media, Washburn also reveals the power and persistence of aesthetic forms born out of sound and multi-media technologies – including remix.

One of the ironies of *Mr. Burns* is that, despite its insistence on the power of "live" theater in a post-electric world, Anne Washburn used sound recording technology to write the play. In the notes on the play in the print edition (Oberon 2014), Washburn reveals that much of the first act, and part of the second, were written using recorded transcripts from a 2008 workshop with the Civilians, a New York-based investigative theater group – a group that included actor Matthew Maher, among others.[9] Even the choosing of the "Cape Feare" episode happened entirely by chance. As Washburn recalls, she wanted to pursue the question of "what would happen to a pop culture narrative pushed past the fall of civilization" and so tasked the actors "with remembering *Simpsons* episodes, and the dialogue around the remembering of the episode in the first act (and the small section of the episode rehearsed in the second act) is largely verbatim from those sessions" (8). Although Washburn notes that the resemblance between the characters and the actors is "passing" at best, when the play was produced in New York, nearly all of the original actors (including Maher) returned for the production.

When adapting the workshop sessions for *Mr. Burns*, Washburn claimed in an interview that she "wrote it with their voices in [her] head the whole time" – in particular, because Matt's words "dominate a lot of the first act the character of Matt has a lot in common with Matt [Maher], in terms of cadence, but is actually, though more subtly, a rather different person" (Sanford). This connection between character and *cadence*, the sonic affect of Matt's speech, seems especially pertinent given that the actor Matt Maher's own speech is so unique. The hesitating qualities of the character Matt's speech are thus inextricably tied to the hesitating cadences of the actor Matt's body. Washburn samples not only his words, but his voice. Because so much of the play was written from audio transcripts, the mode of composition is even more closely tied to the audio-roots of remix as a rebalancing and reworking of the original recorded tracks than one might initially realize. Although Washburn transforms the characters and shapes their stories into something more stage-able, ultimately, she is wielding their words like a DJ, and as a result, she relies quite heavily on precisely the kinds of audio technology that the setting of her own play makes obsolete.

As a playwright, Washburn is particularly attuned to the voices and acoustic spaces of her plays. "I think of theater as ultimately an aural form, rather than a visual one," she remarked in an interview, "and I think that time taught me to hear stories in that way, so when I tried to write a play text I immediately felt that this was the form my brain was geared for" (Sanford). This aural-emphasis is apparent in her other plays as well – for example, *10 out of 12* (2015) is a "play staged through a mixture of bodies and voices," and much of the action is heard through voice-over alone, as the audience wears headsets (Washburn, *Mr. Burns and Other Plays* 235). The emphasis on theater as an aural medium is especially evident in the ways *Mr. Burns* moves between high realism in which speech is written and performed with a kind of transcriptive naturalism and the exaggerated musical elements, such as the mashups and the opera in the third act. These juxtapositions, which move deftly between speech and song, amplify the ways that sounds play upon the memory.

Mr. Burns is just one more example of a literary work that reveals the extent to which our audio technologies continue to shape the creative practices of writers and inform the broader aesthetic markers of the digital era. Washburn need not explicitly call her play a remix for audiences to recognize it as one. Likewise, few audiences would question her technique of using recordings and transcripts to write dialogue. And yet, in her insistence on live performance, on *staging* and making present and embodied our most contemporary aesthetic forms (like mashup), Washburn offers audiences the chance to hear our most technologically mediated forms – animated television shows, pop recordings and remixes – from new angles. These performances highlight the portability of recording and remix aesthetic forms across media and modes, even as their technologically mediated qualities might seem like their most distinguishing feature. Like so many of the texts this book has explored, *Mr. Burns* does not merely imitate recording technologies, but reveals how literature itself records, replays, remixes, and reimagines the ways we listen to the world around us.

Notes

Introduction Resonant Reading

1. When her suitor, Jeff, asks Melanctha if she loves him, she repeatedly tells him: "Yes I love you, sure, Jeff, though you don't any way deserve it from me. Yes, yes I love you. Yes Jeff I say it till I certainly am very sleepy. Yes I love you now Jeff, and you certainly must stop asking me to tell you" (Stein, *Writings* 194). In the passage, Melanctha repeats the phrase nearly a dozen times, but although Jeff heard her "and he tried hard to believe her. He did not really doubt her but somehow it was wrong now, the way Melanctha said it" (195).

2. See Mark Amerika, *Remix the Book* (2011), Lawrence Lessig, *Remix: Making Art and Commerce Thrive in the Hybrid Economy* (2008), Jonathan Lethem, "The Ecstasy of Influence" (2007), Eduardo Navas, *Remix Theory the Aesthetics of Sampling* (2012), and DJ Spooky (aka Paul D. Miller), *Rhythm Science* (2004).

3. See *Vibratory Modernism* (2013), ed. Anthony Enns and Shelley Trower, and *Sounding Modernism: Rhythm and Sonic Mediation in Modern Literature and Film* (2017), ed. Hone, Groth, and Murphet.

4. In a 1929 letter to Stein from Nella Larsen enclosing a copy of her novel *Quicksand*, Larsen praised "Melanctha," stating, "I never cease to wonder how you came to write it and just why you and not some one of us should so accurately have caught the spirit of this race of mine" (qtd. in Blackmer 230).

5. Stein's use of the English language was often characterized as "foreign" by others. See Richard Bridgman, *Gertrude Stein in Pieces*. Oxford University Press, 1971, 6.

6. In an NBC radio interview from November 12, 1934, Stein remarked on the issue of intelligibility: "You mean by understanding that you can talk about it in the way that you have the habit of talking ... putting it in other words ... but I mean by understanding enjoyment." Gertrude Stein. "A

Radio Interview." *The Paris Review*, Issue 115, Fall 1990. www.theparisreview.org /miscellaneous/2282/a-radio-interview-gertrude-stein.

7. Katherine Biers writes about Stein's attentiveness to listening in *Four in America*: "Rather than working hard to replicate her intentions in the minds of her hearers, Stein promises to help her audience make a habit out of listening to language in such a way that they can recognize what underlies or allows for linguistic habits" (190). Relatedly, Sarah Wilson argues that radio significantly influenced Stein's post-WWII writings, such as *Brewsie and Willie*. See Wilson, Sarah. "Gertrude Stein and the Radio." *Modernism/Modernity*, vol. 11, no. 2, Apr. 2004, pp. 261–78. doi:10.1353/mod.2004.0048.

8. The desire to record and broadcast Gertrude Stein's works is also at the heart of the Radio Free Stein project, hosted by the University of British Columbia at www.radiofreestein.com/.

9. See Jonathan Sterne's *The Audible Past*, 74; also, Friedrich A. Kittler's *Gramophone, Film, Typewriter*, 74.

10. For an account of Edison's invention, see Stross 455–506. For a detailed history of inscriptive technologies, see Gitelman's *Scripts, Grooves, and Writing Machines*.

11. Edison was hoping to find a way to record telegraph and phone messages.

12. The name was settled on after assembling (with his employees' assistance) a lengthy list of possible names, most of which emphasized sound (e.g., acoustophone, otophone, palmetophone, ecophone, etc.), but many of which also referenced writing, such as auto-electrograph and ekograph. Thomas A. Edison, *Lists and Inventories – Cylinder Phonograph*, 1877, The Thomas Edison Papers at Rutgers University, [D7702] Document File Series – 1877: (D-77-02) Edison, T.A. – General. http://edison.rutgers.edu/NamesSea rch/SingleDoc.php?DocId=D7702ZEO.

13. Benjamin Pitman's institute and publications helped to popularize phonetic shorthand in America, and in the latter part of the nineteenth century the term phonograph and phonography became nearly synonymous with stenography. Several publications promoting phonography emerged, including trade journals, such as *Browne's Phonographic Monthly* (1875–1879), which were aimed at stenographers. Pittman, who also worked as a journalist and stenographer, would become the court stenographer during the trials related to the assassination of President Lincoln.

14. "Edison and Mark Twain – The Edison Papers." *Thomas A. Edison Papers at Rutgers University*, October 28, 2016, http://edison.rutgers.edu/twain.htm.

15. Twain was known for his interest in new technologies, from the typewriter and the phonograph to the telephone. See Sean Keck. "Literary Regionalism and Mark Twain's Telephone," *The Mark Twain Annual*, vol. 15, no. 1, 2017, pp. 106–25. www.jstor.org/stable/10.5325/marktwaij.15.1.0106.

16. For an excellent reading of the phonograph's role in *Dracula*, see John M. Picker. "The Victorian Aura of the Recorded Voice." *New Literary History*, vol. 32, no. 3, 2001, pp. 769–86.

17. For histories of recording related to music, see Greg Milner's *Perfecting Sound Forever: An Aural History of Recorded Music* (Faber & Faber, 2009), David Suisman's *Selling Sounds: The Commercial Revolution in American Music* (Harvard, 2012), and Susan Schmidt Horning's *Chasing Sound: Technology, Culture & the Art of the Studio Recording from Edison to the LP* (Johns Hopkins, 2013). There are also several anthologies on related topics, including *Audio Culture: Readings in Modern Music* (Bloomsbury, 2004), ed. Christopher Cox and Daniel Warner; *Sound Unbound* (MIT, 2008), ed. Paul D. Miller; and *The Sound Studies Reader* (Routledge, 2012), ed. Jonathan Sterne.

18. Matthew Rubery's *The Untold Story of the Talking Book* (Harvard, 2016) offers a helpful history of audiobooks from the Edison era to the present.

19. Several peer-reviewed journals and blogs devoted to the field have been established, including *Sound Studies* (since 2016), *Resonance: The Journal of Sound and Culture* (since 2020), and the groundbreaking *Sounding Out!* soundstudiesblog.com (since 2009).

20. For more on modernism and media studies, see Mark Goble's *Beautiful Circuits: Modernism and the Mediated Life* (Columbia, 2010) and Katherine Biers's *Virtual Modernism: Writing and Technology in the Progressive Era* (Minnesota, 2013). See also Jessica Pressman's *Digital Modernism: Making It New in New Media* (Oxford, 2014), which takes a slightly different tack, exploring how electronic literature reimagines modernist aesthetics. T. Austin Graham's *The Great American Songbooks: Musical Texts, Modernism, and the Value of Popular Culture* (Oxford, 2013) looks at the relationship between popular song and American modernist novels. For works in radio studies, see Rebecca P. Scales's *Radio and the Politics of Sound in Interwar France, 1921–1939* (Cambridge, 2018), IanWhittington's *Writing the Radio War: Literature, Politics and the BBC, 1939–1945* (Oxford, 2018), and Tom McEnaney's *Acoustic Properties: Radio, Narrative, and the New Neighborhood of the Americas* (Northwestern, 2017). Excellent edited collections include *Sounding Modernism: Rhythm and Sonic Mediation in Modern Literature and Film* (Edinburgh, 2017), ed. Hone, Groth, and *Murphet, and Vibratory Modernism* (Springer, 2013), ed. Enns and Trower.

21. See Keeling and Kun 6–7. Their introduction to *Sound Clash,* the 2011 special issue of *American Quarterly,* offers an excellent critical overview of the implications of sound and listening for American studies. See also *Social Text's* 2010 special issue, "The Politics of Recorded Sound."

22. There are more excellent works on Black sound studies than can be named here, but notable examples include Fred Moten's *In the Break* (Minnesota, 2003), Emily Lordi's *Black Resonance: Iconic Women Singers and African American Literature* (Rutgers, 2013), Carter Mathes's *Imagine the Sound: Experimental African American Literature after Civil Rights* (Minnesota, 2015), and Tsisi Ella Jaji *Africa in Stereo: Modernism, Music, and Pan-African Solidarity* (Oxford, 2014).

23. Sound artist Pauline Oliveros's *deep listening* combines musical practice, meditation, and healing. Poet and editor Craig Dworkin assembled *A Handbook of Protocols for Literary Listening* as part of an exhibition at the 2012 Whitney Biennial in New York, which included a kind of A-Z survey of terms and examples of listening in radical conceptual writing.

24. Scholars like Mark McGurl also make the case for the voice's centrality to post-war American fiction; see "Find Your Voice," *The Program Era*, 128–272.

25. The term *resonant reading* was recently taken up by Katie Dyson in a special cluster of short essays on anxious pedagogies. For Dyson, resonant reading is a response to the limits of critical reading practices. Taking a page from Rita Felski in *The Limits of Critique* (2015), Dyson advocates for reading practices that embrace "the full range of attachments and orientations to the texts we read" through practices such as collaborative reading (539). Katie Dyson. "Resonant Reading: From Anxiety to Attunement." *Pedagogy*, vol. 19 no. 3, 2019, pp. 537–542. muse.jhu.edu/article/733105.

26. The term extended technique comes from music and describes the phenomena that emerged in the twentieth century when musicians needed to learn new ways of playing their instruments to accommodate the demands of contemporary composers. Examples of this include reaching inside the piano to pluck the strings or blowing air through wind instruments without actually playing notes.

27. For more about the pedagogical implications of teaching listening, see Steph Ceraso's excellent *Sounding Composition: Multimodal Pedagogies for Embodied Listening* (University of Pittsburgh Press, 2018).

28. This is a possibility that John Mowitt, in *Sounds: The Ambient Humanities* (2015), argues for explicitly: "Sounds, whether in the world or on the page, are Text, that is provocations to reading, especially readings that find problems not only in or with other readings but with the conditions and limits of reading itself" (2). Mowitt's attention to nonverbal vocal sounds, such as whistles, whispers, and gasps, points to the margins of sound's symbolic capacity.

29. Veit Erlmann argues that, despite the tendency to think of the history of modernity as ocular-centric and to treat hearing as the "less rational" sense, the "histories of reason and resonance" are intertwined, in part because resonance was at the core of scientific understanding of hearing until the 1920s (11–14).

30. In her essay on Conrad, Napolin explores the vibratory sense of resonance as the "outer limits of perception" and even as "subaural" (73).
31. See Ellison, *Living with Music* ed. Robert G. O'Meally, 139; Weheliye, *Phonographies*, 47–48.
32. See Goble, 159; O'Meally, 139; Stoever, 3–4.
33. In *Beautiful Circuits: Modernism and the Mediated Life* (2010), Mark Goble has pointed to this "scene of maximum technology" as marked by "terrific irony" in its appeals to Ford, Edison, and Franklin (159).
34. In *Listening and the Voice* (1976), Don Ihde describes how "listening makes the invisible *present* in a way similar to the presence of the mute in vision" (51). As Alexander Weheliye puts it, listening cuts through "the opacities of the sonic" (50).
35. Ellison's sound system included "a fine speaker system, a first-rate AM-FM tuner, a transcription turntable and a speaker cabinet. I built half a dozen or more preamplifiers and record compensators before finding a commercial one that satisfied my ear, and finally we acquired an arm, a magnetic cartridge, and – glory of the house – a tape recorder" (Ellison *Living with Music* 10–11).
36. Footage of Ellison recording and listening to himself on tape as he dictated passages that would later appear in his posthumous novel *Juneteenth* is available. See Oklahoma Historical Society (OHS) Film and Video Archives. "The Novel – Ralph Ellison on Work in Progress 1966." Item Number: F2009.117.003. *YouTube*, May 29, 2012. www.youtube.com/watch?v=LgCozZ3okh8

1 Ears Taut to Hear

1. Brandt and Brandt Correspondence 1929–1957 (Box 18, Folder 4 of 11), Papers of John Dos Passos, Accession #5950, Special Collections, University of Virginia Library, Charlottesville, VA.
2. In their 1929 sociological study *Middletown: A Study in American Culture*, Helen Merrell Lynd and Robert S. Lynd found that 59 percent of the homes they surveyed in thirty-six cities had a phonograph (Suisman 249).
3. See Jack Weaver, *Joyce's Music and Noise: Theme and Variation in His Writings* (University Press of Florida, 1998), and Brian Reed, "Hart Crane's Victrola," *Modernism/Modernity* 7.1 (2000): 99–125. See also Jean Cocteau. "The Eiffel Tower Wedding Party (Les Mariés de La Tour Eiffel)," *The Infernal Machine, and Other Plays*, translated by Dudley Fitts, New Directions, 1964 (1921), 151–78.
4. The disembodied voice is discussed at length in Allen Weiss, *Breathless: Sound Recording, Disembodiment, and the Transformation of Lyrical Nostalgia* (Wesleyan University Press, 2002).

5. For an extended discussion of sound in the Victorian era and its connection to death, see Mark M. Smith, *Listening to Nineteenth-Century America* (University of North Carolina Press, 2001).

6. See Barry Maine and Robert DeMott (Penguin Introduction xiv), *Working Days: The Journals of the Grapes of Wrath 1938–1941* Introduction, footnote 4.

7. As the archival drafts and notebooks that John Dos Passos made between 1932 and 1936 reveal, he began sketching drafts of the opening prose-poem early in the process of writing *The Big Money* (1936), the third book of his *U.S.A.* trilogy. Fragments of these early versions of the prologue litter the drafts of *The Big Money*; even in the publisher's setting copy, Dos Passos was making substantial revisions. See Box 29 – *The Big Money* (1936) – Later Drafts and Revisions ca. 1932–1956 (Folder 1 of 6), Papers of John Dos Passos, Accession #5950, Special Collections, University of Virginia Library, Charlottesville, VA.

8. In *The Noises of American Literature 1890–1985: Toward a History of Literary Acoustics* (2006), Philipp Schweighauser has suggested that "modernist formal experimentation and innovation can be seen as responses to problems of representing the noise of modernity not only in its metaphorical but also in its literal, acoustic sense. Literature, already severely challenged in its claims to verisimilitude by photography, film, and the phonograph, entered a crisis of representation, and modernist experimental forms are a response to that crisis" (24).

9. In Alexander Graham Bell's 1874 experiments with telephonic technology, for example, he used actual ears from human cadavers as the sound-reproducing agent, literally gluing a makeshift straw stylus to the small bones of the ear (Kittler 74, Stern 53).

10. Dos Passos's claim that U.S.A. is the speech of the people has affinities with Benedict Anderson's theory of nationalism in *Imagined Communities* (1983, 1991), which expands the definition of communities to extend beyond face-to-face interaction.

11. Although Emile Berliner introduced his disc recording machines in 1888, it was not until 1894 that the first disc records reached the public. 1912, by contrast, was the last year that Edison's company released cylinder recordings, having made the transition to discs. "Gramophone," Emile Berliner and the Birth of the Recording Industry, Library of Congress Digital Collections. www.loc.gov/collections/emile-berliner/articles-and-essays/gramophone/

12. In the 1890s pre-recorded discs became a business opportunity. Berliner's introduction of disc recording allowed for the mass production of recordings through a process of stamping. By 1899 the disc began to eclipse the popularity of the cylinder, and by 1913 the cylinder was obsolete. See David J. Morton, *Sound Recording*, 31–39.

13. As Susan Schmidt Horning, Mark Katz, and other historians of the music industry have pointed out, the combined sensitivities of electrical recordings, the loudspeaker, and film soundtracks of the 1920s and 30s led to new styles of vocalization – such as crooners like Bing Crosby and Mel Torme – and the prevalence of saxophone sections like those of Duke Ellington's band (Horning 45; Katz 83).

14. Susan Schmidt Horning's *Chasing Sound* offers a detailed account of how the development of the microphone benefited from Bell Labs' in-depth study of all aspect of the recording process, from studio design to desired frequency range. The new recordings not only had a better dynamic range, but also better "room tone" – they seemed louder too. However, playback remained an issue because the phonograph itself was still acoustic. The first phonograph designed for it was the "Orthophonic Victrola." See Horning 35–37. For more about amplified phonographs, see also Morton 66.

15. See Alexander Woollcott's 1922 review of Eugene O'Neill's *The Hairy Ape*. "Second Thoughts on First Nights." *The New York Times*, Apr. 16, 1922, p. 80.

16. Regarding Dos Passos's portrayal of voices, see Schweighauser 23.

17. The disclaimer accompanying the "ethnic characterizations" notes that: "The National Jukebox is a project of the Library of Congress Packard Campus for Audio Visual Conservation. The goal of the Jukebox is to present to the widest audience possible early commercial sound recordings, offering a broad range of historical and cultural documents as a contribution to education and lifelong learning. These selections are presented as part of the record of the past. They are historical documents which reflect the attitudes, perspectives, and beliefs of different times. The Library of Congress does not endorse the views expressed in these recordings, which may contain content offensive to users" (www.loc.gov/jukebox/).

18. Meta DuEwa Jones offers a helpful reading of Dunbar's poem and Meyers's 1909 recording of it, noting the problematic appropriation of female voices. See *The Muse Is Music: Jazz Poetry from the Harlem Renaissance to Spoken Word* (8–12).

19. Of course, accented language may well be one of modernism's defining features. Joshua L. Miller in *Accented America* argues that writers like Jean Toomer and Gertrude Stein "play out the logic that exact phonological reproductions of immigrant or African American speech are impossible. Instead their idioms call readers' attention to the system of communication itself" (22).

20. A caveat is required here. Despite the great variety of characters depicted in *U.S.A.*, there are few African Americans or other people of color. Many ethnicities are represented, but the majority of them are European. All of the central characters, though they include women and people from different class backgrounds, are notably white.

21. In *Accented America,* Joshua L. Miller finds that Dos Passos recontextualizes the literary experiment of national language that one sees in the works of Henry James, Gertrude Stein, Ernest Hemingway, and F. Scott Fitzgerald, but ultimately finds Dos Passos's attempts at literary pluralism are a failure (178).

22. Box 79 *Nineteen Nineteen* (1932) ca. 1932 – Manuscript drafts, ca. 1932 (Folder 1 of 4), Papers of John Dos Passos, Accession #5950, Special Collections, University of Virginia Library, Charlottesville, VA.

23. Writing about Dos Passos and the radio, Tom McEnaney points to what he calls the "New Deal Acoustics" of Dos Passos's accounts of the convention in Chicago, which are also included in a slightly different form in *In All Countries*. See McEnaney, 25–29.

24. This image is provided courtesy of the estate of John Dos Passos and originally appeared in Pizer, *Paintings and Drawings*, Figure 42. Special thanks to Lisa Nanney for her assistance.

25. These subtitles and character lists can be found in Dos Passos's early manuscript drafts for *The Garbage Man* in the John Dos Passos Collection at the Small Special Collections Library at the University of Virginia, MSS 5950, Box 48.

26. I am citing the 1926 Harper & Brothers edition of *The Garbage Man*; however, it is worth noting that Dos Passos made quite a few changes to the play when it was re-published in *Three Plays* in 1934.

27. For more about Dos Passos and the visual, *see* Justin Edwards, "The Man with a Camera Eye: Cinematic Form and Hollywood Malediction in John Dos Passos's 'The Big Money,'" *Literature/Film Quarterly* 27.4 (1999): 245–254; and Michael Spindler, "John Dos Passos and the Visual Arts," *Journal of American Studies* 15 (1981): 391–405.

28. Stephen Hock rightly acknowledges that in contrast to the Newsreels, critics have "often ignored the relation of the Camera Eye to the cinema" in part because the section causes "critical confusion, disagreement, and outright derision" (20). The title of Hock's article is telling: "Stories Told Sideways Out of the Big Mouth" reminds us of the ways aural the qualities pervade Dos Passos's Camera Eye sections.

29. As media theorist Friedrich Kittler has put it, the phonograph is "a machine that records noises regardless of so-called meaning" (85).

30. Friedrich Kittler has remarked that the phonograph "draws out those speech disturbances that concern psychiatry" (86).

31. Austin Graham speaks to this phenomena at a number of junctures in his book, *The Great American Songbooks,* where he suggests that "when audiences can be depended on to know of and even 'play' a song in the mind upon receiving a written cue, a range of possibilities opens up for authors" (23). See Graham 23–25, 65–66.

32. Friedrich Kittler asserts that Edison's invention ushered in an "epoch of nonsense" and that "nonsense is always already the unconscious" (86).

33. See John Trombold, 289.

34. The record collection, which only contains records made starting around the year 1950, consists primarily of classical and Spanish guitar recordings, but also contains a few records by Harry Bellafonte. See Box 122 in the Papers of John Dos Passos, Accession #5950, Special Collections, University of Virginia Library, Charlottesville, VA.

35. See Dos Passos, *The Fourteenth Chronicle*. For example, in a letter dated Midnight, January 15, 1918, "Reading Butler. Someone is playing the *Seraphina* on the phonograph – There's a festival brass in it that makes me think of health resorts – a continental watering place on a warm summer's night with lights & crowds walking about & sharing cafés and a ship – a long string of lights – coming into the harbor from the sea" (128). Elsewhere he even describes mortars blasting with "the twang of fragments like a harp broken in the air" (95).

36. See Box 8 – Letters – Gerald and Sara Murphy (ca. 1925–1964), Papers of John Dos Passos, Accession #5950, Special Collections, University of Virginia Library, Charlottesville, VA.

37. Gerald Murphy and Cole Porter had been good friends at Yale, and many claim Murphy helped launch Porter's music career (Carr 197).

38. John Trombold had created an excellent index of all the songs referenced in the Newsreel sections of *U.S.A.*, including the names of composers and lyricists as well as publication dates (see "Popular Songs as Revolutionary Culture").

39. See manuscript drafts of *U.S.A* in Box 48 – *The 42nd Parallel* (1930) ca. 1930, ca. 1956, 1964, Papers of John Dos Passos, Accession #5950, Special Collections, University of Virginia Library, Charlottesville, Va.

40. "Alexander's Ragtime Band" has been recorded dozens of times over the years, but it was first recorded in 1911 by Arthur Collins and Byron Harlan (Victor 16908). It became a hit yet again in 1927 when Bessie Smith recorded it (Columbia 14219-D). Irving Berlin himself claimed that the lyrics "'were an *invitation* to 'come,' to join in, and 'hear' the singer and his song. And that idea of *inviting* every receptive auditory within shouting distance became a part of the happy ruction . . . [and] was the secret of the song's tremendous success'" (qtd. in Furia 511).

41. Philip Furia has argued that "'Alexander's Ragtime Band' redefined the nature of American popular songs. Most nineteenth-century songs were strophic, consisting of verses that outlined a narrative." By contrast, with "'Alexander's Ragtime Band,' Berlin established a song pattern that would dominate popular music for the next fifty years. Although he began with a verse[. . .],

it was very brief and, rather than relating a narrative, it simply introduced the refrain, or, as it came to be called, the chorus" (510).

42. The repetitions and rhymes built into the songs themselves worked as mnemonic devices that helped people to memorize them, but with phonographic recordings, the process of memorizing songs changed. Friedrich Kittler asserts that, "Records turn and turn until phonographic inscriptions inscribe themselves into brain physiology. We all know hits and rock songs by heart precisely because there is not reason to memorize them anymore" (80). Studies of the relationship between music and memory by neurologist Oliver Sacks and others have tended to reinforce this assertion. See Oliver Sacks, *Musicophilia: Tales of Music and the Brain* (Knopf, 2010); and D. J. Levitin, *This Is Your Brain on Music: The Science of a Human Obsession* (Penguin, 2006).

43. Interestingly, while the January 14, 1925, recording of St. Louis Blues for Columbia was one of Smith's last acoustical recordings, the recording made for the 1929 film would have been fully electrical.

44. In *Black Resonance: Iconic Women Singers and African American Literature* (2013), Emily Lori explores the affinities, appropriations, and resonances between Black male writers such as Richard Wright and James Baldwin and singers like Bessie Smith, noting the complex gender dynamics of male writers whose writing aspires toward the lyricism of female blues singers. See Lordi, 100.

45. See Box 27 – Big Money – Early Manuscript Drafts ca. 1932–1936 (Folder 3 of 4), Papers of John Dos Passos, Accession #5950, Special Collections, University of Virginia Library, Charlottesville, VA.

46. Caedmon Audio was founded in 1952 by Barbara Holdridge (neé Cohen) and Marianne Roney. Holdridge and Roney hoped to record every living writer and the label – which was staunchly aimed at middle-class audiences – was the first to market spoken-word recordings, laying the foundation for audiobook industry. For a history of Caedmon, see Matthew Rubery, *The Untold Story of the Talking Book* (2016), chapter 7: Caedmon's Third Dimension.

47. Caedmon's *U.S.A.* readers include Ed Begley, George Grizzard, Rip Torn, and John Dos Passos; the Newsreels were performed by Edward Bishop, John Brandon, David Healy, Helen Horton, and Gordon Tanner; it was directed by Howard Sackler.

48. In the 2010 audiobook version of the trilogy for Tantor Audio, David Drummond not only performs the many voices of the characters, he also performs the Newsreels, even singing the song lyrics. More than one listener review on Audible.com points out Dos Passos's realist ear; as one listener notes, "The audible parts of the writing, especially newspaper headlines, radio messages, and popular songs, make this a wonderful choice for a book to be listened to as opposed to being read" Michael G. Price. "A Diego Rivera

Painting in Written Form (Review)." January 3, 2013. *The 42nd Parallel*. www.audible.com/pd/The-42nd-Parallel-Audiobook/B0040H5JYG.

2 Ethnographic Transcription and the Jazz Auto/Biography

1. According to Susan Horning, "Presto Recording Corporation pioneered high-quality disc recorders and introduced the lacquer-coated aluminum disc in 1934, which revolutionized recording practice" (53). The presto discs were also especially popular with radio transcription services (61).

2. The term "oral history" is usually attributed to historian Allan Nevins, who founded The Columbia Center for Oral History in 1948.

3. Morton had begun to conceive of his own autobiography several years earlier and had even appeared on Radio WOL, Washington, DC, in 1936 to tell the history of jazz.

4. One of the earliest attempts at a comprehensive jazz history was the French critic Hugues Panassié's *Le jazz hot* (1934), translated for American readers as *Hot Jazz* (1936), which distinguished jazz from European styles and attempted to define "hot" jazz in relation to other emerging styles. Other early histories include Herbert Asbury's colorful *The French Quarter: An Informal History of the New Orleans Underworld* (1936), and Charles Edward Smith and Frederic Ramsey Jr.'s *Jazzmen* (1939). For an overview of these early jazz histories, see Scott Deveaux, "Constructing the Jazz Tradition," in *The Jazz Cadence of American Culture*, ed. Robert G. O'Meally, 483–511.

5. Christopher Harlos and Holly E. Farrington both offer useful critiques of the genre of jazz autobiography. In separate works, Brent Edwards, Daniel Stein, and Gerald Early suggest helpful links between jazz autobiographies and broader literary practices. Early has suggestively proposed that these forms of writing "reestablish and renew the tradition of jazz as a music that must be rhetorically rehearsed, even rhetorically realized" (133).

6. Marybeth Hamilton notes that "the years preceding the Morton interview had seen intensifying interest in autobiographical testimony, both among social scientists (particularly those linked to the University of Chicago and Yale's Institute of Human Relations) and, more recently, within the Federal Writers' Project. Researchers gathered the life stories of the unlettered" (727).

7. See Brady 55. Recordings of Native American languages and music were of particular interest to late nineteenth-century Americans who romanticized the disappearing tribes as the last vestigial traces of a wild American frontier. As the interest in primitivism grew, increased attention was paid to African American culture as well, which was naively viewed as harnessing this raw energy.

8. For example, Judith C. Lapadat and Anne C. Lindsay argue that the persistent assumption of transcription's transparency is problematic and that those who are treating language as data must make greater efforts to document transcription methodology (70).

9. As Paul Benzon has pointed out, "the typewriter builds error into the act of writing," and in the process of dictation in particular, "technological efficiency and dispersive textual uncertainty were intertwined" (94, 92). For Benzon, this fact is nowhere more evident than in Andy Warhol's *A: A Novel* (1968), which is constituted of unedited transcripts of tape recordings.

10. Brent Hayes Edwards has argued that transcription was a central concern for Harlem Renaissance writers. See his illuminating discussion of James Weldon Johnson's poetics of transcription in *Epistrophies*, 61–80.

11. For letters from Hurston to the Lomaxes, see "Zora Neale Hurston," www.culturalequity.org/alan-lomax/friends/hurston.

12. In *Louisiana* (1994), a loosely fictionalized novel based on Zora Neale Hurston's ethnographic expeditions, Erna Brodber highlights the Hurston-esque protagonist's use of a tape recorder not only to record her subjects but to commune with the dead.

13. See Richard Wright's review of *Their Eyes Were Watching God*, "Between Laughter and Tears," *New Masses*, October 5, 1937, pp. 22–23.

14. In Hurston's "Works in Progress for The Florida Negro," she privileges not language or music but sound: "Way back there when Hell wasn't no bigger than Maitland, man found out something about the laws of sound. . . . He found out that sounds could be assembled and manipulated and that such a collection of sound forms could become as definite and concrete as a war-axe or a food-tool. So he had language and song. Perhaps by some happy accident he found out about percussion sounds and spacing the intervals for tempo and rhythm. Anyway, it is evident that the sound-arts were the first inventions and that music and literature grew from the same root" (*Folklore* 876).

15. In *The Sonic Color Line,* Jennifer Stoever writes extensively about dialect as re-performance in her chapter on "Preserving 'Quare Sounds,' Conserving the 'Dark Past' The Jubilee Singers and Charles Chesnutt Reconstruct the Sonic Color Line." See 134–37.

16. Quoted in Evan Eisenberg's *The Recording Angel*, 102.

17. See Van Wyck Brooks, "On Creating a Usable Past," *Dial* 64 (April 11, 1918): 337–41.

18. In 2012, Lomax's foundation, the Association for Cultural Equity, began making Lomax's recordings available to the public on its website, www.culturalequity.org.

19. For more about the complex legacy of Lomax and the problematic politics behind projects like the Global Jukebox, see the special series "100 Years of

Lomax," ed. Tanya Clement, *Sounding Out! The Sound Studies Blog,* June 8, 2015, https://soundstudiesblog.com/category/100-years-of-lomax/.

20. Other recorded autobiographies include: Louis Armstrong's *A Musical Autobiography* (Decca, 1957), Lil Armstrong's *Satchmo and Me* (Riverside), Baby Dodds's *Talking and Drum Solos: Footnotes to Jazz, Vol. I* (Folkways, 1951), Art Hodes's *Recollections from the Past* (Solo Arts Records); Bunk Johnson's *This is Bunk Johnson Talking, Explaining to You the Early Days of New Orleans* (American Music), and Willie "the Lion" Smith's "Reminiscing the Piano Greats" (Vogue, 1959).

21. As Christopher Harlos argues, the genre question was already an issue for jazz autobiography, and "some of the handy and traditional distinctions (i.e., fiction/ nonfiction, biography/autobiography, written/oral) when superimposed on contemporary critical issues of race, class, and gender leave an array of alternatives to ponder" (161).

22. See Szwed 178.

23. See Lomax, *Mister Jelly Roll* 222–24.

24. Morton claimed to have written the song about 1905, but others credit Robert Hoffman 1909; Lead Belly was also known for the song.

25. For more on rhapsody, see Ong 23.

26. The records contained notes by Rudi Blesh, who also wrote the preface to Bechet's *Treat It Gentle.* Blesh compared the set of twelve albums to "chapters" in a book (Szwed "Liner Notes: Doctor Jazz" 24). It is worth noting that the tracks were edited into a new narrative order by historian Harriet Janis, with some titles edited, and some of the more obscene or violent tracks omitted. Blesh helped bring about the transfer of the recordings to LP in the early 1950s, and they were released again, in the same edited format, by Riverside in 1959. For a more complete account of the reissue history, see Szwed's "Doctor Jazz" liner notes to the Complete Library of Congress Recordings: Jelly Roll Morton (2005).

27. Later in this book, we will see that William S. Burroughs also uses this strange two-dot ellipsis. Walt Whitman also used two dot ellipses in his preface to *Leaves of Grass* (1855).

28. The description "gravel-throat" first appeared in 1942 in the *American Thesaurus of Slang.* See "Gravel" and "Gravelly" in the OED.

29. See Roland Barthes, "The Grain of the Voice," *Image, Music, Text.* Hill and Wang, 1977.

30. As Jennifer Stoever argues, however, such distinctions of the sonic color line are more often indicative of the cultural expectations of the white "listening ear" than of the sound itself (7).

31. I am using the term intermedia to delineate the status of *Mister Jelly Roll* as neither a record nor a book. The term has been used variously, but it has been

used most frequently to describe interdisciplinary genres of art, and especially 1960s neo-Dadaist new-media performance art by groups such as Fluxus and Hans Breder. See Hans Breder, Klaus-Peter Busse, *Intermedia: Enacting the Liminal* (2005).

32. See Lomax 115–18. The links between the two books are numerous, from Rudi Blesh's involvement in promoting both projects to the fact that both books were illustrated by the jazz album-cover artist David Stone Martin.

33. Bechet appeared on several of Lomax's radio programs over the years, including the "Hootenany" radio program on CBS on March 10, 1947. See "Sidney Bechet," www.culturalequity.org/alan-lomax/friends/bechet.

34. In consulting with Bechet experts who have searched for these tapes over the years, I was met with a general sense of despair and even speculation that perhaps the tapes are themselves a myth. And yet, evidence from the Charles Delaunay archive at the Bibliothèque Nationale de France confirms that the tapes indeed exist (or existed), though their present whereabouts remain unknown. It is worth noting, however, that after searching the catalogs, I have determined that these interviews are *not* located at the following archives: The John D. Reid Collection at the Arkansas Art Center, The John Ciardi collection at the Library of Congress, The John Ciardi Papers at Syracuse University, and the Charles Delaunay Papers at the Bibliothèque Nationale de France.

35. See letters between Ciardi, Bechet, and Delaunay 1951–52 located in the Charles Delaunay Collection, Département de l'audiovisuel, Bibliothèque nationale de France, boîte n° 26–27. See also John Chilton's *Sidney Bechet: Wizard of Jazz* (290–92); and Edward M. Cifelli's *John Ciardi: A Biography* (153–55).

36. From a letter from Charles Delaunay to Mark Patterson of Twayne Publishers Inc. dated April 8, 1959. Located in the Charles Delaunay Collection, Département de l'audiovisuel, Bibliothèque nationale de France, boîte n° 26.

37. In Paris, where he spent the latter part of his life in the 1950s, Bechet was a celebrity – even bigger than Elvis. As a result, a number of interviews were conducted for French radio with Bechet, and many of these recordings still exist, including a two-disc set rereleased by Sony Music in France titled *L'Histoire De Sidney Bechet* (2009). This collection includes interviews with Yves Salques, Frank Ténot, and Daniel Filipacchi (of radio Europe No. 1) from 1957 in which Bechet talks about his early life, covering much of the same material found in *Treat It Gentle*, interspersed with some of his most famous recordings for the Vogue record label. Transcripts of these interviews are located in the BnF's Charles Delaunay Archive, boîte n° 26.

38. There is a slight discrepancy between Flower's account of Reid's role and that described by Bechet's biographer, John Chilton. Flower says of Reid: "Sidney Bechet was first persuaded to tell his story some years ago by Miss Joan Reid, who succeeded in getting a very considerable amount of material on to tape" (v).

Chilton says: "With the help of Joan Williams ... Bechet began transferring his memoirs to paper, usually from recollections he had recorded on tape" (290). From Chilton's description, it is somewhat ambiguous whether Bechet may have made some of the recordings himself, without the aid of an interviewer. By 1951, it is presumed that a significant portion of the manuscript was complete (including the chapter about Bechet's grandfather Omar), and Bechet began talking to the poet John Ciardi about the possibility of publishing the book. Upon hearing of Bechet's project, Ciardi brought the book to the publishing house, Twayne, who subsequently hired him as editor (Cifelli 153). According to Ciardi's biography, the manuscript by Joan Reid was colored by her purple prose and intervening remarks. Ciardi felt that Reid's writing distracted from Bechet's unique voice, and he undertook the task of reworking Reid's transcripts by erasing her voice and conducting further interviews with Bechet. As Ciardi stated in a letter to his biographer about the manuscript he edited, "It's all Sidney's talk and talk I have put into his mouth" (154). Ciardi may have been somewhat bitter about his work on Bechet's book, given that Reid attempted to claim authorship and, for a while, halted the progress of the publication with a lawsuit; this may account for what at times seems like an exaggerated claim of influence over Bechet's text. When Reid threatened to sue, Twayne shelved the project and it was not until Cassell & Company Ltd. (Hill & Wang in the United States) picked up the manuscript and assigned Desmond Flower as editor that the book was finished.

39. The story was written most likely between 1955 and 1957 based on letters from the time.

40. The tendency of jazz musicians to acknowledge their multiple identities is not unique to Bechet. Charles Mingus would famously assert "I am three" in his autobiography *Beneath the Underdog* (Knopf, 1971).

41. My transcript draws from tape 071 in the Sidney Bechet collection at the Hogan Jazz Archives at Tulane University.

42. Jean-Luc Nancy writes that "to be listening is always to be on the *edge* of meaning ... as if the sound were precisely nothing else than this edge, this fringe, this margin." Meaning made of sound is thus "a meaning whose *sense* is supposed to be found in resonance, and only in resonance" (7).

43. Bryan Wagner, "Disarmed and Dangerous: The Strange Career of Bras-Coupé" (136–37).

44. Interestingly, the High John the Conqueror root was often used for hoodoo sexual spells, not unlike the one that Bechet describes in the Omar chapter.

45. Bechet was notorious among studio engineers; in a 1945 radio interview, he remarked, "'When it got to my chorus the needle would jump. I couldn't play the way I wanted to. The engineers would almost go crazy when they saw me coming into the studios. They'd say, 'Here comes trouble itself'" (qtd. in Chilton 61).

46. Instead, the Original Dixieland Jazz Band (an all-white ensemble) is credited with making the first jazz recording in 1917.

47. African Americans were frequently denied their lawful rights, and musical ownership was a legitimately contentious issue. Sheet music had only come under copyright in 1897, and the protection of recordings did not become codified into law until shockingly late in 1972. Unknown artists were frequently paid a flat fee of as little as $25 to make a recording and received no residuals. For a detailed history, see Tim Brooks, *Lost Sounds: Blacks and the Birth of the Recording Industry 1890–1919* (University of Illinois Press, 2004).

48. "Multitracking" as we currently think of it was not technically feasible until the use of tape recording in the studios in the late 1940s. Even then, it was not until 1956 when Les Paul helped develop the Ampex tape recorder (which was capable of recording eight parallel tracks) that multitracking became truly possible. (See David L. Morton Jr.'s *Sound Recording*, 141–51.) What Bechet talks about as making a "trick" record requires recording alongside the other record playing (a rather low-tech effect).

49. During the same recording session he also recorded a one-man-band version of "Blues of Bechet" but only recorded four instruments. For whatever reason, this recording seemed less controversial than the six-track "Sheik."

50. In the interview with Flower, Bechet does an amusing impression of Fats' signature voice that does not quite register on the page.

51. Moreover, since Bechet could not read or write music, he was improvising the arrangement as he went along. In an interview about the recording for *Afro-American,* he joked: "Man! that ends three months of torture, thinking about this session was giving me nightmares; I dreamed I was playing the whole Duke Ellington band." See "Sid Bechet Uses Six Instruments." *Afro-American (1893–1988)*, July 5, 1941, p. 13.

52. In her essay on Lomax's recording sessions with Morton, Marybeth Hamilton similarly conjectures whether we ought to call his recording session an "aural" history (*New Literary History* 728).

3 Press Play

1. Note that a wire recorder, as mentioned here, was an early form of magnetic recording and the precursor to tape and was introduced commercially in the United States in 1948.

2. See "On the Road: Present at the Creation," *Morning Edition*, NPR, September 9, 2002, https://seamus.npr.org/programs/morning/features/patc/ontheroad/index.html.

3. As McGurl details, "The Voice Project" and similar programs were used in places like the San Francisco Bay Area to affirm Black vernacular expression

and language. These community projects, along with neoslave narratives of the 1960s and 1970s, had ties to progressive education and the politics of self-expressive liberation (260–67). For writers of color, claiming a voice is a political response to silencing (236).

4. N. Katherine Hayles points to the paradox of tape as "a mode of voice inscription at once permanent and mutable" (77).

5. Karin Bijsterveld and Annelies Jacobs have written, "Prior to the 1950s, tape recorders were almost exclusively made for professional and semi-professional markets" (Bijsterveld and Jacobs 28). However, 1953 was a watershed year for tape as it reached one million users – it was also the year RCA Victor introduced a consumer tape recorder. See "Brew Disk-To-Tape Revolution – 1,000,000 Homes Have Machines," *Variety*, September 16, 1953, p. 1, www.archive.org/s tream/variety191-1953-09#page/n144/mode/1up.

6. Magnetic recording was first developed by Valdemar Poulsen of Denmark in 1898.

7. Karin Bijsterveld notes that the tape recorder was a failure in terms of sales and marketing, "since its actual use significantly diverged from the use promoted by manufacturers. It simply did not become the sound souvenir device its makers originally had in mind. Only one of the uses of the tape recorder – to record and replay music – fostered the later rise and success of the compact cassette recorder" (40).

8. In the course of developing tape, a number of different media for making magnetic recordings were tested, including steel drums and steel wire (Morton 114).

9. Tape recording speeds work in multiples or submultiples of $7\frac{1}{2}$ inches per second (ips), thus $^{15}/_{16}$ ips was an economical tape speed appropriate for speech, $1^7/_8$ for music, $7\frac{1}{2}$ for professional use, or up to 30 for master recordings (Staab 20).

10. In his 1950 tape manual, A. C. Shaney made a number of arguments in favor of tape, even asserting that magnetic tape recorders were better for editing sound than film because the splices were silent and did not have to be specially treated and edited out (10).

11. By passing the wire or tape over a similar magnet head, "the varying magnetic patterns generate a corresponding current in the coil of the electro-magnet, thus giving us once again an electrical signal which we can convert into sound, by passing it through an amplifier unit and into a loudspeaker" (Staab16).

12. Frank da Cruz, "IBM 701: The First Magnetic Tape Drive for Computer Data Storage," July 2003, www.columbia.edu/cu/computinghistory/701-tape.html.

13. For more about play, see Pierre Schaeffer's concept of *jouer* in *In Search of Concrete Music*, trans. Christine North and John Dack (2012).

14. See Cage, 3; Eisenberg 107. Cage borrowed the concept of "organization of sound" from Edgard Varèse, who was in turn inspired by Ferruccio Busoni.

15. As Neal told his wife Carolyn Cassady, he "bought a tape recorder because . . . both he and Jack 'understood the power of voices'" (C. Cassady 125).

16. The Webster Electric Ekotape pamphlet recommends uses for the Ekotape, including "rehearsing and recording speeches, radio shows, auditions, broadcasts. Teaching languages, speech correction, music appreciation, voice training. Sales training and sales presentations; meetings and conferences." See "Webster Ekotape 101," Tapeheads.net, September 23, 2012, www .tapeheads.net/showthread.php?p=261059.

17. The only recordings that survived this period amount to little more than 15 minutes of tape fragments made at the Cassady's San Jose, California, house in 1952. A cassette tape copy of this tape made by Carolyn Cassady is located at the British Museum in their "Beats and Friends" Audio-Visual Collection. Excerpts from these recordings were played on NPR in 2002 as part of a special segment about *On the Road*: www.npr.org/programs/morning/fea tures/patc/ontheroad/. See also O'Hagen, "Kerouac Crosses the Line," *New York Review of Books*, March 21, 2013, p. 17; and Shapcott, 232.

18. The original typed transcripts are located in the Jack Kerouac Papers at the New York Public Library's Henry W. and Albert A. Berg Collection of English and American Literature. With very few exceptions, the transcripts are included verbatim in *Visions of Cody*. Exceptions include explicitly sexualized stories about public figures, including Billie Holiday and the daughter of the editor of the *New York Times*.

19. In Ginsberg's letter to Kerouac, he softens the tone considerably, but still tells Jack that the new *On the Road* was unpublishable. See Kerouac, *Selected Letters, Volume I*, 179.

20. *Visions of Cody* was not published in full until 1972, after Kerouac's death. New Directions had released a limited edition 120-page excerpt from *Visions of Cody* in 1960, but as the dust jacket explained, the full-length version was deemed "unpublishable" at the time. Other excerpts from *Cody* appeared in *Playboy* (December 1959), the *Transatlantic Review 9* (1962), and elsewhere.

21. In *Action Writing: Jack Kerouac's Wild Form* (2006), Michael Hrebeniak wrote that *Cody* was "the consummation of [Kerouac's] search" for his own form, and argues that, "what emerges is a work that cannot be subsumed into a single interpretative position or philosophy" (61–62).

22. Kerouac's "Spontaneous Prose" draws on a number of poetic lineages, from Ezra Pound's imagism to Charles Olson's projective verse.

23. For more about Warhol's transcription practices, see Paul Benzon, "Lost in Transcription: Postwar Typewriting Culture, Andy Warhol's Bad Book, and

the Standardization of Error," *PMLA: Publications of the Modern Language Association of America*, vol. 125, no. 1, 2010, pp. 92–106, 264.

24. Justin Thomas Trudeau argues that Kerouac's transcription "fails to capture the immediacy of the relationship as it is transferred to the written page" (339).

25. In a letter to Allen Ginsberg, Kerouac described the process of sketching, saying, "You just have to purify your mind and let it pour the words (which effortless angels of the vision fly when you stand in front of reality) and write with 100% personal honesty both psychic and social, etc. and slap it all down shameless, willy-nilly, rapidly until sometimes I got so inspired I lost consciousness I was writing" (qtd. in Johnson 419). This desire to lose consciousness, to enter a trancelike state, to escape writing, is also in line with what Ann Charters says about how Kerouac's drug use was a way to get at "the center of the universe and reduce it to vibrations" (Charters 144).

26. Belletto views the hybrid text as a negotiation between historical objectivity and radical subjectivity and asserts that Kerouac "thought tapes would allow him to be a better historian" (196). See also Charters 145.

27. "Completely Verbatim" transcripts of the tapes (30.11–30.15) are available in the Jack Kerouac Papers, Henry W. and Albert A. Berg Collection of English and American Literature, New York Public Library.

28. "Crazy Rhythm" (1937, Victor) with Coleman Hawkins (tenor), Benny Carter (alto), Django Reinhardt (guitar), Stephane Grappelli (piano), and saxophonists Andre Ekyan (alto) and Alix Combelle (tenor), Tommy Benford (drums), Eugène d'Hellemes (bass).

29. The recording of "Crazy Rhythm" is notable for the way it anticipates the distinctive sounds of bebop, and one could argue that part of what Jack and Cody are listening for is bop's origin moment. Coleman Hawkins recorded "Crazy Rhythm" in 1937 in Paris with Benny Carter and an all-star lineup that included Django Reinhardt. The record was cut two years before the official beginning of bebop – which was, incidentally, the year Kerouac arrived in New York and began frequenting Minton's and other Harlem jazz clubs. It was a time when big bands were still the most popular configuration, but the stripped-down band on this recording is more akin to the smaller ensembles that would drive the new sound.

30. According to the *New Grove Dictionary of Jazz*, "to play 'outside' or 'out' is to depart, in improvisation, from the harmonic structure of the theme. The term came into use in the early 1960s, in conjunction with its antonym, 'inside,' to describe the playing of musicians who brought into performances of hard bop and modal jazz some of the harmonic license of free jazz; the outstanding exponent of playing outside was Eric Dolphy." See "Outside," *The New Grove Dictionary of Jazz*, 2nd ed., ed. Barry Kernfeld. Oxford University Press, 2002.

31. These particular "riffing" sessions are located on disc 10B, John Clellon Holmes recordings, 1949–51 and 1968, Kent State University Library Special Collections, Kent, Ohio.

32. Derrida would later write about Hamlet's ghost as the *revenant* in *Spectres* (1989).

33. This ritual quality of recorded speech is something Ginsberg knew something about. On disc 11A, he and Kerouac riff and rhyme semi-sensically on the open "o" and plosive "p" and "b" sounds of the words "*a piccione*" (Italian for pigeon) and "a boney type bird." (Disc 11A, John Clellon Holmes recordings, 1949–51 and 1968, Kent State University Library Special Collections, Kent, OH.)

34. Earlier in "Imitation of the Tape," the repetition of "moan" takes on biblical proportions: "Go thou across the ground; go moan for man; go moan, go groan, go groan alone go roll your bones, alone; go thou and be little beneath my sight; go thou, and be minute and as seed in the pod, but the pod the pit, world a Pod, universe a Pit; go thou, go thou, die hence; and of Cody report you well and truly" (295).

35. During his stay, Kerouac wrote *Doctor Sax*, an early version of which he is said to have composed entirely in taped monologue. According to Ann Charters, while Kerouac was living with the Cassadys, "into the machine he delivered a two-hour taped monologue about being thirteen years old in Lowell. One hour of the tape was the entire tale of *Doctor Sax*" (148).

36. Robin Lydenberg asserts, "Individual identity is not destroyed in the cut-up text but expanded; depersonalization of the text is viewed as a necessary step toward a liberation from the isolation and immobility of individual ownership" (427).

37. All citations of *The Ticket That Exploded* refer to the 1994 Grove Press edition.

38. Whereas Kerouac's scatology echoed jazz, Burroughs's implies actual excrement.

39. The possible racial underpinnings of this group are made explicit when the narrator Lee points out the White Hunters are an "equivocal" group: "Were they white supremacists or an anti-white movement . . . ? The extreme right or the far left . . . ?" They were, by their own definition, a *nonorganization* (9).

40. Timothy Murphy compares "Silver Smoke of Dreams" to the works of Babbit and Stockhausen, and especially the children's voices in Stockhausen's "Gesang" (Murphy 217).

41. Here is the passage as it appears in *Ticket*: "toneless voice in San Francisco? . . belong to the wind . . silver morning smoke in the desolate markets . . sure you dream up Billy who bound word for it . . in the beginning there was no Iam . . stale smoke of dreams it was Iam . . haunted your morning and will you other stale morning smell of other Iam . . no Iam there . . no one silences . . There

was no morning .. sure late Billy .. Iam the stale Billy .. I lived your life a long
time ago .. sad shadow whistles" (202).

42. See Lydenberg and Skerl, 4–5.

43. Robin Lydenberg compares Burroughs's attitudes toward language to those of
Roland Barthes (in *Mythologies* and *S/Z*) (415–19).

44. Marshall McLuhan's theory also helps to explain reading the *text* versus
reading the *message:* "The message, it seemed, was about the 'content,' as
people used to ask what a painting was *about.* Yet they never thought to ask
what a melody was about, nor what a house or dress was about. In such
matters, people retained some sense of the whole pattern, of form and
function as unity" (*Understanding Media* 13).

45. Burroughs's interest in unsettling *word locks* has been connected to his
interest in the work of Alfred Korzybski, the semanticist. In 1939,
Burroughs heard Korzybski's lectures on semantics in Chicago, where he
warned of the psychological problems that could arise from the misuse of
language and language's mediating role in our experience of reality. See
Russell 66–67.

46. "You can cut into *Naked Lunch* at any intersection point. .... I have written
many prefaces" (*Naked Lunch* 203).

47. Timothy Murphy makes a similar observation about the trilogy, noting that
"many passages, both of cut-ups and of linear narrative, are repeated
throughout all three novels and act like refrains or choruses to unify, to
some small extent, the fractured story" (107).

48. Some of the songs that are immediately recognizable in the passage are: "Do
you love me?" (1962, recorded by The Contours for Motown), "Auld Lang
Syne" (traditional, poem by Robert Burns 1788), "Stardust" (1927, a Hoagy
Carmichael standard considered to be one of the most popular songs of the
twentieth century), "Tell Laura I Love Her" (1960, a pop-ballad made popular
by Ray Peterson), "My Blue Heaven" (1924, a standard by Walter Donaldson,
popularized by Fats Domino in 1956), "St. Louis Blues" (1914, a traditional
blues by W. C. Handy).

49. "I spent a year as a copywriter in this small advertising agency. .... I've recently
thought a great deal about advertising. After all, they're doing the same sort of
thing. They are concerned with the precise manipulation of word and image"
(http://theparisreview.org).

50. In a 1969 interview with Danie Odier, Burroughs acknowledged, "Of course,
you can do all sorts of things on tape-recorders which can't be done anywhere
else – effects of simultaneity, echoes, speed-ups, slow-downs, playing three
tracks at once, and so forth. There are all sorts of things you can do on a tape
recorder that cannot possibly be indicated on a printed page. The concept of
simultaneity cannot be indicated on a printed page except very crudely

through the use of columns, and even then the reader must follow one column at a time. We're used to reading from left to right and then back, and this conditioning is not easy to break down" (*The Job* 13).

51. Burroughs had different views about the relationship between traditional literary forms like the novel and new media forms. In 1969 he commented, "I think that the novelistic form is probably outmoded and that we may look forward perhaps to a future in which people do not read at all or read only illustrated books and magazines or some abbreviated form of reading matter" (*The Job* 11).

52. The 2013 Grove Press "restored" edition of *The Ticket That Exploded* cut the "invisible generation" epilogue for reasons that editor Oliver Harris acknowledges are idiosyncratic, citing only that it was added in the 1967 edition. This seems a rather unfortunate decision given that Burroughs himself had suggested the addition of the piece in his own revision, and it has become critical to the reception of that novel.

53. Burroughs was also interested in a phenomenon called "infrasound," which was explored by the military as a possible weapon, but Burroughs thought it had implications for music as well. Infrasound, he offered in his 1972 *Rolling Stone* interview, could be used "to produce very definite psycho-physiological effects in the audience, reader, viewer, as the case may be" (Palmer 52).

54. Burroughs read excerpts from *Naked Lunch* and *Nova Express* on *Saturday Night Live* on November 7, 1981, www.openculture.com/2012/02/william_s_burroughs_on_saturday_night_live_1981.html.

55. As Evan Eisenberg rightly points out George Martin, the producer and arranger credited with crafting the Beatles' recorded sound, helped give "dramatic continuity" to albums like *Sgt. Pepper's* – albums that elevated "kitsch into Dada" (104).

56. See Victor Bockris, *With William Burroughs: A Report from the Bunker*: "Burroughs: ... This was when the Beatles were just getting into the possibilities of overlaying, running backward, the full technical possibilities of the tape recorder. And Ian was a brilliant technician along those lines.

   Ian met Paul McCartney and Paul put up the money for this flat which was at 34 Montagu Square ... I saw Paul several times. The three of us talked about the possibilities of the tape recorder. He'd just come in and work on his 'Eleanor Rigby.' Ian recorded his rehearsals. I saw the song taking shape. Once again, not knowing much about music, I could see that he knew what he was doing. He was very pleasant and very prepossessing. Nice-looking young man, hardworking" (72).

57. In a recorded interview, Barry Miles also remembered Burroughs' presence while Paul McCartney was writing "Eleanor Rigby" and Paul's feelings that

Burroughs was a "mentor" figure. www.lawrence.com/audioclips/4831/. See Barry Miles, *El Hombre Invisible*, 148.

4 The Stereophonic Poetics of Langston Hughes and Amiri Baraka

1. This chapter is derived in part from an article titled "Black Sonic Space and the Stereophonic Poetics of Amiri Baraka's *It's Nation Time*," published in *Sound Studies* on February 1, 2016.

2. See Auslander, 60.

3. Caroline Bassett writes about this phenomenon as it relates to mobile phone technology in "How Many Movements?," *The Auditory Culture Reader*, ed. Michael Bull and Les Back, 343–55, Berg, 2003.

4. See Lowney, 562–64.

5. In a conversation in *Small Axe* from July 2014, Alex Weheliye has rightly reemphasized the need to acknowledge the centrality of Black culture to scholarly conceptions of modernity "not by removing the specificity of black life but by using the liminal yet integral spatiotemporal positioning of blackness as a way to call into question modernity as such" (181).

6. See *Small Axe*'s discussion of Black sound studies in Nyong'o, Henriques, Weheliye, 171–90.

7. Jaji does offer illuminating thoughts on the unique uses of stereo in the *son et lumière* show staged off the coast of Dakar during the World Festival of Negro Arts (Festival Mondial des Arts Nègres) in 1966, which used light and stereo sound to illuminate the stories of historic sites of the slave trade (89–92).

8. In 1948, Columbia records released the 33⅓ rpm long-playing disc, and, in 1949, RCA Victor released its 45 rpm seven-inch disc; both claimed to be "high fidelity."

9. In the introduction to their collection of essays *Living Stereo: Histories and Cultures of Multichannel Sound* (2015), Paul Théberge, Kyle Devine, and Tom Everett claim the term "sound stage" to define stereophonic space because "staging places an emphasis on the ways in which we might think of stereo not simply as a static space in which sounds are represented (or reproduced), but as a more performative space that is produced through a variety of social and technical practices and, also, a space in which other cultural practices are enabled" (5). For further reading on the sound image and sound localization, see Damaske 5–10; Goldstein 376–90; and Yost 173–84.

10. Rick Altman chronicles this period in the history of cinema, noting J. P. Maxfield of Western Electric's assertion that "sound scale must always match image scale" (49).

11. Andrew R. Boone reported that the development of the sound for *Fantasia* was in many ways the brainchild of the conductor Leopold Stokowski (65). Just the year before, Stokowski had collaborated with Bell Labs to host a demonstration at Carnegie Hall of stereo recordings of the Philadelphia Symphony Orchestra.

12. Jean Baudrillard defines simulacra against simulation because simulation presupposes reality. Simulacra are "models of a real without origin or reality: a hyperreal" (3). For more on the stereo and the sublime, see Barry 116–18.

13. See, e.g., Hughes's illustrated children's book *Rhythm* (1954).

14. A recording of the concert is available, see Goodbye Newport Blues, July 3, 1960, Wolfgang's, www.wolfgangs.com/music/goodbye-newport-blues/audi o/20020381-17613.html.

15. When large crowds (est. 3000) were turned away from the festival on July 2, 1960, with a lineup featuring Oscar Peterson, Lambert, Hendricks, and Ross, Ray Charles, and others, they began to tear down the fences and oust patrons from their seats. The police began blasting the crowd with fire hoses and called in the National Guard to try to quiet the rioters. See Rampersad, *The Life of Langston Hughes,* 2:315–16.

16. These and other early drafts of *Ask Your Mama* are part of the Langston Hughes Collection at Yale's Beineke Rare Book and Manuscript Library, JWJ MSS 26, Boxes 271–72.

17. See references to Hughes's travels with his record player in *I Wonder as I Wander*, pp. 12, 21, 131, 133.

18. Hughes recorded a series of albums for Folkways in the 1950s, including *The Story of Jazz* (1954) and *The Dream Keeper* (1955). He also recorded an album for Black Forum, *Writers of the Revolution,* with Margaret Danner, that was released posthumously in 1970.

19. Langston Hughes Papers, James Weldon Johnson Collection in the Yale Collection of American Literature, Beinecke Rare Book and Manuscript Library.

20. In the press materials, the use of color is described more explicitly: "Langston Hughes, the author of *Ask Your Mama: 12 Moods for Jazz,* says that his poetry is influenced by both traditional and contemporary jazz. He has certainly been a partisan of Duke Ellington, whose *Black, Brown and Beige* he admires. Since the moods of his poetry are in those three Ellington colors, and also incorporate the blues, the format of the new Hughes book published this month by Knopf is one of alternating brown and blue ink on beige paper, with a kaleidoscopic dustjacket and a cubistic six-color binding. Visually it is one of the most striking books of the fall season. Its design is by Vincent Torre" (Press Material from the Langston Hughes Papers. James Weldon

Johnson Collection in the Yale Collection of American Literature, Beinecke Rare Book and Manuscript Library. JWJ MSS 26, Boxes 271–72, folder 4472).

21. Press Material from The Langston Hughes Collection at Yale's Beineke Rare Book and Manuscript Library, JWJ MSS 26, Boxes 271–72, folder 4472.

22. Hughes said the music was a description of what he heard while writing the poem. However, as early drafts show, the musical descriptions were only conceived as a second column at the point when Hughes was attempting to put together a first reading of the poem with musicians at The Market Place in New York, February 1961. Initially, what Hughes called "Musical Themes" were listed at the very end of the poetic text. The "Music Cues" were added to the right hand margin, it would seem, for the purposes of the musicians following the "score" at The Market Place reading. Interestingly, a copy of this early iteration of the poem with the music cues was sent to Amiri Baraka along with the musicians involved in the performance. The musical themes first appear in Draft 11, January 18–20, 1961. See Langston Hughes Papers. James Weldon Johnson Collection in the Yale Collection of American Literature, Beinecke Rare Book and Manuscript Library. JWJ MSS 26, Box 271–72.

23. In 1962, Dave Brubeck worked with Louis Armstrong and created a musical about the state department tours and the civil rights movement called *The Real Ambassadors*, which included a song called "Cultural Exchange."

24. As John Lowney has noted, Hughes was increasingly involved in promoting cultural production from the African diaspora during the 1960s through his editorial work and by participating in festivals such as the 1961 American Society of African Culture Festival in Lagos (Lowney 565).

25. Our understanding of auditory space is also a function of the acoustical architecture and the way our ears process the resonance of sounds as they reflect off different surfaces (including our ear canal and the pinna). See Goldstein, 392–93.

26. Although Hughes never explicitly identifies Dinah as Dinah Washington in the poem's text, in the files for the book's publicity, he includes a list of "Persons Named" as a glossary of who each name "could be," including "Dinah–could be Dinah Washington" (Box 272, Folder 4473). Of course, the insistence on "could be" implies a desire to leave the reference open to other possibilities as well – for instance, "Dinah" in the Louis Armstrong song, or "someone's in the kitchen with Dinah" from the folk tune "I've Been Working on the Railroad." After all, *Dinah* was not Dinah Washington's real name – it was Ruth Jones. Dinah was most likely chosen for her by producer Joe Glaser.

27. Hughes's fears of the whitewashing of Black culture were first expressed in his essay "The Negro Artist and the Racial Mountain," which he wrote for *The*

Nation in 1926. Remarking upon his encounter with a young man who told him "I want to be a poet, not a Negro poet," Hughes answers that African Americans should embrace their identity and find value in Black vernacular forms.

28. Austin Graham suggests that Hughes's use of the popular AAB form of the blues in his poems invited his readers to sing (141–45).

29. Contemporary performances of *Ask Your Mama* have incorporated actual remix into the piece. Laura Karpman's 2009 composition in collaboration with Jesse Norman and the Roots, for example, incorporates the Buddah Records recording of Hughes reading *Ask Your Mama*, as well as samples of recordings Hughes references in the poem.

30. See Scanlon 48, 62.

31. "Ça ira. *The Concise Oxford Dictionary of Music*, 5th ed., 2007.

32. Karpman spoke in detail about the piece in a feature for the PBS News Hour. "Jessye Norman, the Roots Team Up for Langston Hughes' 'Ask Your Mama,'" *PBS News Hour*, August 27, 2009, www.pbs.org/newshour/arts/jes sye-norman-the-roots-team-up-for-langston-hughes-ask-your-mama.

33. The title essay of Joan Didion's *The White Album* (1979) is notable for deriving its title from the Beatles' 1968 self-titled album without ever actually talking about it, and yet, the form of the essay, which comprises loosely related chapters or *tracks* clearly operates much the way an album does.

34. The founding of the Black Arts Repertory Theatre and School by Amiri Baraka in 1965 is considered by most to be the catalyzing moment for the Black Arts movement. This same year, Baraka wrote "Black Art," which he also recorded with Sonny Murray on *Sonny's Time Now* (Jihad Records 1967).

35. Folkways Records, established in 1948 by Moses Asch, promoted spoken word as well as folk music, but Caedmon Records, founded in 1952, is generally thought responsible for popularizing the poetry LP as a mainstream, middle-class commodity.

36. The eroding distinction between recording and text was even more evident in jazz circles where recordings had already gained status as texts, especially for the purposes of learning music. See Monson, 126; Bayley, 4.

37. See Collins and Crawford, 9–11.

38. According to Lorenzo Thomas, "among the factors that influenced the developmental direction of Black Arts poetry were (1) the model of African American music – particularly jazz; (2) an interest in finding and legitimizing an 'authentic' African American vernacular speech; and (3) the material or physical context of Black Arts poetry readings" ("Neon Griot" 310).

39. Some of the albums included Maya Angelou's *The Poetry of Maya Angelou* (1969); Jayne Cortez's *Celebrations and Solitude* (1974) with bassist Richard

Davis; Nikki Giovanni's *Truth Is on Its Way* (1971) and *Like a Ripple on the Pond* (1973); and Sarah Webster Fabio's *Boss Soul* (1972).

40. Pat Thomas's *Listen, Whitey! The Sights and Sounds of the Black Power Movement* (2012) recounts this period in some detail and notes that Gaye's "What's Going On" was initially blocked by Motown's Berry Gordy as too controversial and was released only at Gaye's insistence (12).

41. *It's Nation Time* had been out of print for 46 years until its vinyl reissue by Motown in 2018. The reissue was newly mixed in stereo by engineer and producer Russell Elevado.

42. From the track "All in the Street" on *It's Nation Time* (1972).

43. Rev. Jesse Jackson, for instance, advocated a Black political party. The Black Panther Party's Platform (1966) called for "a United Nations-supervised plebiscite to be held throughout the black colony in which only black colonial subjects will be allowed to participate for the purpose of determining the will of black people as to their national destiny." See *Ten-Point Program and Platform of the Black Panther Party*, October 1966, www2.iath.virginia.edu/sixties/HTML_docs/Resources/Primary/Manifestos/Panther_platform.html.

44. In *Imagined Communities* Benedict Anderson defines the nation as "an imagined political community – and imagined as both inherently limited and sovereign" (6). Such communities are *imagined* "because the members of even the smallest nation will never know most of their fellow-members, meet them, or even hear of them, yet in the minds of each lives the image of their communion" (6).

45. For more about the decline of CAP and the internal battles between the Marxists and the cultural nationalists, see Woodard, 219–54; Smethurst, 87–88.

46. See Larry Neal's description of Black Arts as it relates to Black Power in Collins and Crawford, 7.

47. On the album, *It's Nation Time,* the track is located on side A at minute 3:05.

48. For more about the disorienting effects of these recordings, see Ian MacDonald's *Revolution in the Head: The Beatles' Records and the Sixties* (Penguin Random House, 2007).

49. Like many moments on this album, the space is inherently gendered, and female voices are relegated to the background (not surprising, given the well-known misogyny of Black Nationalism in the 1970s).

50. For more about Sun Ra and issues of space, see Wald, 673–96, 862.

51. *The Black Mass* (1966) is a play that explores the Jacoub myth in which Jacoub creates a Frankenstein-esque white monster whose greatest flaw is an awareness of time. See Baraka, *Four Black Revolutionary Plays*. See also Woodard, 209.

52. *It's Nation Time*, side A, 5:59.

53. *It's Nation Time,* side A, 8:10.
54. *It's Nation Time,* side A, 10:59.
55. *It's Nation Time,* side A, 17:04.
56. Rev. Jesse Jackson recalled, "I had drawn much of the strength of Nationtime from a poem written by LeRoi Jones, Amiri Baraka at that time. The sense of people saying, 'What's Happening?' . . . Say, . . . 'It's Nationtime, it's time to come together. It's time to organize politically" (Woodard 209).
57. *It's Nation Time,* side B, 12:35.
58. Lytle Shaw also notes that Baraka's sounds here also recall the SAC air-raid sirens he would have encountered as Seargent Jones. See Lytle Shaw, *Narrowcast: Poetry and Audio Research*, Stanford, 2018, pp. 175–77.
59. *It's Nation Time,* side B, 14:58.

5 From Cut-up to Mashup

1. See Mark Amerika, *Remix the Book* (2011), Lawrence Lessig, *Remix: Making Art and Commerce Thrive in the Hybrid Economy* (2008), Jonathan Lethem, "The Ecstasy of Influence" (2007), Eduardo Navas, *Remix Theory the Aesthetics of Sampling* (2012), DJ Spooky (aka Paul D. Miller), *Rhythm Science* (2004).
2. The *Oxford English Dictionary* defines *Remix* (n) first as "1. Sound Recording. A new version of a recording in which the separate instrumental or vocal tracks are rebalanced or recombined; (now also) a reinterpretation or reworking, often quite radical, of an existing music recording, typically produced by altering the rhythm and instrumentation; a commercial release of such a recording." The Merriam-Webster Dictionary similarly defines *Remix* (n) as "a variant of an original recording (as of a song) made by rearranging or adding to the original."
3. The distinctions made between the terms remix and mashup are somewhat nebulous and continue to be debated, with mashup generally considered a subset of remix. For those who distinguish between the two, the difference is primarily one of how many recordings are incorporated – remix referring to a new version of a single song with mashup comprising two or more recordings.
4. Margie Borschke has similarly argued that "[remix] has come to be used as shorthand for many modes of digital expression; it can be used to describe media that is made from existing media and it can also be offered to explain the influence of digital technologies on cultural practices and artifacts" (35). Margie Borschke, "Rethinking the Rhetoric of Remix," *Media International Australia*, vol. 141, no. 1, 2011, pp. 17–25.
5. For a more thorough discussion of the inter- and intratextual qualities of remix, see Walter Everett, "'If You're Gonna Have a Hit': Intratextual Mixes and Edits of Pop Recordings," *Popular Music*, vol. 29, no. 2, 2010, pp. 229–50.

6. This anecdote is important to how Questlove talks about the history of the music, and he has repeated it elsewhere in interviews and in chapter 5 of his recent book *Creative Quest* (2018).

7. Questlove's riff on Roland Barthes is more impressionistic than accurate, echoing Barthes' collapse of writer and reader in *S/Z*. Barthes argues, for example, that "the goal of literary work (of literature as work) is to make the reader no longer a consumer, but a producer of the text" (4). What Questlove calls a brick, Barthes calls a block: "We shall therefore star the text, separating, in the manner of a minor earthquake, the blocks of signification of which reading grasps only the smooth surface, imperceptibly soldered by the movement of sentences, the flowing discourse of narration, the 'naturalness' of ordinary language" (13).

8. During the period that the Roots were working on *Things Fall Apart* at Electric Lady Studios, Questlove was also collaborating with Common on his album *Like Water for Chocolate* (2000), which takes its title from the 1989 novel (and 1993 film) by Mexican author Laura Esquivel.

9. Some claim that the term disc jockey was coined by radio personality Walter Winchell in 1935 to describe radio host Martin Block, but the first printed use of the term was in *Variety* in 1941 (OED). According to the OED, the shortened appellation "DJ" (or deejay), referring to a radio host, appeared in *Billboard* in 1946.

10. "The process of stripping songs down to their essential components must be understood as substantially intertwined with the practice of deejaying; while studio engineers were beginning to use the mixing board to open songs up from the inside, their work was clearly prefigured by the deejays who destroyed song form from the outside" (Veal 55–56).

11. For a provocative assessment of 1970s disco and remix as avant-garde artistic practice, see Tan Lin, "Disco as Operating System, Part One," *Criticism*, vol. 50, no. 1, 2008, pp. 83–100.

12. For a thoughtful meditation on the mixtape form, see Javon Johnson's editorial introduction to *The End of Chiraq: A Literary Mixtape* (Northwestern, 2018).

13. One of the first lawsuits to contest sampling was *Grand Upright Music, Ltd v. Warner Bros. Records Inc.*, 780 F. Supp. 182 (SDNY 1991). In this case, Gilbert O'Sullivan (of Warner Bros.) sued Biz Markie for sampling "Alone Again (Naturally)."

14. Zara Dinnen has argued that Jonathan Lethem's essay "The Ecstasy of Influence" offers a possible model for this new type of configurable literature. See Dinnen, "In the Mix: The Potential Convergence of Literature and New Media in JonathanLethem's 'The Ecstasy of Influence,'" *Journal of Narrative Theory*, vol. 42, no. 2, 2012, pp. 212–30.

15. Although I have limited my examples of literary remix to two case studies that actively borrow the term remix, one can find elements of sampling and other

forms of remix aesthetics across a range of contemporary works of literature, from Kathy Acker's novel *Blood and Guts in High School* (1984), which samples from *The Scarlet Letter*, to the Flarf poetry of writers such as Kenneth Goldsmith, whose book *The Weather* (2005) features poetry taken from radio weather reports.

16. Reviews of the earlier edition frequently commented on the bloated form of *To Repel Ghosts*. One such review in *The Nation* called the 300-page volume "overstuffed," finding its "riffs" repetitive and the rhythms of its tercets "monotonous" (Palatella 32).

17. As John Taylor's review in *Poetry* notes, "Young employs obscure biographical details that only insiders can comprehend" (97). John Taylor. "Short Reviews: To Repel Ghosts," *Poetry*, vol. 180, no. 2, 2002, pp. 96–97.

18. James Van der Zee's photo of Basquiat appears on the back cover of Kevin Young's *To Repel Ghosts: The Remix*.

19. "Most Kingz" (2011) by Jay-Z featured Chris Martin and was written in collaboration with DJ Green Lantern. Notably, it samples Run DMC's "Down with the King" (1993) – a song which itself famously samples "Where Do I Go" from the Broadway musical *Hair*.

20. Most of the extant criticism about *Invisible Monsters* (and the Remix) focuses on the role of identity in the novel, and in particular the narrator's struggle to find a stable sense of identity. See *Chuck Palahniuk: Fight Club, Invisible Monsters, Choke*, ed. Francisco Collado-Rodríguez (Bloomsbury, 2013); David McCracken, *Chuck Palahniuk, Parodist: Postmodern Irony in Six Transgressive Novels*, McFarland, 2016; Rfuardo Mendieta, "Surviving American Culture: On Chuck Palahniuk," *Philosophy and Literature*, vol. 29 no. 2, 2005, pp. 394–408.

21. That reviews refer to the novel remix as a "director's cut" stems in part from the promotion materials released for the book by the publisher W. W. Norton. See http://books.wwnorton.com/books/Invisible-Monsters-Remix/.

22. See, e.g., the Electronic Literature Organization's (ELO) collected volumes of electronic literature (Volume 3, February 2016 includes several "remixes"). https://eliterature.org/.

23. In an interview with *Rolling Stone*, Madonna recalls writing the song while working on the movie *Dick Tracy* and also going to the club Sound Factory. A gay club that specialized in underground music, Sound Factory also featured a Runway, where dancers performed the stylized moves of runway models (Scaggs). For more about runway and vogueing at the Sound Factory, see MTV, *Runway at the Sound Factory – NYC 1993*, www.youtube.com/wat ch?v=AoauLqqD9c8.

24. These lyrics and others are from "Vogue" on Madonna's *I'm Breathless* (Warner Bros., 1990).

25. In Butler's formulation, "interiority is an effect and function of a decidedly social discourse," which is to say, a kind of illusion (2548). Just as drag performance is an important aspect of Butler's concept of gender performativity, drag features as an important element in the novel. While Brandy Alexander is not in drag *per se* as a result of undergoing gender reassignment surgery (partially anyway), her performative approach to gender and the self borrows from drag aesthetics. David McCracken also draws the connection between Butler's gender performativity and *Invisible Monsters*, arguing that Shannon ultimately gives her role to her brother Shane/Brandy Alexander (122). See Judith Butler, "Gender Trouble," *The Norton Anthology of Theory and Criticism*, 2nd ed., ed. Vincent B. Leitch, W. W. Norton, 2010, and David McCracken, *Chuck Palahniuk, Parodist: Postmodern Irony in Six Transgressive Novels*, McFarland, 2016.

26. Ingrid Lunden, "Storytelling App Wattpad Raises $51M at a $398M Valuation," http://social.techcrunch.com/2018/01/17/storytelling-app-wattpad -raises-51m-at-a-398m-valuation/.

27. "In 2013, Amazon launched Kindle Worlds, a program in which fans could write and sell fic with the permission of, and according to, guidelines set by the original creators or copyright holders. Any sales are split three ways between the fan, the brand owner, and Amazon. Kindle Worlds is widely considered a bust, partly because the participating properties are not very enticing" (Miller "Fanfiction"). According to Amazon's website, the program is now defunct.

28. "We Invented the Remix . . . Redux – Fanlore," https://fanlore.org/wiki/W e_Invented_the_Remix . . . _Redux.

29. Lawrence Lessig has been one of the chief activists of the "copyleft," urging the reform of copyright laws in the United States.

A Post-Electric Postscript: Recording and Remix Onstage

1. For examples of reviews that discuss *Mr. Burns* as a remix or mashup, see Jane Howard, "'Mr Burns' Is The Wild and Loving Theatre Production," and Lauren Smart, "In Mr. Burns: A Post-Electric Play, It's Marge and Homer at the End of the World."

2. The play debuted in 2012 at the Wooly Mammoth Theatre in Washington, DC, followed by a very successful extended run at the Playwrights Horizon Theatre in New York in 2013. According to Ben Brantley and Jesse Green of the *New York Times*, Washburns' *Mr. Burns* ranks number four on a list of the twenty-five best plays since *Angels in America* (Brantley and Green).

3. *Mr. Burns* was performed at the Cockroach Theatre in Las Vegas as part of the 2014–15 season at the Art Square Theater, directed by Troy Heard.

4. Note that for all references to the text, I will be citing the 2014 Oberon Books edition of *Mr. Burns*.

5. I was able to view of a video of the Playwrights Horizons 2013 New York Production at the New York Public Library's Theater on Film and Television Archive. However, this particular scene is also available in abridged form as a video on the *New York Times* blog. See Erik Piepenburg, "In Performance: Matthew Maher of 'Mr. Burns, a Post-Electric Play,'" *New York Times*, September 24, 2013, http://artsbeat.blogs.nytimes.com/2013/09/24/in-performance-matthew-maher-of-mr-burns-a-post-electric-play/.

6. Matthew Maher has discussed his childhood surgery to correct a cleft palate in various interviews; see Linda Buchwald, "Matthew Maher Plays a Part Written for Him in Annie Baker's 'The Flick,'" *Backstage,* March 6, 2013, www.backstage.com/magazine/article/matthew-maher-plays-part-written-annie-bakers-flick-47140/.

7. Interestingly, the choice of the "Chart Hits" that Michael Friedman would "remix" were given to Washburn by the actors, whom she surveyed for a "general soundtrack of the last ten years" (Sanford).

8. For example, Ben Brantley of the *New York Times* writes, "The vital instinct to pass on and share stories, inevitably reshaping them along the way, is what this show celebrates" ("Stand Up Survivors"). See also Dee Jefferson, "Mr Burns, a Post-Electric Play"

9. In addition to director Steve Cosson, the Civilians actors included: Quincy Bernstin, Maria Dizzia, Gibson Frazier, Matt Maher, Jenny Morris, Sam Wright, and Colleen Werthmann (Washburn 8).

Works Cited

Abel, Marco. "Speeding across the Rhizome: Deleuze Meets Kerouac on the Road." *MFS: Modern Fiction Studies*, vol. 48, no. 2, 2002, pp. 227–56.

Adorno, Theodor W. "The Curves of the Needle." *October*, translated by Thomas Y. Levin, vol. 55, Dec. 1990, pp. 49–55.

"The Form of the Phonograph Record." *October*, translated by Thomas Y. Levin, vol. 55, Dec. 1990, pp. 56–61.

Towards a Theory of Musical Reproduction: Notes, a Draft and Two Schemata. Edited by Henri Lonitz. Wiley, 2006.

Afro-American. "Sid Bechet Uses Six Instruments." July 5, 1941, p. 13.

Alfonso, Barry. "William S. Burroughs Interview 1984." *Conversations with William S. Burroughs*, edited by A. Hibbard, pp. 152–9, University Press of Mississippi, 1999.

Altman, Robert B. *Sound Theory/Sound Practice*. Taylor & Francis, 1992.

Amerika, Mark. *Remix the Book*. University of Minnesota Press, 2011.

Anderson, Benedict. *Imagined Communities: Reflections on the Origin and Spread of Nationalism*. Verso, 2006.

Association for Cultural Equity. "Sidney Bechet," www.culturalequity.org/alan-lomax/friends/bechet.

Attali, Jaques. *Noise: The Political Economy of Music*. Manchester University Press, 1985.

Auslander, Philip. *Liveness: Performance in a Mediatized Culture*. Taylor & Francis, 2008.

Avon Comedy Four. *Hungarian Restaurant Scene*. Victor 35602, Nov. 8, 1916, www.loc.gov/jukebox/recordings/detail/id/4970.

Baldwin, Davarian L. "Black Empires, White Desires: The Spatial Politics of Identity in the Age of Hip-Hop." *That's the Joint!: The Hip-Hop Studies Reader*, edited by Mark Anthony Neal and Murray Foreman, pp. 159–76, Psychology Press, 2004.

Baraka, Amiri. *The Autobiography of LeRoi Jones*. Chicago Review Press, 2012.

Home: Social Essays. Akashic Books, 2009.

It's Nation Time: African Visionary Music. Black Forum/Motown, 1972.

Real Song. Enja, 1995.

Baraka, Imamu Amiri. *Spirit Reach*. Jihad Productions, 1972.

Black Music. W. Morrow, 1967.

Four Black Revolutionary Plays: All Praises to the Black Man. Bobbs-Merrill, 1969.

It's Nation Time. Third World Press, 1970.

Wise, Why's, Y's. Third World Press, 1995.

Barry, Eric D. "High-Fidelity Sound as Spectacle and Sublime, 1950–1961." *Sound in the Age of Mechanical Reproduction,* edited by David Suisman and Susan Strasser, pp. 115–40, University of Pennsylvania Press, 2011.

Barthes, Roland, and Roland Havas. "Listening." *The Responsibility of Forms: Critical Essays on Music, Art, and Representation,* translated by Richard Howard, pp. 245–60, University of California Press, 1991.

Barthes, Roland. "The Grain of the Voice." *Image-Music-Text,* pp. 179–89. Hill and Wang, 1978.

S/Z: An Essay. Translated by Richard Miller. Farrar, Straus and Giroux, 1974.

Basie, Count, and Albert Murray. *Good Morning Blues: The Autobiography of Count Basie.* Da Capo Press, 2002.

Bassett, Caroline. "How Many Movements: Mobile Telephones and Transformations in Urban Space." *The Auditory Culture Reader,* edited by Michael Bull and Les Back, pp. 343–54. Berg, 2003.

Baudrillard, Jean. *Simulacra and Simulation.* Translated by Sheila Faria Glaser. University of Michigan Press, 1994.

Bayley, Amanda, editor. *Recorded Music: Performance, Culture and Technology.* Cambridge University Press, 2010.

Bechet, Sidney. *Treat It Gentle: An Autobiography.* Da Capo Press, 1962.

Belkind, Allen, editor. *Dos Passos, the Critics, and the Writer's Intention.* Southern Illinois University Press, 1971.

Belletto, Steven. "Kerouac His Own Historian: Visions of Cody and the Politics of Historiography." *Clio,* vol. 37, no. 2, Spring 2008, p. 193.

Benjamin, Walter. *The Work of Art in the Age of Its Technological Reproducibility, And Other Writings on Media.* Translated by M. W. Jennings et al. Belknap Press of Harvard University Press, 2008.

Benzon, Paul. "Lost in Transcription: Postwar Typewriting Culture, Andy Warhol's Bad Book, and the Standardization of Error." *PMLA: Publications of the Modern Language Association of America,* vol. 125, no. 1, 2010, pp. 92–106, 264.

Bernstein, Charles. *Close Listening: Poetry and the Performed Word.* Oxford University Press, 1998.

Berrigan, Ted. "The Art of Fiction No. 41, Jack Kerouac." *The Paris Review,* no. 43, Summer 1968, www.theparisreview.org/interviews/4260/the-art-of-fiction-no-41-jack-kerouac.

Biers, Katherine. *Virtual Modernism: Writing and Technology in the Progressive Era.* University of Minnesota Press, 2013.

Bijsterveld, Karin, and Annelies Jacobs. "Storing Sound Souvenirs: The Multi-Sited Domestication of the Tape Recorder." *Sound Souvenirs: Audio Technologies, Memory and Cultural Practices,* edited by Karin Bijsterveld and José van Dijck, pp. 25–42, Amsterdam University Press, 2009.

Bill, Edward Lyman, editor. *Talking Machine World (Jan–Dec 1906).* Edward Lyman Bill, 1906, http://archive.org/details/talkingmachinewo2bill.

Bingham, Ralph. Mrs. Rastus at the Telephone. Victor 17818, April 9, 1915, www.loc.gov/jukebox/recordings/detail/id/2016.

Blackmer, Corinne E. "African Masks and the Arts of Passing in Gertrude Stein's 'Melanctha' and Nella Larsen's 'Passing.'" *Journal of the History of Sexuality*, vol. 4, no. 2, Oct. 1993, pp. 230–63.

Blesser, Barry, and Linda-Ruth Salter. *Spaces Speak, Are You Listening?* MIT Press, 2007.

Bolter, Jay David, and Richard Grusin. *Remediation: Understanding New Media*. MIT Press, 2000.

Bolton, Micheal Sean. "Get Off the Point: Deconstructing Context in the Novels of William S. Burroughs." *Journal of Narrative Theory*, vol. 40, no. 1, Winter 2010, pp. 53–79, 129.

Boone, Andrew R. "Mickey Mouse Goes Classical." *Popular Science*, Jan. 1941, p. 66.

Brackett, David. "James Brown's 'Superbad' and the Double-Voiced Utterance." *Popular Music*, vol. 11, no. 3, Oct. 1992, pp. 309–24.

Brady, Erika. *A Spiral Way: How the Phonograph Changed Ethnography*. University Press of Mississippi, 2012.

Brantley, Ben. "Stand Up, Survivors; Homer Is with You." *New York Times*, Sept. 16, 2013, p. C1.

Brantley, Ben, and Jesse Green. "The Great Work Continues: The 25 Best American Plays since 'Angels in America.'" *New York Times*, May 31, 2018, www.nytimes.com/interactive/2018/05/31/theater/best-25-plays.html.

Breit, Harvey. "Talk with Alan Lomax." *New York Times*, June 23, 1950, p. BR7.

Brooks, Tim. *Lost Sounds: Blacks and the Birth of the Recording Industry, 1890–1919*. University of Illinois Press, 2004.

Brown, James. James Brown Live at the Apollo. King Records, 1963.

Brown, Sterling. "On Dialect Usage." *The Slave's Narrative*, edited by Henry Louis Gates Jr., pp. 37–39, Oxford University Press, 1991.

Buchart, Dieter. "Basquiat's Notebooks: Words and Knowledge Scratched and Sampled." *Basquiat: The Unknown Notebooks*, edited by Dieter Buchhart and Tricia Laughlin Bloom, pp. 27–48, Skira Rizzoli, 2015.

Buchwald, Linda. "Matthew Maher Plays a Part Written for Him in Annie Baker's 'The Flick,'" Mar. 6, 2013, www.backstage.com/magazine/article/matthew-maher-plays-part-written-annie-bakers-flick-47140/.

Bull, Michael, and Les Back, editors. *The Auditory Culture Reader*. Berg, 2003.

Burroughs, William S. *Break through in Grey Room*. Sub Rosa, 2008.

Nothing Here Now but the Recordings. Industrial Records, 1981.

Rub Out the Words: The Letters of William S. Burroughs 1959–1974. HarperCollins, 2012.

The Job: Interviews with William S. Burroughs. Grove Press, 1974.

The Ticket That Exploded. 1967. Grove Press, 1992.

Burroughs, William S., and Victor Bockris. *With William Burroughs: A Report from the Bunker*. St. Martin's Press, 1996.

Burroughs, William S., and Brion Gysin. *The Third Mind*. Viking Press, 1978.

Burroughs, William S., and Jack Kerouac. *And the Hippos Were Boiled in Their Tanks*. Perseus Books Group, 2009.

Burton, Antoinette, editor. *Archive Stories: Facts, Fictions, and the Writing of History*. Duke University Press, 2006.

Cage, John. *Silence: Lectures and Writings*. 1961. Wesleyan University Press, 2010.

Carr, Virginia Spencer. *Dos Passos: A Life*. Northwestern University Press, 2004.

Cassady, Carolyn. *Off the Road*. Overlook, 2008.

Chanan, Michael. *Repeated Takes: A Short History of Recording and Its Effects on Music*. Verso, 1995.

Chang, Jeff. *Can't Stop Won't Stop: A History of the Hip-Hop Generation*. 1st ed. Picador, 2005.

Charters, Ann. *Kerouac: A Biography*. St. Martin's Press, 1994.

Chilton, John. *Sidney Bechet: The Wizard of Jazz*. Da Capo Press, 1996.

Cifelli, Edward M. *John Ciardi: A Biography*. University of Arkansas Press, 1998.

Collins, Lisa Gail, and Margo Natalie Crawford, editors. *New Thoughts on the Black Arts Movement*. Rutgers University Press, 2006.

Coltrane, John. *Coltrane Live at Birdland*. Impulse!, 1968.

Cortazar, Julio. *Hopscotch: A Novel*. Translated by Gregory Rabassa. 1st Pantheon pbk. ed. Pantheon, 1987.

Cortez, Jayne. *Celebrations and Solitudes*. Strata-East, 1974.

Cosson, Steve. Mr. Burns, a Post-Electric Play [Videorecording] / Playwrights Horizons. New York Public Library, Theatre on Film and Television Archive, 2013.

Cox, Christoph, and Daniel Warner. *Audio Culture: Readings in Modern Music*. Bloomsbury Academic, 2004.

Cult, The. "The Cult: The Official Fan Site of Chuck Palahniuk." https://chuck palahniuk.net/home.

Damaske, Peter. *Acoustics and Hearing*. Springer, 2008.

Davis, Charles T., and Henry Louis Gates Jr. *The Slave's Narrative*. Oxford University Press, 1991.

Denny, Harold Norman. "One Soldier on 'Three Soldiers.'" *New York Times*, 1921, p. 37.

Derrida, Jacques. *Of Grammatology*. Translated by Gayatri C. Spivak. Johns Hopkins University Press, 1998.

Dimock, Wai-Chee. *Through Other Continents: American Literature across Deep Time*. Princeton University Press, 2008.

Dos Passos, John. *1919 (U.S.A.)*. 1932. Houghton Mifflin, 2000.

John Dos Passos: The Major Nonfictional Prose. Edited by Donald Pizer. Wayne State University Press, 1988.

The 42nd Parallel (U.S.A.). 1930. Houghton Mifflin Harcourt, 2000.

The Best Times: An Informal Memoir. New American Library, 1968.

The Big Money (U.S.A.). 1936. Houghton Mifflin Harcourt, 2000.

The Garbage Man: A Parade with Shouting. Harper & Brothers, 1926.

Three Plays: The Garbage Man, Airways, Inc., Fortune Heights. Harcourt Brace, 1934.

Three Soldiers. George H. Doran, 1921.

Dos Passos, John, and Townsend Ludington. *The Fourteenth Chronicle: Letters and Diaries of John Dos Passos.* Gambit, 1973.

Dos Passos, John, with Ed Begley, George Grizzard, and Rip Torn. *John Dos Passos U.S.A. Selections from The 42nd Parallel.* Caedmon, 1968.

Du Bois, W. E. B. *The Souls of Black Folk: Authoritative Text, Contexts, Criticism.* Edited by H. L. Gates and T. H. Oliver. W. W. Norton, 1999.

Dworkin, Craig. "A Handbook of Protocols for Literary" *Jacket2,* 2012, https://jacket2.org/commentary/handbook-protocols-literary-listening-ed-craig-dworkin-2012-pdf.

Dyson, Frances. *Sounding New Media: Immersion and Embodiment in the Arts and Culture.* University of California Press, 2009.

Dyson, Katie. "Resonant Reading: From Anxiety to Attunement." *Pedagogy,* vol. 19, no. 3, Sept. 2019, pp. 537–42.

Early, Gerald. "The Lives of Jazz." *American Literary History,* vol. 5, no. 1, 1993, pp. 129–146.

Edison, Thomas A. *Lists and Inventories – Cylinder Phonograph.* 1877, http://edison.rutgers.edu/NamesSearch/SingleDoc.php?DocId=D7702ZEO.

"The Perfected Phonograph." *North American Review,* vol. 146, no. 379, 1888, pp. 641–50.

"The Phonograph and Its Future." *North American Review,* vol. 126, no. 262, May 1878, pp. 527–36.

"Thomas Alva Edison's 'Treatise on National Economic Policy and Business.'" *Business History Review,* vol. 59, no. 3, Oct. 1985, pp. 433–64.

Edwards, Brent Hayes. *Epistrophies: Jazz and the Literary Imagination.* Harvard University Press, 2017.

"The Literary Ellington." *Representations,* vol. 77, 2002, pp. 1–29.

Edwards, Justin. "The Man with a Camera Eye: Cinematic Form and Hollywood Malediction in John Dos Passos's 'The Big Money.'" *Literature/Film Quarterly,* vol. 27, no. 4, Oct. 1999, pp. 245–54.

Eisenberg, Evan. *The Recording Angel: Music, Records and Culture from Aristotle to Zappa.* 2nd ed. Yale University Press, 2005.

Eliot, T. S. "The Waste Land." *The Norton Anthology of American Literature,* 9th ed., vol. B, edited by Robert S. Levine, pp. 365–78, W. W. Norton, 2017.

Ellison, Ralph. *Invisible Man.* 1952. Random House, 1995.

Living with Music: Ralph Ellison's Jazz Writings. Edited by Robert G. O'Meally. Modern Library, 2002.

Elsdon, Peter. "Jazz Recordings and the Capturing of Performance." *Recorded Music: Performance, Culture and Technology,* edited by Amanda Bayley, pp. 146–166, Cambridge University Press, 2010.

Enns, Anthony, and Shelley Trower. *Vibratory Modernism.* Palgrave Macmillan, 2013.

Enock, Joseph. "Stereophonic Reproduction." *Gramophone,* Dec. 1956, p. 101.

Erlmann, Veit. *Reason and Resonance: A History of Modern Aurality.* Zone Books, 2014.

Farrington, Holly E. "Narrating the Jazz Life: Three Approaches to Jazz Autobiography." *Popular Music and Society*, vol. 29, no. 3, 2006, pp. 375–86.

Faulkner, William. *Light in August*. Knopf Doubleday, 2011.

Feather, Leonard. *The Jazz Years: Earwitness to an Era*. Da Capo Press, 1987.

Fitzgerald, F. Scott. "Head and Shoulders." *F. Scott Fitzgerald: Novels and Stories 1920–1922*, pp. 310–44, Library of America, 2000.

Ford, Phil. *Dig: Sound and Music in Hip Culture*. Oxford University Press, 2013.

Frattarola, Angela. "The Phonograph and the Modernist Novel." *Mosaic: A Journal for the Interdisciplinary Study of Literature*, vol. 43, no. 1, Mar. 2010, p. 143.

Fremont-Smith, Eliot. "Books of The Times; While There Is Pain There Is Hope." *New York Times*, July 21, 1967, p. 22.

Furia, Philip. "Alexander's Ragtime Band, 1911." *A New Literary History of America*, edited by Greil Marcus and Werner Sollors, pp. 507–12, Belknap Press of Harvard University Press, 2009.

Gabbard, Krin, editor. *Jazz among the Discourses*. Duke University Press, 1995.

——. editor. *Representing Jazz*. Duke University Press, 1995.

Garner, Lori Ann. "Representations of Speech in the WPA Slave Narratives of Florida and the Writings of Zora Neale Hurston." *Western Folklore*, vol. 59, no. 3/4, July 2000, pp. 215–31.

Gebhardt, Nicholas. *Going for Jazz: Musical Practices and American Ideology*. University of Chicago Press, 2001.

Gibson, William. "God's Little Toys." *Wired*, July 2005, www.wired.com, www.wired.com/2005/07/gibson-3/.

Gilroy, Paul. "Between the Blues and the Blues Dance: Some Soundscapes of the Black Atlantic." *Audio Culture: Readings in Modern Music*, edited by Michael Bull and Les Back, pp. 381–97, Bloomsbury Academic, 2003.

——. *The Black Atlantic: Modernity and Double Consciousness*. Harvard University Press, 1993.

Ginsberg, Allen. *Howl and Other Poems: Pocket Poets Number 4*. City Lights, 1956.

Gitelman, Lisa. *Scripts, Grooves, and Writing Machines: Representing Technology in the Edison Era*. Stanford University Press, 1999.

Goble, Mark. *Beautiful Circuits: Modernism and the Mediated Life*. Columbia University Press, 2010.

Goldstein, E. Bruce. *Sensation and Perception*. Wadsworth Cengage Learning, 2010.

Gould, Glen. "The Prospects of Recording." 1966. *Audio Culture: Readings in Modern Music*, edited by D. Warner and C. Cox, pp. 115–26, Bloomsbury Academic, 2004.

Graham, T. Austin. *The Great American Songbooks: Modernism, Musical Texts, and the Value of Popular Culture*. Oxford University Press, 2013.

——. "The Literary Soundtrack: Or, F. Scott Fitzgerald's Heard and Unheard Melodies." *American Literary History*, vol. 21, no. 3, 2009, pp. 518–49.

Griffin, Farah Jasmine. "Children of Omar: Resistance and Reliance in the Expressive Cultures of Black New Orleans Cultures." *Journal of Urban History*, vol. 35, no. 5, May 2009, pp. 656–67.

Hamilton, Marybeth. "1938, May: Jelly Roll Morton Speaks." *A New Literary History of America*, edited by Greil Marcus and Werner Sollors, pp. 724–8, Belknap Press of Harvard University Press, 2009.

Harlos, Christopher. "Jazz Autobiography: Theory, Practice, Politics." *Representing Jazz*, edited by Krin Gabbard, pp. 131–68, Duke University Press, 1995.

Harris, Joel Chandler. "A Queer Experience with the Phonograph." *Uncle Remus and His Friends: Old Plantation Stories, Songs, and Ballads*, pp. 292–300, Houghton, Mifflin, 1892.

Harris, William J. *The Poetry and Poetics of Amiri Baraka: The Jazz Aesthetic*. University of Missouri Press, 1985.

Hassan, Ihab. "The Subtracting Machine: The Work of William Burroughs." *William S. Burroughs at the Front: Critical Reception, 1959–1989*, edited by Jennie Skerl and Robin Lydenberg, p. 53, Southern Illinois University Press, 1991.

Hayles, N. Katherine. *How We Became Posthuman: Virtual Bodies in Cybernetics, Literature, and Informatics*. University of Chicago Press, 2008.

Heble, Ajay. *Landing on the Wrong Note: Jazz, Dissonance, and Critical Practice*. Routledge, 2000.

Henriques, Julian. "Dread Bodies: Doubles, Echoes, and the Skins of Sound." *Small Axe*, vol. 18, no. 2, 2014, pp. 191–201.

Hersch, Charles. *Subversive Sounds: Race and the Birth of Jazz in New Orleans*. University of Chicago Press, 2007.

Hill, George W. *The Phonograph Witness, a Drama in Five Acts*. Harvard University Press, 1883.

Hock, Stephen. "'Stories Told Sideways Out of the Big Mouth': Dos Passos's Bazinian Camera Eye." *Literature/Film Quarterly*, vol. 33, no. 1, 2005, pp. 20–27.

Hoffman, Frank. *Encyclopedia of Recorded Sound*. Taylor & Francis, 2004.

Hoffman, Michael J., editor. *Critical Essays on Gertrude Stein*. G. K. Hall, 1986.

Hoover, Elizabeth. "Kevin Young on 'Ardency.'" *The Paris Review*, Feb. 15, 2011, www.theparisreview.org/blog/2011/02/15/kevin-young-on-'ardency'/

Hopkins, David. "Middle Eight: To Be or Not to Bop: Jack Kerouac's 'On the Road' and the Culture of Bebop and Rhythm 'n' Blues." *Popular Music*, vol. 24, no. 2, May 2005, pp. 279–86.

Horning, Susan Schmidt. *Chasing Sound: Technology, Culture, and the Art of Studio Recording from Edison to the LP*. Johns Hopkins University Press, 2013.

Howard, Jane. "'Mr Burns' Is the Wild and Loving Theatre 'The Simpsons' Deserves." *Junkee*, May 7, 2017, https://junkee.com/mr-burns-simpsons-review/104576.

Hrebeniak, Michael. *Action Writing: Jack Kerouac's Wild Form*. Southern Illinois University Press, 2006.

Hubert, Philip G. "The New Talking Machines." *Atlantic Monthly*, Feb. 1889, www.theatlantic.com/magazine/archive/1889/02/the-new-talking-machines/3 08356/.

Hughes, Langston. *Ask Your Mama: 12 Moods for Jazz*. 1961. Alfred A. Knopf, 2009.
   I Wonder as I Wander: An Autobiographical Journey. 1934. Paw Prints, 2008.
   Montage of a Dream Deferred. Holt, 1951.
   The Big Sea: An Autobiography. 1940. Edited by Arnold Rampersad. Farrar, Straus and Giroux, 1993.
   The Collected Poems of Langston Hughes. Edited by Arnold Rampersad. 1st Vintage classics ed. Vintage, 1995.
   The Poems 1951–1967 (LH3). Edited by Arnold Rampersad. University of Missouri Press, 2001.

Hume, Kathryn. "William S Burroughs's Phantasmic Geography." *Contemporary Literature*, vol. 40, no. 1, Spring 1999, pp. 111–35.

Hurston, Zora Neale. "Zora Neale Hurston," Aug. 30, 1935, www .culturalequity.org/alan-lomax/friends/hurston.
   "Letters – Zora Neale Hurston," 2008, www.culturalequity.org/alan-lomax/fri ends/hurston.
   Folklore, Memoirs, and Other Writings. Edited by C. A Wall. Library of America, 1995.

Ihde, Don. *Listening and Voice: Phenomenologies of Sound*. 2nd ed. State University of New York Press, 2007.

Jacobs, Karen. *The Eye's Mind: Literary Modernism and Visual Culture*. Cornell University Press, 2001.

Jaji, Tsitsi Ella. *Africa in Stereo: Modernism, Music, and Pan-African Solidarity*. Oxford University Press, 2014.

Jefferson, Dee. "Mr Burns, a Post-Electric Play." *Time Out Sydney*, May 21, 2017, www.timeout.com/sydney/theatre/mr-burns-a-post-electric-play#tab_panel_1.

Johnson, Joyce. *The Voice Is All: The Lonely Victory of Jack Kerouac*. Penguin, 2012.

Jones, Meta DuEwa. "Politics, Process & (Jazz) Performance: Amiri Baraka's 'It's Nation Time.'" *African American Review*, vol. 37, no. 2/3, Summer 2003, pp. 245–52.
   The Muse Is Music: Jazz Poetry from the Harlem Renaissance to Spoken Word. University of Illinois Press, 2011.

Kahn, Douglas, and Gregory Whitehead. *Wireless Imagination: Sound, Radio, and the Avant-Garde*. MIT Press, 1994.

Kalaidjian, Walter B. *American Culture between the Wars: Revisionary Modernism & Postmodern Critique*. Columbia University Press, 1993.

Kalamu ya Salaam. "Amiri Baraka Analyzes How He Writes." *African American Review*, vol. 37, no. 2/3, Summer 2003, pp. 211–36.

Katz, Mark. *Capturing Sound: How Technology Has Changed Music*. University of California Press, 2010.

Kazin, Alfred. "Dos Passos and the 'Lost Generation.'" *Dos Passos, the Critics, and the Writer's Intention*, edited by Allen Belkind, pp. 1–21, Southern Illinois University Press, 1971.

Keeling, Kara, and Josh Kun, editors. *Sound Clash: Listening to American Studies*. Johns Hopkins University Press, 2012.

Kelly, Kevin. "Remix, Rewind, Reinvent: Predicting the Future of Media." *Wired*, July 13, 2016, www.wired.co.uk/article/kevin-kelly-on-the-future-of-media.

Kerouac, Jack. *Jack Kerouac: Selected Letters, 1940–1956*. Edited by A. Charters. Viking, 1995.

Jack Kerouac: Selected Letters, 1957–1969. Edited by Ann Charters. Diane, 1999.

Jack Kerouac: The Complete Collection. Chrome Dreams, 2012.

On the Road. 1957 Penguin Books, 2003.

On the Road: The Original Scroll. Penguin, 2007.

"The Essentials of Spontaneous Prose." *The Portable Jack Kerouac*, edited by Ann Charters, pp. 484–5, Penguin Books, 2007.

The Unknown Kerouac: Rare, Unpublished, & Newly Translated Writings. Edited by Todd Tietchen. Translated by Jean-Christophe Cloutier. Library of America, 2016.

Visions of Cody. 1972. Penguin, 2012.

Windblown World: Journals of Jack Kerouac 1947–1954. Edited by D. G. Brinkley. Penguin Putnam, 2006.

Kerouac, Jack, and Allen Ginsberg. *Jack Kerouac and Allen Ginsberg: The Letters*. Edited by Bill Morgan and David Stanford. Penguin, 2010.

Kirkus Reviews. "Invisible Monsters Remix (Review)." Vol. 80, no. 11, June 2012, p. 1116.

"The Ticket That Exploded." June 1967, www.kirkusreviews.com/book-reviews/william-s-burroughs/ticket-exploded/916893884.

Kittler, Friedrich A. *Gramophone, Film, Typewriter*. Stanford University Press, 1999.

Knickerbocker, Conrad. "The Art of Fiction No. 36, William S. Burroughs." *Paris Review*, no. 35, Fall 1965, www.theparisreview.org/interviews/4424/the-art-of-fiction-no-36-william-s-burroughs.

Kun, Josh. *Audiotopia: Music, Race, and America*. University of California Press, 2005.

Lamar, Kendrick. "DAMN." *Aftermath*, Apr. 14, 2017.

Landsberg, Melvin. *Dos Passos' Path to U.S.A.: A Political Biography*. Associated University Press, 1972.

Lapadat, Judith C., and Anne C. Lindsay. "Transcription in Research and Practice: From Standardization of Technique to Interpretive Positionings." *Qualitative Inquiry*, vol. 5, no. 1, 1999, pp. 64–86.

Lefebvre, Henri. *Rhythmanalysis: Space, Time and Everyday Life*. Translated by Gerald Moore and S. Elden. Bloomsbury, 2013.

Lessig, Lawrence. *Remix: Making Art and Commerce Thrive in the Hybrid Economy*. 8/30/09 ed. Penguin Books, 2008.

Lethem, Jonathan. "The Ecstasy of Influence." *Harper's Magazine*, Feb. 2007, https://harpers.org/archive/2007/02/the-ecstasy-of-influence/.

Levine, Caroline. *Forms: Whole, Rhythm, Hierarchy, Network*. Princeton University Press, 2017.

Lin, Tan. "Disco as Operating System, Part One." *Criticism*, vol. 50, no. 1, 2008, pp. 83–100.

Lomax, Alan. *Mister Jelly Roll Morton: The Fortunes of Jelly Roll Morton, New Orleans Creole and "Inventor of Jazz."* University of California Press, 2001.

Lomax, Allen. *Alan Lomax, Assistant in Charge: The Library of Congress Letters, 1935–1945*. Edited by Ronald D. Cohen. University Press of Mississippi, 2010.

Lordi, Emily J. *Black Resonance: Iconic Women Singers and African American Literature*. Rutgers University Press, 2013.

Lowney, John. "Jazz, Black Transnationalism, and the Political Aesthetics of Langston Hughes's Ask Your Mama." *American Literature*, vol. 84, no. 3, Sept. 2012, p. 563.

Ludington, Townsend. *John Dos Passos: A Twentieth Century Odyssey*. Dutton, 1980.

Lydenberg, Robin. "Cut-Up: Negative Poetics in William Burroughs and Roland Barthes." *Comparative Literature Studies*, vol. 15, no. 4, 1978, p. 414.

Lynd, Robert S., and Helen Merrell Lynd. *Middletown: A Study in Contemporary American Culture*. Harcourt, Brace, 1929.

Mackey, Nathaniel. "The Changing Same: Black Music in the Poetry of Amiri Baraka." *boundary 2: A Journal of Postmodern Literature and Culture*, vol. 6, no. 2, 1978, pp. 355–86.

Madonna. *I'm Breathless*. Sire–Warner Brothers, May 22, 1990.

Maine, Barry, editor. *Dos Passos, the Critical Heritage*. Routledge, 1988.

"Steinbeck's Debt to Dos Passos." *The Critical Response to John Steinbeck's "The Grapes of Wrath,"* edited by Barbara A. Heavilin, pp. 151–60, Greenwood Press, 2000.

Malcolm, Douglas. "'Jazz America': Jazz and African American Culture in Jack Kerouac's 'On the Road.'" *Contemporary Literature*, vol. 40, no. 1, 1999, pp. 85–110.

Marcus, Greil, and Werner Sollors, editors. *A New Literary History of America*. Belknap Press of Harvard University Press, 2009.

Marcus, Greil, and Sean Wilentz, editors. *The Rose & the Briar: Death, Love and Liberty in the American Ballad*. W. W. Norton, 2005.

Marinetti, F. T. "The Founding and Manifesto of Futurism (1909)." *Futurism: An Anthology*, edited by Lawrence Rainey et al., pp. 49–53, Yale University Press, 2009.

McEnaney, Tom. *Acoustic Properties: Radio, Narrative, and the New Neighborhood of the Americas*. 1st ed. Northwestern University Press, 2017.

McGinn, Robert E. "Stokowski and the Bell Telephone Laboratories: Collaboration in the Development of High-Fidelity Sound Reproduction." *Technology and Culture*, vol. 24, no. 1, 1983, pp. 38–75.

McGurl, Mark. *The Program Era: Postwar Fiction and the Rise of Creative Writing.* Harvard University Press, 2009.

McLeod, Kimbrew. "An Oral History of Sampling." *The Routledge Companion to Remix Studies*, edited by Eduardo Navas et al., pp. 83–95, Taylor & Francis, 2014.

McLuhan, Marshall. "Review." *William S. Burroughs at the Front: Critical Reception, 1959–1989*, edited by Jennie Skerl and Robin Lydenberg, p, 69, Southern Illinois University Press, 1991.

Understanding Media: The Extension of Man. Routledge Classics, 2001.

Melia, Mike. "Jessye Norman, the Roots Team Up for Langston Hughes' 'Ask Your Mama,'" Aug. 27, 2009, www.pbs.org/newshour/art/blog/2009/08/jessye-norman-the-roots-team-up-for-langston-hughes-ask-your-mama.html.

Mendieta, Eduardo. "Surviving American Culture: On Chuck Palahniuk." *Philosophy and Literature*, vol. 29, no. 2, 2005, pp. 394–408.

Miles, Barry. *William Burroughs: El Hombre Invisible.* Random House UK, 2002.

Millard, Andre. *America on Record: A History of Recorded Sound.* Cambridge University Press, 2005.

Miller, Joshua L. *Accented America: The Cultural Politics of Multilingual Modernism.* Oxford University Press, 2011.

Miller, Laura. "Fanmade World: Your Guide to the Fanfiction Explosion." *Vulture*, Mar. 11, 2015, www.vulture.com/2015/03/fanfiction-guide.html.

Miller, Paul D. (DJ Spooky). "In through the Out Door: Sampling and the Creative Act." *Sound Unbound: Sampling Digital Music and Culture*, edited by Paul D. (DJ Spooky) Miller, pp. 5–20, MIT Press, 2008.

Rhythm Science. Mediawork/MIT Press, 2004.

Miller, R. Baxter. "Framing and Framed Languages in Hughes's Ask Your Mama: 12 Moods for Jazz." *MELUS*, vol. 17, no. 4, Winter 1991, pp. 3–13.

Milner, Greg. *Perfecting Sound Forever: An Aural History of Recorded Music.* Farrar, Straus, and Giroux, 2009.

Monson, Ingrid. *Saying Something: Jazz Improvisation and Interaction.* University of Chicago Press, 1997.

Moore, Nathan. "Nova Law: William S. Burroughs and the Logic of Control." *Law and Literature*, vol. 19, no. 3, Fall 2007, pp. 435–70, 544.

Moore, Rich. "Cape Feare." The Simpsons, episode 83, aired Oct. 7, 1993.

Morgan, Ted. *Literary Outlaw: The Life and Times of William S. Burroughs.* W. W. Norton, 2012.

Morris, Adalaide Kirby, editor. *Sound States: Innovative Poetics and Acoustical Technologies.* University of North Carolina Press, 1997.

Morton, David L. *Sound Recording: The Life Story of a Technology.* Johns Hopkins University Press, 2006.

Morton, Ferdinand (Jelly Roll), and Alan Lomax. The Complete Library of Congress Recordings of Jelly Roll Morton. Rounder Records, 1938, 2005.

Moten, Fred. *In the Break: The Aesthetics of the Black Radical Tradition.* University of Minnesota Press, 2003.

Mowitt, John. *Sounds: The Ambient Humanities.* University of California Press, 2015.

Murphy, Timothy S. *Wising Up the Marks: The Amodern William Burroughs.* University of California Press, 1997.

Mustazza, Chris. "New Gertrude Stein Recordings at PennSound." *Jacket 2,* Mar. 17, 2015, https://jacket2.org/commentary/new-gertrude-stein-recordings-pennsound.

Myers, J. A. *When Malindy Sings.* Victor 35097, Dec. 9, 1909, www.loc.gov/juke box/recordings/detail/id/1816.

Nancy, Jean-Luc. *Listening.* Translated by Charlotte Mandell. Fordham University Press, 2007.

Nanney, Lisa, and Donald C. Pizer. *John Dos Passos Revisited.* Twayne, 1998.

Napolin, Julie Beth. *The Fact of Resonance: Modernist Acoustics and Narrative Form.* Fordham University Press, 2020.

"'A Sinister Resonance': Vibration, Sound, and the Birth of Conrad's Marlow." *Qui Parle,* vol. 21, no. 2, 2013, pp. 69–100.

Navas, Eduardo, et al., editors. *Keywords in Remix Studies.* Routledge, 2017.

Remix Theory: The Aesthetics of Sampling. Springer, 2012.

editors. *The Routledge Companion to Remix Studies.* Taylor & Francis, 2014.

New York Times. "Sound Waves 'Rock' Carnegie Hall As 'Enhanced Music' Is Played." Apr. 10, 1940, p. 25.

Nitaraj, Nirmala, editor. *Mr. Burns: A Post-Electric Play: Insight into the Play, Playwright, and Production.* Words on Plays – American Conservatory Theatre, 2015, www.act-sf.org/content/dam/act/2014-15_Season/wop/AC T_MrBurns_WOP_color_final.pdf.

North, Michael. *Camera Works: Photography and the Twentieth-Century Word.* Oxford University Press, 2005.

The Dialect of Modernism: Race, Language, and Twentieth-Century Literature. Oxford University Press, 1994.

Novak, David, and Matt Sakakeeny, editors. *Keywords in Sound.* Duke University Press, 2015.

Nyong'o, Tavia. "Afro-Philo-Sonic Fictions: Black Sound Studies after the Millennium." *Small Axe,* vol. 18, no. 2, 2014, pp. 173–79.

Oliveros, Pauine. *Deep Listening: A Composer's Sound Practice.* iUniverse, 2005.

Olson, Charles. "Projective Verse." 1950, www.poetryfoundation.org/learning/es say/237880.

O'Meally, Robert G., editor. *The Jazz Cadence of American Culture.* Columbia University Press, 1998.

O'Neill, Eugene. "The Hairy Ape." *Three Great Plays,* pp. 97–140, Dover Thrift, 2005.

Ong, Walter J. *Orality and Literacy: The Technologizing of the Word.* Taylor & Francis, 2002.

Palahniuk, Chuck. "Bait: Off-Color Stories for You to Color (Press Release)." *The Cult,* https://chuckpalahniuk.net/books/bait-off-color-stories-for-you-to-color.

Invisible Monsters: A Novel. W. W. Norton, 1999.

Invisible Monsters Remix. W. W. Norton, 2012.

Palatella, John. "Patrimony." *Nation,* May 2005, pp. 28–32.

Palmer, Robert, and William S. Burroughs. "'William Burroughs: Rolling Stone Interview' 1972." *Conversations with William S. Burroughs*, edited by Allen Hibbard, pp. 51–79, University Press of Mississippi, 1999.

Panic! at the Disco. *Fever You Can't Sweat Out*. Decaydance/Atlantic, 2005.

Piazza, Tom. *Setting the Tempo: Fifty Years of Great Jazz Liner Notes*. Anchor Books, 1996.

Piepenburg, Erik. "In Performance: Matthew Maher of 'Mr. Burns, a Post-Electric Play.'" ArtsBeat, Sept. 24, 2013, https://artsbeat.blogs.nytimes.com/2013/09/2 4/in-performance-matthew-maher-of-mr-burns-a-post-electric-play/.

Pitman, Benjamin. *The Manual of Phonography*. Phonographic Institute, 1860.

Pizer, Donald. *Toward a Modernist Style: John Dos Passos*. Bloomsbury, 2013.

Dos Passos' U.S.A.: A Critical Study. University Press of Virginia, 1988.

"John Dos Passos in the 1920s: The Development of a Modernist Style." *Mosaic: A Journal for the Interdisciplinary Study of Literature*, vol. 45, no. 4, Dec. 2012, pp. 51–67.

The Paintings and Drawings of John Dos Passos: A Collection and Study. Clemson University Press, 2016.

Plant, Deborah G. *"The Inside Light": New Critical Essays on Zora Neale Hurston*. Praeger, 2010.

Pressman, Jessica. *Digital Modernism: Making It New in New Media*. Oxford University Press, 2014.

Punday, Daniel. "Word Dust: William Burroughs's Multimedia Aesthetic." *Mosaic: A Journal for the Interdisciplinary Study of Literature*, vol. 40, no. 3, Sept. 2007, pp. 33–49.

Railton, Reid A. "Stereo Seen Personally." *Gramophone*, August 1958, p. 69.

Rampersad, Arnold. *The Life of Langston Hughes: Vol. I. 1902–1941, I, Too, Sing America*. Oxford University Press, 2002.

The Life of Langston Hughes: Vol. II. 1914–1967, I Dream a World. Oxford University Press, 2002.

Reed, Brian. "Hart Crane's Victrola." *Modernism/modernity*, vol. 7, no. 1, 2000, pp. 99–125.

Reed, Ishmael. "Ishmael Reed on the Life and Death of Amiri Baraka." *Wall Street Journal*, Jan. 12, 2014, http://blogs.wsj.com/speakeasy/2014/01/12/ishmael-reed-on-the-life-and-death-of-amiri-baraka/.

Reid, John, et al. *The John Reid Collection 1940–1944*. Arkansas Arts Center, 1994.

RePass, Richard. "Review: Mister Jelly Roll." *Tempo*, no. 25, Oct. 1952, pp. 37–38.

Rhodes, Richard. "Cutting-Up." New York Times, 1967, p. 241.

Rubery, Matthew. *The Untold Story of the Talking Book*. Harvard University Press, 2016.

Russell, Jamie. *Queer Burroughs*. Palgrave Macmillan, 2001.

Sanford, Tim. "Tim Sanford and Anne Washburn on Mr. Burns, Interview." *Playwrights Horizons*, www.playwrightshorizons.org/shows/trailers/tim-sanford-and-anne-washburn-mr-burns/.

Sartre, Jean-Paul. "John Dos Passos and 1919." *Dos Passos, The Critics and the Writer's Intention,* edited by Allen Belkind, pp. 70–80, Southern Illinois University Press, 1971.

Savage, James R. "Jelly Roll's Full Life in a Half World." *Chicago Daily Tribune,* July 2, 1950, p. H4.

Scaggs, Austin. "Madonna Looks Back: Interview." *Rolling Stone,* Oct. 29, 2009, www.rollingstone.com/music/music-news/madonna-looks-back-the-rolling-stone-interview-197575/.

Scanlon, Larry. "News from Heaven: Vernacular Time in Langston Hughes's Ask Your Mama." *Callaloo: A Journal of African-American and African Arts and Letters,* vol. 25, no. 1, 2002, pp. 45–65.

Schaeffer, Pierre. "Acousmatics." *Audio Culture: Readings in Modern Music,* edited by Daniel Warner and Christoph Cox, pp. 76–81, Continuum, 2004.

In Search of a Concrete Music. Translated by John Dack and Christine North. University of California Press, 2012.

Schafer, R. Murray. *The Soundscape: Our Sonic Environment and the Tuning of the World.* Destiny Books, 1993.

Schoenherr, Steven. "Recording Technology History." July 6, 2005, http://history.sandiego.edu/gen/recording/notes.html.

Schweighauser, Philip. *The Noises of American Literature, 1890–1985: Toward a History of Literary Acoustics.* University Press of Florida, 2006.

Scientific American. "The Talking Phonograph." Vol. XXXVII, no. 25, 1877, p. 384.

Scott-Heron, Gil. *Small Talk at 125th and Lenox.* Flying Dutchman, 1970.

Shaney, A. C. *Elements of Single and Dual Track Magnetic Tape Recording and 1001 Applications.* Amplifier Corporation of America, 1950.

Shapcott, John. "'I Didn't Punctuate It': Locating the Tape and Text of Jack Kerouac's Visions of Cody and Doctor Sax in a Culture of Spontaneous Improvisation." *Journal of American Studies,* vol. 36, no. 2, 2002, pp. 231–48.

Sinnreich, Aram. *Mashed Up: Music, Technology, and the Rise of Configurable Culture.* University of Massachusetts Press, 2010.

Skerl, Jennie, and Robin Lydenberg, editors. *William S. Burroughs at the Front: Critical Reception, 1959–1989.* Southern Illinois University Press, 1991.

Smart, Lauren. "In Mr. Burns: A Post-Electric Play, It's Marge and Homer at the End of the World." Dallas Observer, Aug. 11, 2015, www.dallasobserver.com/arts/in-mr-burns-a-post-electric-play-its-marge-and-homer-at-the-end-of-the-world-7473716.

Smethurst, James.*African American Roots of Modernism: From Reconstruction to the Harlem Renaissance.* University of North Carolina Press, 2011.

The Black Arts Movement: Literary Nationalism in the 1960s and 1970s. University of North Carolina Press, 2005.

Smith, Mark M. *Listening to Nineteenth-Century America.* University of North Carolina Press, 2001.

Sobieszek, Robert A., and William S. Burroughs. *Ports of Entry: William S. Burroughs and the Arts.* Los Angeles County Museum of Art, 1996.

Sonvilla-Weiss, Stefan. *Mashup Cultures*. Springer, 2010.

Spindler, Michael. "John Dos Passos and the Visual Arts." *Journal of American Studies*, vol. 15, Dec. 1981, pp. 391–405.

Staab, Joachim G. *Fun with Tape*. Focal Press, 1967.

Stein, Daniel. "The Performance of Jazz Autobiography." *Genre: Forms of Discourse and Culture*, vol. 37, no. 2, 2004, pp. 173–200.

Stein, Gertrude. *Portraits and Prayers*. Random House, 1934.

———. *Three Lives: Stories of the Good Anna, Melanctha, and The Gentle Lena*. Grafton Press, 1909.

———. *Writings, 1903–1932*. Library of America, 1998.

———. *Writings, 1932–1946*. Library of America, 1998.

Stein, Gertrude, and Carl Van Vechten. *The Letters of Gertrude Stein and Carl Van Vechten, 1913–1946*. Edited by E. Burns. Columbia University Press, 1986.

Steinbeck, John. *The Grapes of Wrath*. Edited by Robert DeMott. Penguin Books, 2006.

Sterne, Jonathan. *The Audible Past: Cultural Origins of Sound Reproduction*. Duke University Press, 2003.

———. "The Stereophonic Spaces of Soundscape." *Living Stereo: Histories and Cultures of Multichannel Sound*, edited by P. Théberge et al., pp. 65–84. Bloomsbury, 2015.

Stoever, Jennifer Lynn. *The Sonic Color Line: Race and the Cultural Politics of Listening*. NYU Press, 2016.

Stoker, Bram. *Dracula*. Archibald Constable, 1899.

Stross, Randall E. *The Wizard of Menlo Park: How Thomas Alva Edison Invented the Modern World*. Crown, 2008.

Suisman, David. *Selling Sounds: The Commercial Revolution in American Music*. Harvard University Press, 2012.

Suisman, David, and Susan Strasser, editors. *Sound in the Age of Mechanical Reproduction*. University of Pennsylvania Press, 2011.

Sun Ra. Space Is the Place. Blue Thumb Records, 1973.

Szendy, Peter. *Listen: A History of Our Ears*. Fordham University Press, 2009.

Szwed, John. *Alan Lomax: The Man Who Recorded the World*. Penguin, 2010.

———. *Space Is the Place: The Lives and Times of Sun Ra*. Pantheon Books, 1997.

Taylor, David A. *Soul of a People: The WPA Writers' Project Uncovers Depression America*. John Wiley, 2010.

Théberge, Paul, et al., editors. *Living Stereo: Histories and Cultures of Multichannel Sound*. Bloomsbury, 2015.

Thomas, Lorenzo. "Neon Griot: The Functional Role of Poetry Readings in the Black Arts Movement." *Close Listening: Poetry and the Performed Word*. edited by Charles Bernstein, pp. 300–323. Oxford University Press, 1998.

Thomas, Pat. *Listen, Whitey! The Sounds of Black Power 1965–1975*. Fantagraphics Books, 2012.

Thompson, Ahmir "Questlove," and Ben Greenman. *Mo' Meta Blues: The World According to Questlove*. Reprint ed. Grand Central, 2015.

Thompson, Emily Anne. *The Soundscape of Modernity: Architectural Acoustics and the Culture of Listening in America, 1900–1933*. MIT Press, 2002.

Tietchen, Todd. "Language out of Language: Excavating the Roots of Culture Jamming and Postmodern Activism from William S. Burroughs' Nova Trilogy." *Discourse*, vol. 23, no. 3, Fall 2001, pp. 107–29, 132.

Tkweme, W. S. "Blues in Stereo: The Texts of Langston Hughes in Jazz Music." *African American Review*, vol. 42, no. 3/4, Fall 2008, pp. 503–12, 797.

Tongue, Cassie. "Mr Burns: The Simpsons Meets a Post-Apocalyptic World in a Dizzyingly Clever Production." *Guardian*, May 23, 2017, www.theguardian.com/stage/2017/may/23/mr-burns-the-simpsons-meets-a-post-apocalyptic-world-in-a-dizzyingly-clever-production.

Trombold, John. "Popular Songs as Revolutionary Culture in John Dos Passos' 'U.S.A.' and Other Early Works." *Journal of Modern Literature*, vol. 19, no. 2, Oct. 1995, pp. 289–316.

Trudeau, Justin Thomas. "Stooging the Body, Stooging the Text: Jack Kerouac's Visions of Cody." *Text and Performance Quarterly*, vol. 27, no. 4, 2007, pp. 334–50.

Veal, Michael. *Dub: Soundscapes and Shattered Songs in Jamaican Reggae*. Wesleyan University Press, 2007.

Wagner, Bryan. "Disarmed and Dangerous: The Strange Career of Bras-Coupé." *Representations*, vol. 92, no. 1, 2005, pp. 117–51.

Wagner, Linda W. *Dos Passos: Artist as American*. University of Texas Press, 2014.

Wald, Gayle. "Soul Vibrations: Black Music and Black Freedom in Sound and Space." *American Quarterly*, vol. 63, no. 3, Sept. 2011, pp. 673–96.

Walkmen, The. *A Hundred Miles Off*. Record Collection Music, May 23, 2006.

Washburn, Anne. *Mr Burns*. Oberon Books, 2014.

———. *Mr. Burns and Other Plays*. Theatre Communications Group, 2017.

Webster Fabio, Sarah. *Boss Soul*. Folkways Records, 1972.

Weheliye, Alexander G. "Engendering Phonographies: Sonic Technologies of Blackness." *Small Axe*, vol. 18, no. 2, 2014, pp. 180–90.

———. *Phonographies: Grooves in Sonic Afro-Modernity*. Duke University Press, 2005.

Weiss, Allen S. *Breathless: Sound Recording, Disembodiment, and the Transformation of Lyrical Nostalgia*. Wesleyan University Press, 2002.

Weiss, M. Lynn. *Gertrude Stein and Richard Wright: The Poetics and Politics of Modernism*. University Press of Mississippi, 2008.

Wharton, Edith. "The Pelican." Library of America, 1898, http://storyoftheweek.loa.org/2017/01/the-pelican.html.

Wickman, Forrest. "'Jammin' on the One' Is the Most Influential Moment in Hip-Hop History." *Slate*, Dec. 18, 2016, www.slate.com/articles/arts/wonder_week/2016/12/_jammin_on_the_one_is_the_most_influential_moment_in_hip_hop_history.html.

Williams, William Carlos. *Paterson*. New Directions, 1995.

Wilson, John S. "In Old New Orleans You Couldn't Do a Thing without Music." *New York Times*, 1960, p. BR3.

Wolfe, Tom. *The Electric Kool-Aid Acid Test*. Picador, 2008.

Woodard, Komozi. *A Nation within a Nation: Amiri Baraka (LeRoi Jones) and Black Power Politics.* University of North Carolina Press, 1999.

Yost, William A. *Fundamentals of Hearing: An Introduction.* Academic Press, 2007.

Young, Kevin. *The Grey Album: On the Blackness of Blackness.* Graywolf Press, 2012.

⸻. *To Repel Ghosts: Five Sides in B Minor.* Zoland Books, 2001.

⸻. *To Repel Ghosts: The Remix.* Knopf, 2005.

Youngquist, Paul. "The Space Machine: Baraka and Science Fiction." *African American Review*, vol. 37, no. 2/3, Summer 2003, pp. 333–43.

Yow, Valerie Raleigh. *Recording Oral History: A Guide for the Humanities and Social Sciences.* AltaMira Press, 2005.

Zutter, Natalie. "Rainbow Rowell's Harry Potter-Inspired Carry On Is the Ultimate Fanfiction Remix." Nov. 16, 2015, www.tor.com/2015/11/16/carry-on-harry-potter-fanfic-remix/.

Index

Recent Books In This Series *(continued from page ii)*

CPSIA information can be obtained
at www.ICGtesting.com
Printed in the USA
BVHW032304240123
657061BV00002B/16